G000279157

With of Lace

Withof Lace

Trude v.d. Heijden-Biemans
Yvonne Scheele-Kerkhof
Puck Smelter-Hoekstra

B.T. BATSFORD LTD · LONDON

ACKNOWLEDGEMENTS

The patterns in this book have been designed by the authors, except for Patterns 72, 73 and 74, which are traditional Japanese design motifs, and Patterns 67, 68 and 69, the source of which is Hokusai, *c.*1800.

The designs have been worked by Yvonne Scheele-Kerkhof and Trude v.d. Heijden-Biemans, and Patterns 22, 49 and 85 by Truus de Vries-Schrijver.

Yvonne Scheele-Kerkhof wrote the text; Trude v.d. Heijden-Biemans took the photographs; and Puck Smelter-Hoekstra drew the line illustrations.

Thank you, Joy Field, for spending so much of your precious time on reading the text.

First published 1991

ISBN 0 7134 6186 1

Typeset by Servis Filmsetting Ltd, Manchester

And printed by Bath Press Ltd, Bath, Avon

for the Publisher
B. T. Batsford Limited
4 Fitzhardinge Street
London W1H 0AH

Contents

Preface

Withof lace developed from Sluis Duchesse. When I was very young I attended the Royal School of Lace, *Koningin Sophie der Nederlanden*, at Sluis in Zeeuws Vlaanderen. Miss A. Metz was the principal of this school. She taught me how to work Duchesse lace, whilst Mrs Caniere taught me the very special method of handling the bobbins. My tuition followed the course recommended by Mrs Van der Meulen-Nulle's book (see p.155).

When I started teaching this type of bobbin lace, and especially as I began drawing new patterns and studying old lace (including needlepoint), slowly and almost imperceptibly fresh ideas were growing. When one of my youngest students mentioned the words 'Withof Special', the name was born. Withof is the name of our convent in Etten-Leur in the south of the Netherlands. In future our designs would be called 'Withof Lace'.

Withof lace makes significant use of depth and relief, light and shadow. The patterns are mostly of fantasy flowers, stylized birds, leaves and tendrils. As I discussed the patterns with my students and we worked them (sometimes in different ways), new ideas and methods began to emerge.

I am grateful to all those – and there are many of them – who have worked the patterns with so much enthusiasm and dedication. The development of the lace would not have been possible without my students. Their contribution has been extremely valuable and I hope that they will continue to look for further opportunities to revitalize other laces.

I would especially like to thank Yvonne, Puck and Trude, who took the initiative to write this book and have described clearly, drawn and worked each piece of lace. By including some of their own designs, they show just what can be achieved. This book will certainly be a precious guide for anybody who wishes to study Withof lace.

Sister Judith de Kreyger
Withof
Etten-Leur

Please note:
The photographs next to the working instructions are shown greatly enlarged for ease of working. When indicated, photographs are shown on pages 150–3 to show the actual size of the finished piece.

A short history

Withof lace developed from Duchesse lace as it was designed and worked in the Royal School of Lace in the Netherlands. The lace school was founded in Sluis in 1854 in an attempt to fight the poverty caused by the silting up of the harbour and by the deterioration of the fish industry. The school's purpose was to keep girls off the streets and, at the same time, provide them with an education which would enable them to make a living.

The lace they made was sold by the school, and the girls were then paid for it. As the school was a charitable institution, and as such did not make a profit, the entire proceeds could go to the lacemakers. Unfortunately, despite attempts to save it, the school had to be closed in 1872 owing to changing fashions and less demand for handmade lace.

In 1902 *De Nederlandsche Kantwerkschool* was founded in Apeldoorn. A year later Miss L.W. Nulle was appointed as a teacher there and when it moved to The Hague in 1905 she was made Principal. Her special interest was in designing modern lace. By participating in and organizing various exhibitions in the Netherlands and abroad, she succeeded in drawing the attention of the general public to Dutch lace.

In 1907 she published a book *Handleiding tot het Vervaardigen van Duchessekant* (*Guide to Making Duchesse Lace*). Much lace was made in the school in the Hague for the Royal Family, just as it had been in Sluis. In 1909 Queen Wilhelmina became its patron, when it was renamed *Koninklijke Nederlandsche Kantwerkschool* (Royal Dutch Lace School).

In the meantime, Miss Nulle married, and she left the school in 1911. She continued to show her love for lace, though, by holding courses throughout the country. Seven years later, the Royal Dutch Lace School had to be closed because of deteriorating circumstances, not the least of which was the onset of the First World War. On the initiative of the Mayor of Sluis, the Royal School of Lace had been re-opened there in 1910. Mrs Marie Louise Caniere, a student of the original lace school, became Principal. In 1912 Miss J.M. Roos, who had studied at the Royal Dutch Lace School in The Hague, succeeded her. Duchesse lace became the most important type of lace made at the Sluis school.

Detail of Altar cloth, designed and worked in Sluis Duchesse technique by Sister Judith de Kreyger in 1937

Until 1935, the Sluis school prospered but parents then began to choose other avenues for their daughters and the number of students fell below a viable figure. Luckily, this did not mean the end of tuition in lacemaking in the Netherlands. In various places, there were, and still are, lace schools which offer a variety of courses.

Collar and cuffs, worked to an old Duchesse pattern in Withof lace by Yvonne Scheele

FROM DUCHESSE TO WITHOF

In recent years, Sluis Duchesse lace has evolved in such a way through the work of Sister Judith and her students that it has become worthy of a name in its own right: *Withof lace*. Its main characteristics are a dense weave, and the creation of depth and relief, and light and shadow. It is also a remarkably firm lace. The way is now open for using old Duchesse patterns to produce a more lively appearance. Other new developments are being explored in the use of needlepoint techniques together with Withof lace. Sister Judith strongly encourages her students to cultivate lacemaking, especially Dutch lace. It is our intention to promote this movement with the publication of this book.

Modesty, designed by Sister Judith de Kreyger, and worked by Sari Haveman in Withof lace combined with needle point lace

Important hints

Before starting the pattern, study it carefully. First decide on the order of work. This is very important. Start with motifs that are foremost in the design, or parts into which other sections have to be sewn. Although it may look as if parts lie on top of each other, they have actually been joined with sewings (see photograph on p.95, top right). Fillings are worked to fill the spaces within motifs, or, in some patterns, are used only to unite separate sections.

Take care that the line of work flows smoothly with the direction of the motif. Turn the pillow as the work progresses in order to keep the bobbins directly in front of you.

Protect the work with a cover cloth. The lace then stays clean and the pillow can be turned without running the risk of the thread catching on the pins.

Keep all the bobbins the same distance from the work. When starting a piece, always hang the bobbins astride the pin, as shown in the diagrams.

Move the bobbins from one side of the pillow to the other as the work progresses. By doing this the threads will spread more evenly.

Pull both runner bobbins carefully before working the edge stitch. A nice, firm edge stitch is very important. Even by rolling one cannot hide an uneven edge stitch.

The pins are set head to head. For a wider curve, the pins are placed a little further apart, but no further than a pin-head. The use of special Duchesse pins is necessary since the heads of these pins are very small and, therefore, can be set very close to one another. Duchesse pins are also very short which makes it easy to push them right into the pillow.

When making a row of sewings, take care that the spread is even, especially when sewing more than once into one pin-hole.

You can roll and raise as many pairs as you wish for depth and relief. Picots are an optional alternative for a decorative edge. If the gimp is taken into the bundle, keep this against the work.

Always try to carry over pairs from one motif to the next. It saves much tying and sewing and the lace will be more even.

Finally, *take your time*! A good result is well worth an extra few hours spent on the work. Broken threads and having to undo the work take time too!

This book contains basic guidance. Remember that the pattern is a drawing and not a pricking. The number of pairs of bobbins to use has not been stated as this depends on the personal taste of each lacemaker, on the setting of the pins, and on the thickness of thread. The thread used to work the patterns is stated in each case. All the patterns can be either enlarged or reduced, depending on your preference. Choose your thread accordingly. All the patterns shown in the book have been worked in Egyptian cotton.

Equipment

- Flat, firm pillow – 60cm in diameter
- Cover cloth – a square, plain cotton cloth slightly larger than the pillow, with a hole in the centre approximately 5–6cm across
- Smooth, unspangled bobbins (sewings have to be made)
- Thread – Egyptian cotton, 80/2 to 170/2; and for the gimp Fresia linen 80/2 (to go with 120/2) – finer thread needs a thinner gimp
- Duchesse pins – 17.45 × 25mm
- Duchesse needlepin, with curved end. Carefully bend a needle which has been heated in a flame
- A pair of sharp scissors
- A pair of blunt scissors – loose at the pivot to tie the pairs (see diagrams 1–5)
- Matt, coloured, sticky transparent film to make the pattern (which might be a photocopy) firmer. Use the film backing beneath the pattern or photocopy to make it firmer still
- Drawing materials

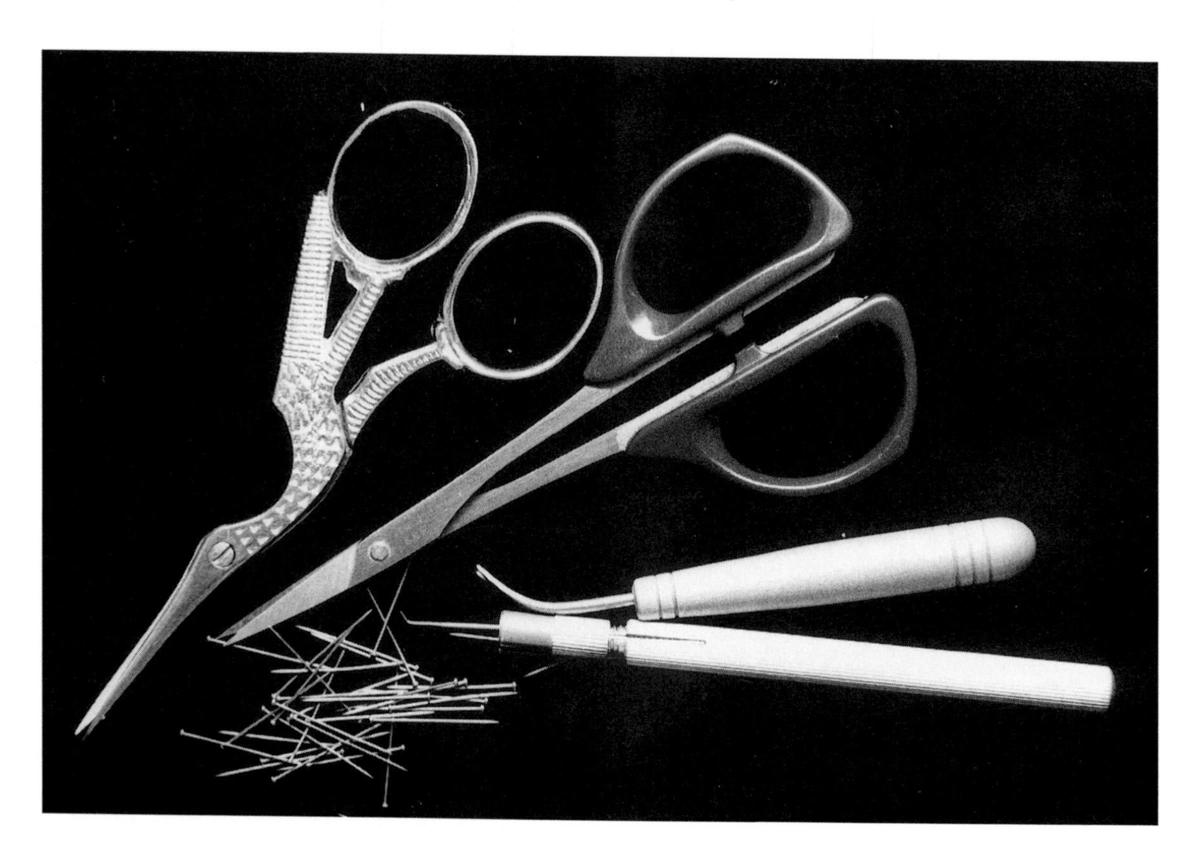

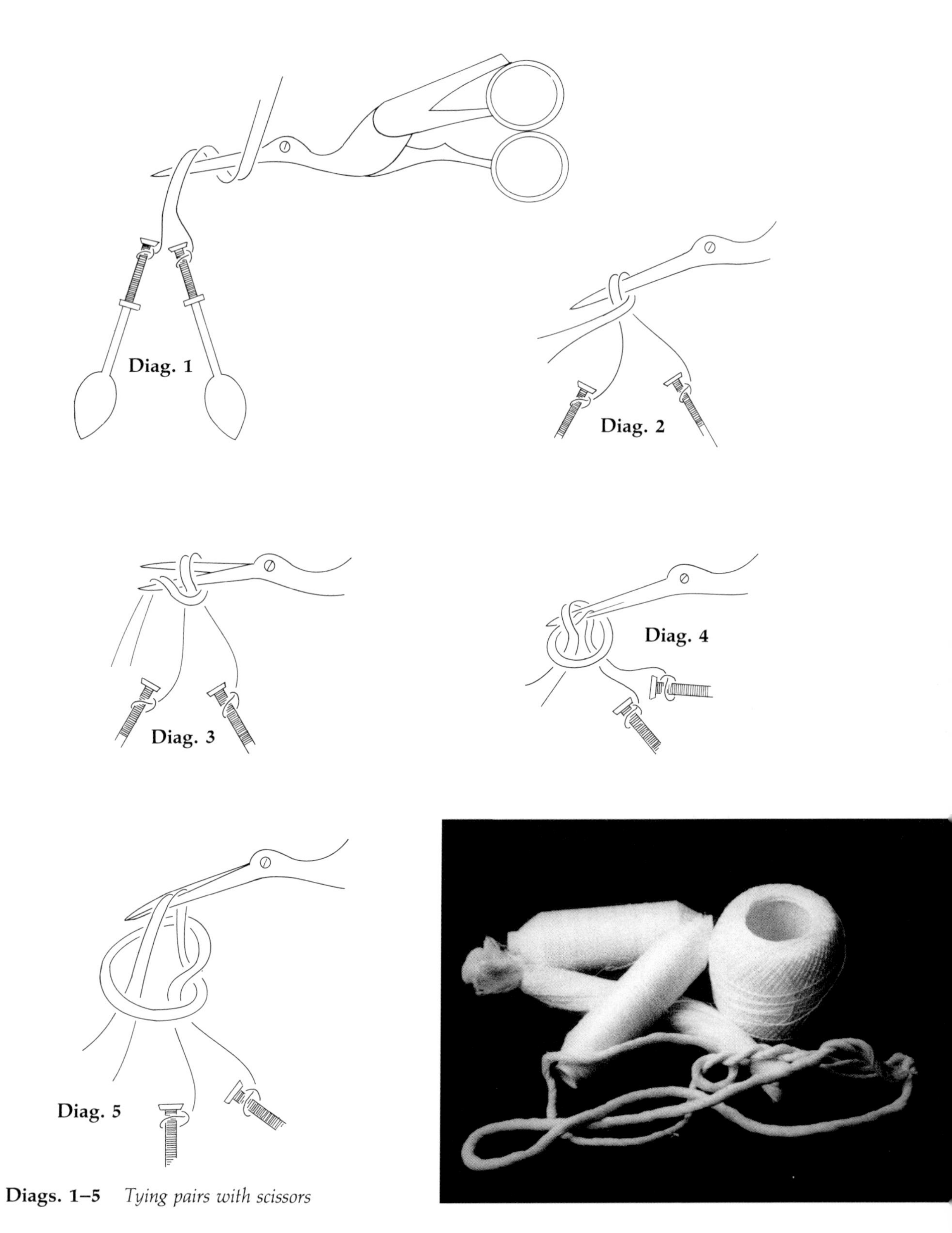

Diags. 1–5 *Tying pairs with scissors*

1. Setting up (or commencing work)

STRAIGHT SETTING UP

Depending on the width, set pins not too close together on the horizontal line (diag. 6).

Hang 4 pairs round the left-hand end pin and 2 pairs round each of the other pins.
Work from left to right. *Always* start with the pin around which the 4 pairs are hung. Thus, if working from right to left, hang 4 pairs on the right-hand end pin (diag. 7).

With 1st and 2nd pairs – work whole stitch and twist both pairs twice.
With 3rd and 4th pairs – work whole stitch and twist both pairs twice.
With 4th and 5th pairs – work whole stitch and twist both pairs twice.
Put 5th pair round the back of the 2nd pin and to the left of 6th pair.

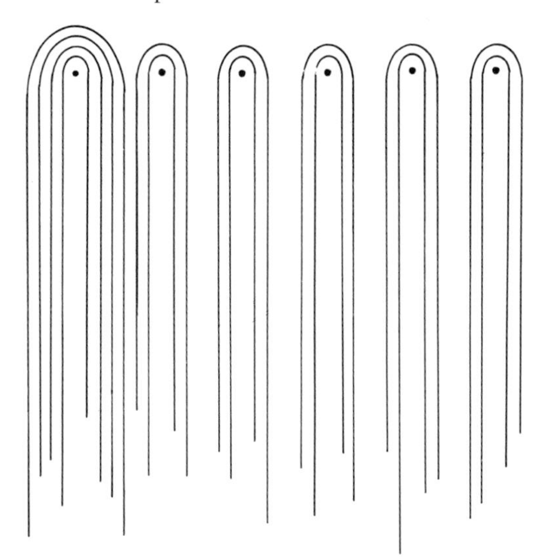

Diag. 6 *Straight setting up from left to right*

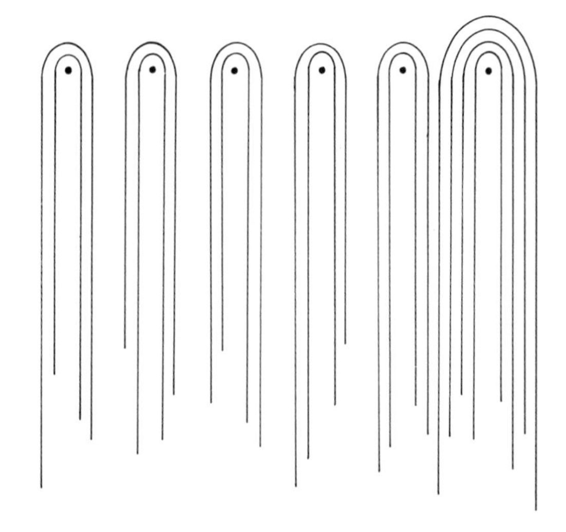

Diag. 7 *Straight setting up from right to left*

With 5th and 6th pairs – work whole stitch and twist both pairs twice.
With 6th and 7th pairs – work whole stitch and twist both pairs twice.
Put 7th pair round the back of the 3rd pin and to the left of 8th pair.
With 7th and 8th pairs – work whole stitch and twist both pairs twice.
With 8th and 9th pairs – work whole stitch and twist both pairs twice.
Put 9th pair round the back of the 4th pin and to the left of 10th pair.

Continue in this manner until all pairs have been used. The pins will still be uncovered with a straight edge across the top of them (diag. 8).

Now start the pattern.
With the 2nd pair from the left work in whole

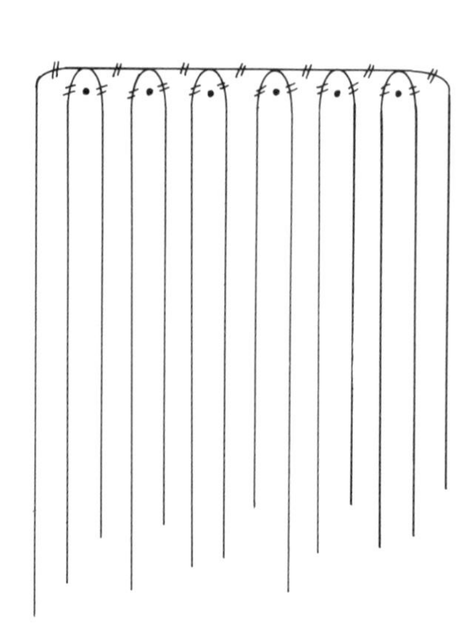

Diag. 8 *Joining pairs, showing a straight edge across the top*

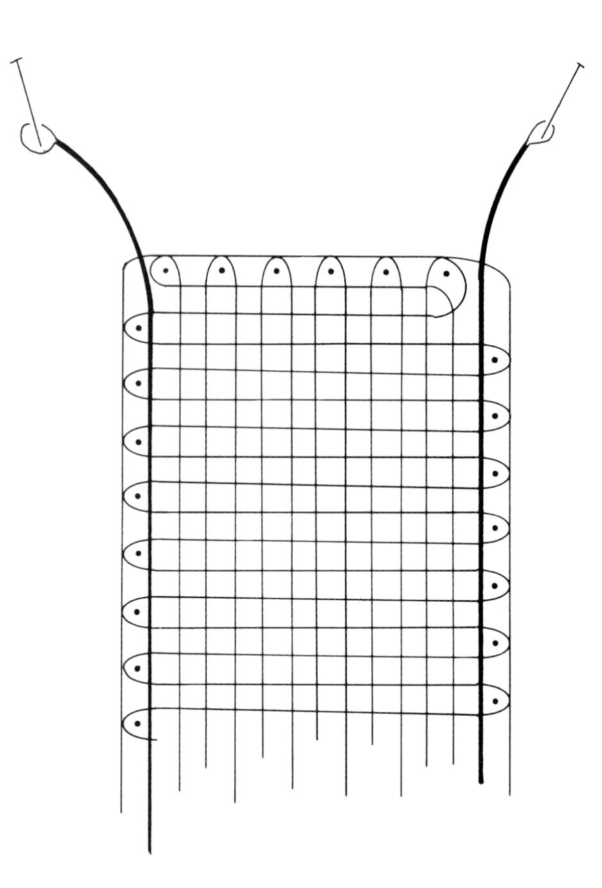

Diag. 10 *A gimp pair is added between 2nd and 3rd pair*

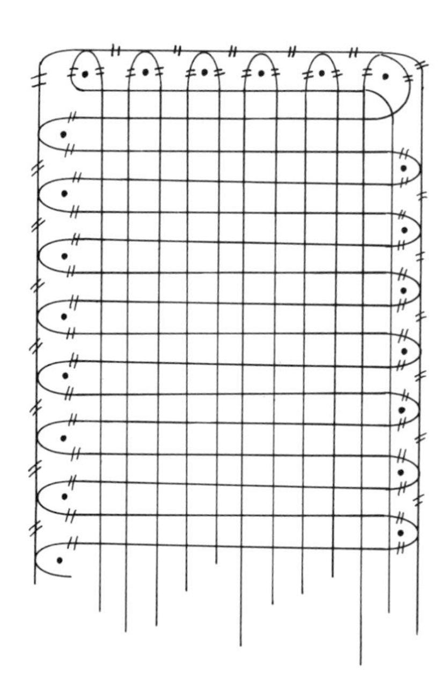

Diag. 9 *Whole stitch 2nd pair through the passives as far as the last pair. Back to the left with the 3rd pair*

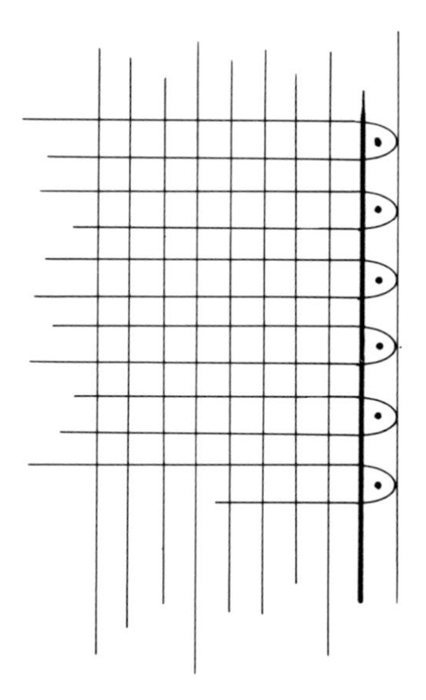

Diag. 11 *A straight edge stitch is used at the sides*

stitch through the passives as far as the last pair and leave. With the 3rd pair from the right work whole stitch back to the left up to the last pair (diag. 9).

If gimp pairs are required, they are now added thus. Hang each gimp pair (one bobbin with gimp thread and one with the main thread you are using) round a pin outside the work, and lay them to the inside of the outermost passive pair, with the thicker thread to the outer edge (diag. 10). Take the workers through this gimp pair. The gimp pair is *always* worked in whole stitch. Now make the edge stitch (whole stitch and twist both pairs twice). Put the pin between the 2nd and 3rd pairs (diag. 11).

If a gimp pair is required across the width of the pattern, work this in whole stitch after the straight edge has been formed and before the first row of whole stitch: In this case a double gimp pair is needed (i.e. a gimp thread pair plus a pair with the main thread) (diag. 12).

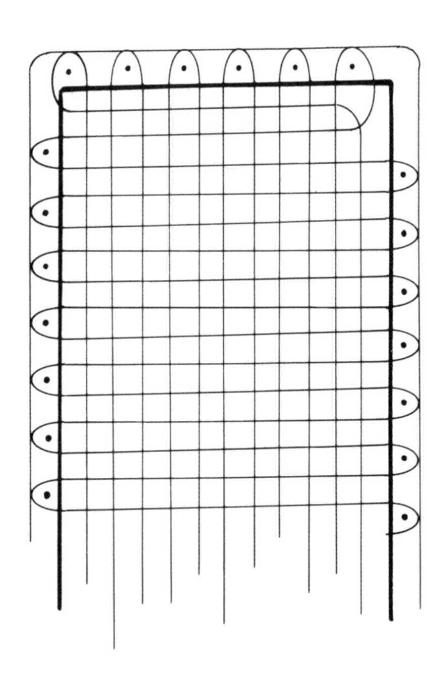

Diag. 12 *Double gimp pairs are whole stitched across the width of the pattern*

Patterns 1a and 1b

Thread 100/2

Sample braids

Work a sample braid twisting the passives and runners as required (Pattern 1a). When you have finished the 1st braid, tie the pairs and cut them. Now work the 2nd one in half stitch. As fewer pairs are needed for this, fewer pins are set.

The centre braid has to be sewn into both sides. Set the pins on the horizontal line and work the setting up now. The runner pair has to be sewn in the corresponding pin-hole of the adjacent braids (for side sewings see diag. 13). When a

Diag. 13 *Side sewing*

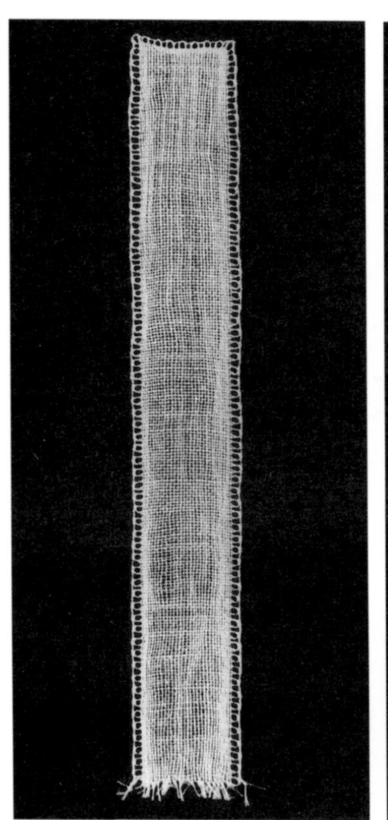

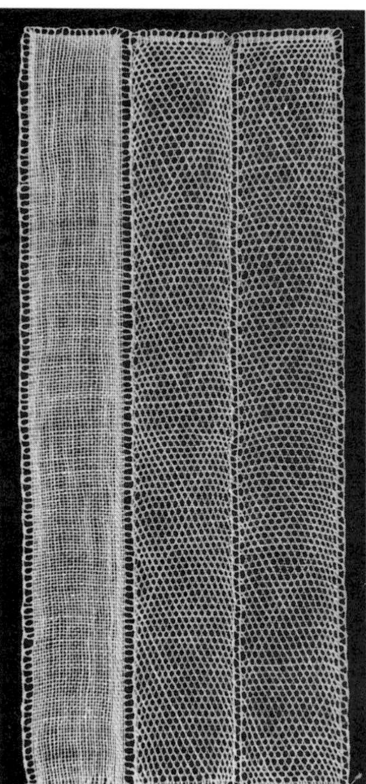

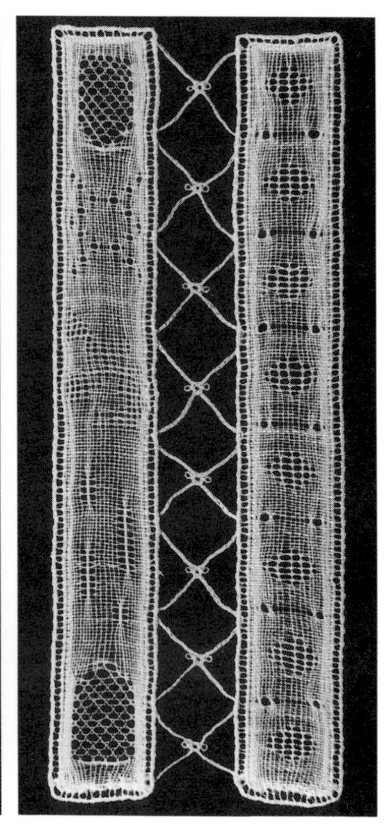

Sample braids

motif is rolled, a raised sewing is needed (see diag. 14) as follows.
Take the pin out of the work and pull one thread of the runners through the pin-hole using the needlepin. Now pass the other bobbin through this loop. Pull the threads tight and twist them (diag. 15). Work to the other side and sew in the same way (diag. 16).

Diag. 14 *Raised or top sewing*

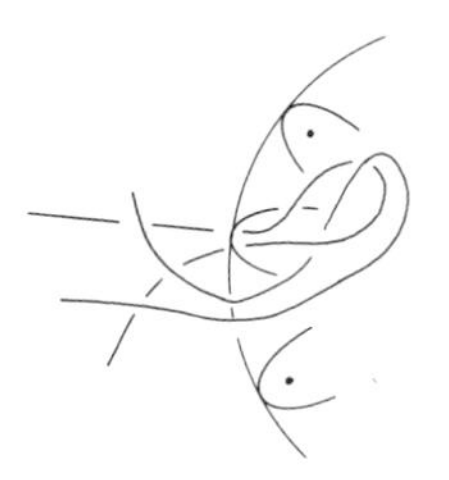

Diag. 15 *A sewing*

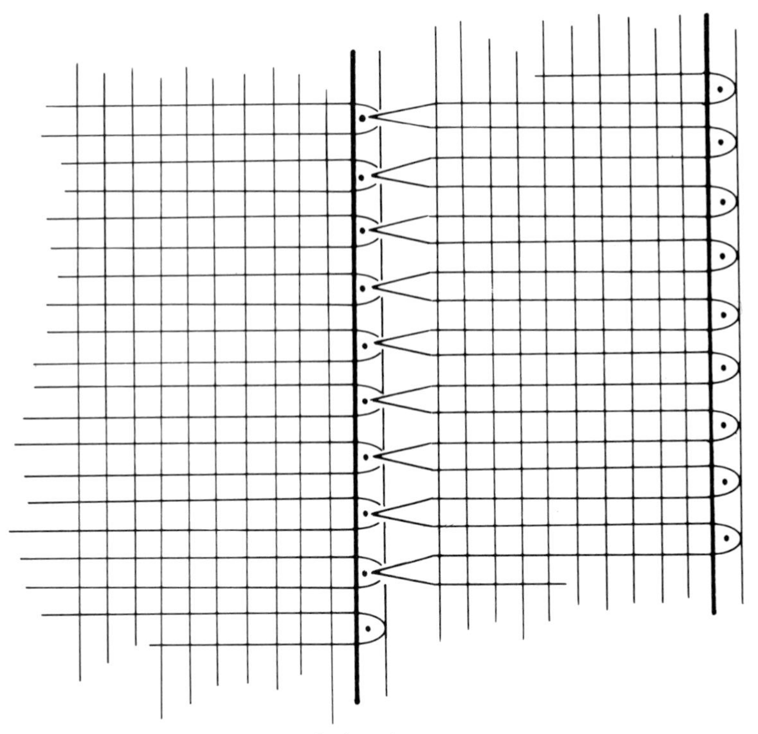

Diag. 16 *Sewings into the braid*

FINISHING A STRAIGHT BRAID

At the end of the braid the runners have to be worked through all the passives up to the gimp pair and taken out. Now work the 1st pair of passives at the other side through the gimp pair. Make the edge stitch, go back through the gimp pair and tie the runners off with the next passives using a reef knot (diag. 17).

Repeat this until there are only 2 edge pairs left. Work a whole stitch with them and bundle them with the gimp pair (diag. 18).

Diag. 17 *Finishing a straight braid*

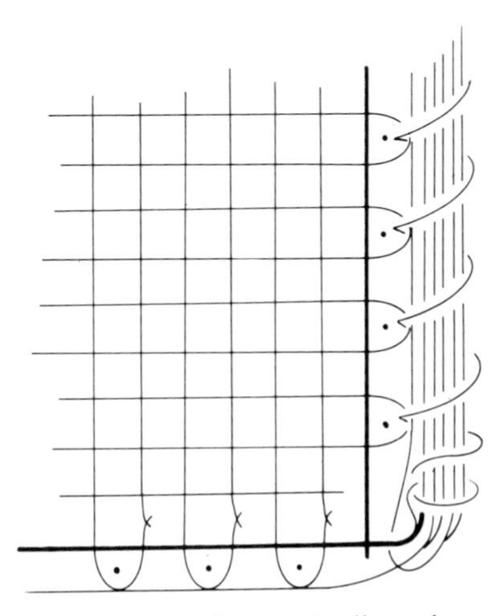

Diag. 18 *Bundling and rolling along a straight edge*

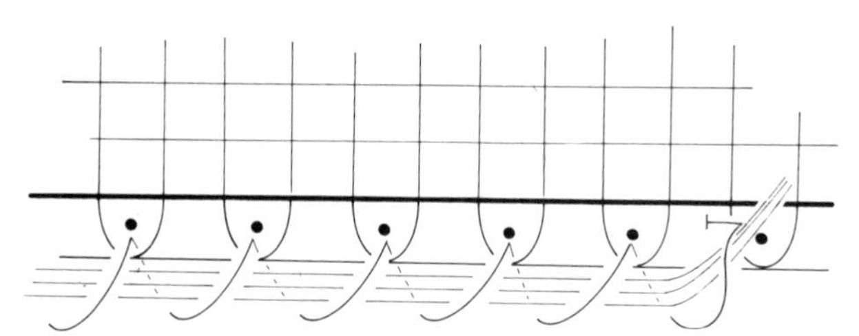

Diag. 19 *Finishing the roll on a straight or curved edge*

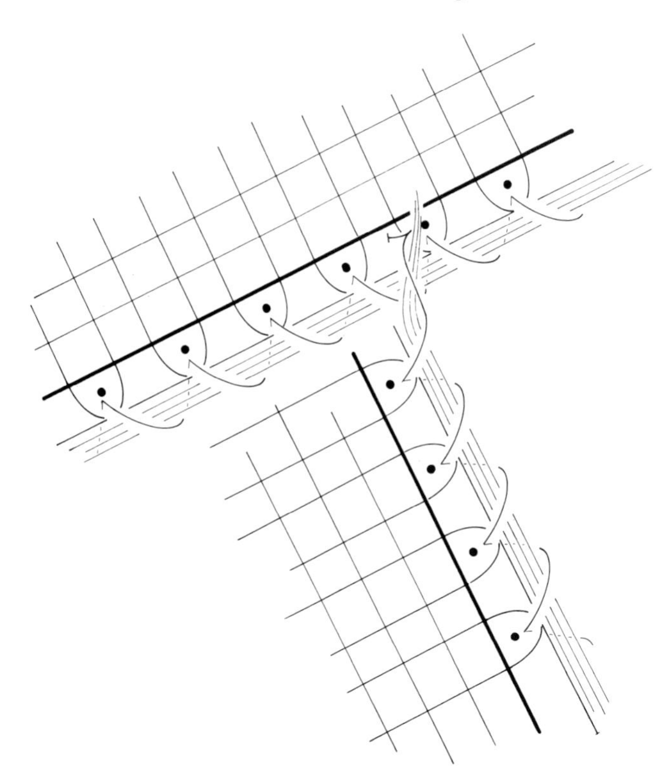

Diag. 20 *Finishing the roll into another motif*

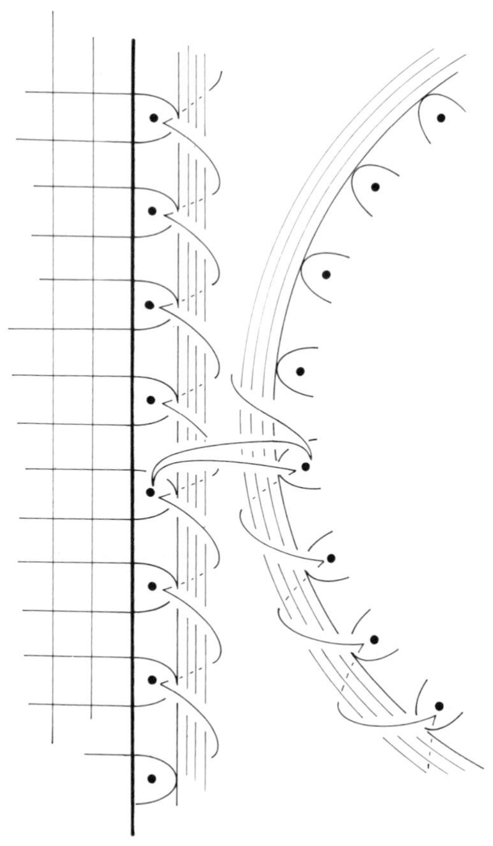

Diag. 21 *Joining motifs*

Take one bobbin out of the bundle. Pass this thread under the other threads, and put the bobbin over the threads through the loop. Roll with this bundle (diag. 18). To finish the roll in the side loop of the pin-hole in which rolling was started see diag. 19; and to finish the roll in another motif, see diag. 20. Diag. 21 shows the process of attaching one motif to another.

Before cutting off the bundle, tie one thread of the bundle with the thread that has been used already for rolling.

ROLLING

Put the needlepin in the pin-hole and pass the thread underneath the bundle, through the pin-hole, and put the bobbin through this loop. Pull carefully so that the knot is on top of the bundle and thus on the wrong side of the work (diag. 18).

ROLLING WITH PICOTS

Work with at least 3 pairs. Use 2 outer pairs for picots and whole stitches; use one bobbin to make the sewings and keep the other bobbin close to the work. After the first sewing, make a picot with the outer pair (diags. 22–23). Then work a whole stitch with the pair next to it and work another sewing (diag. 24).

Diag. 23 *Eye of a picot*

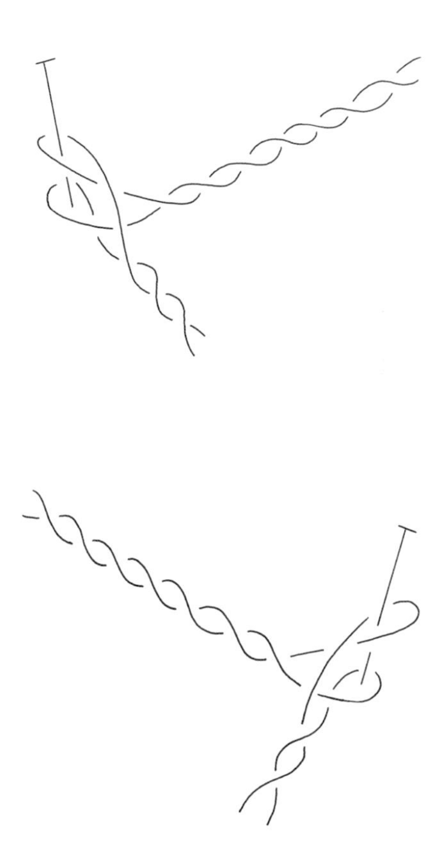

Diag. 22 *Picots, left and right*

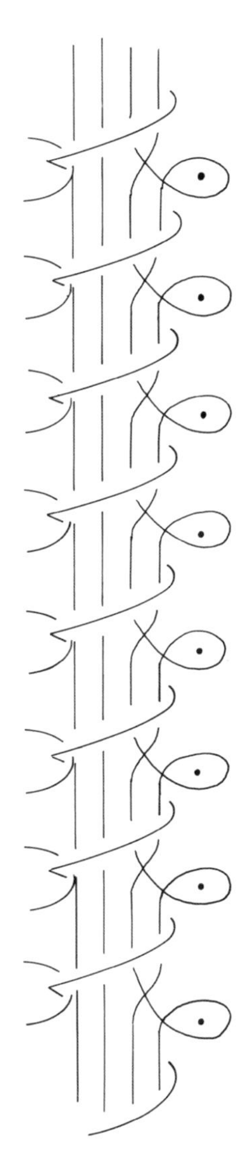

Diag. 24 *Rolling with picots*

NARROW SETTING UP

The narrow setting up may be used when fewer sewings have to be made and where the setting up is in the centre of the work. An example is the scroll but this method may also be used in the round setting up.

Hang the pairs round the pin as for the straight setting up (diag. 25), i.e. 4 pairs on the first pin and 2 pairs on each of the other pins.
With 1st and 2nd pairs work whole stitch and twist both pairs twice (diag. 26).
With 3rd and 4th pairs, twist both pairs twice.
With 4th and 5th pairs work whole stitch and twist both pairs twice.
Put 5th pair round the back of the 2nd and pin to the left of 6th pair.
With 6th and 7th pairs – work whole stitch and twist both pairs twice. Put 7th pair round 3rd pin.
With 8th and 9th pairs – work whole stitch and twist both pairs twice, etc. (diag. 27).

ROUND SETTING UP

Pattern 2
Thread 80/2

Set 3 pins. Hang 4 pairs round the centre pin and 2 pairs round each of the other pins (diag. 28).
Make a straight edge, joining the pairs working from the centre to the right (diag. 6) and from the centre to the left (diag. 7).
Add double gimp pairs and in the same way at least two extra pairs of passives (diag. 29).
Start to work from the centre.
If needed, set new pins on the outline (see Pattern 15, p.38).
If the motif widens straight away, add extra pairs in the middle also, as follows. Set a pin outside

Round setting up

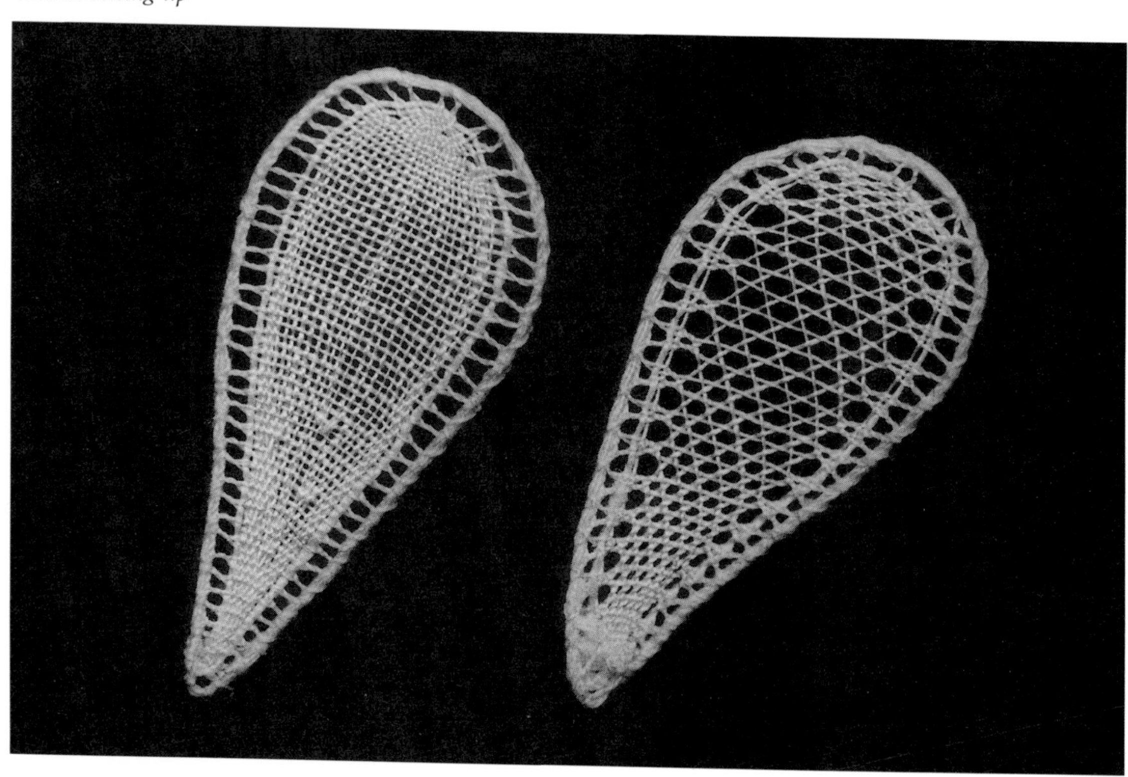

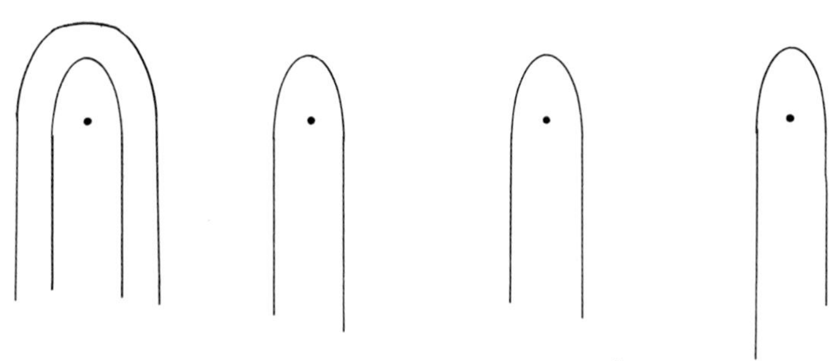

Diag. 25 *Narrow setting up from left to right*

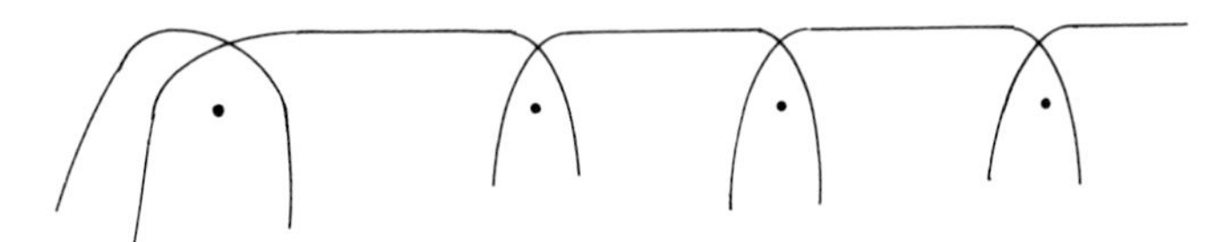

Diag. 26 *Joining of the pairs, showing pairs*

Diag. 27 *Joining of the pairs, showing single threads*

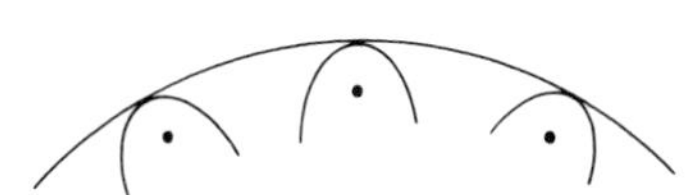

Diag. 28 *Round setting up*

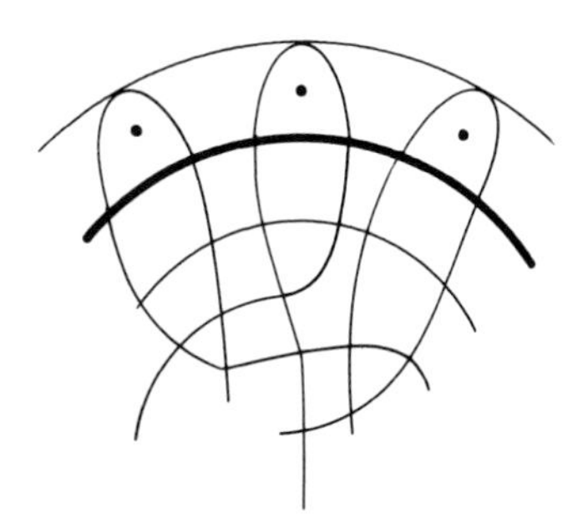

Diag. 29 *Double gimp pairs and passive pairs are added*

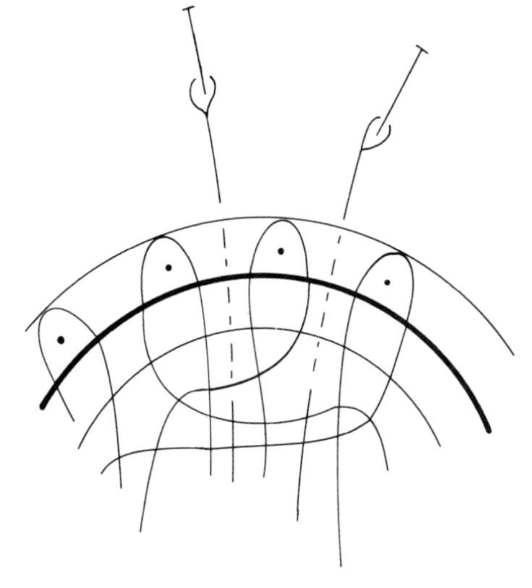

Diag. 30 *New pairs added on a pin outside the work*

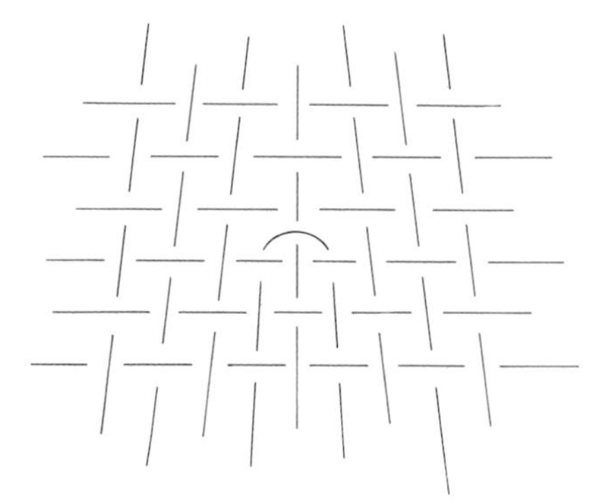

Diag. 31 *Ease the new pair through*

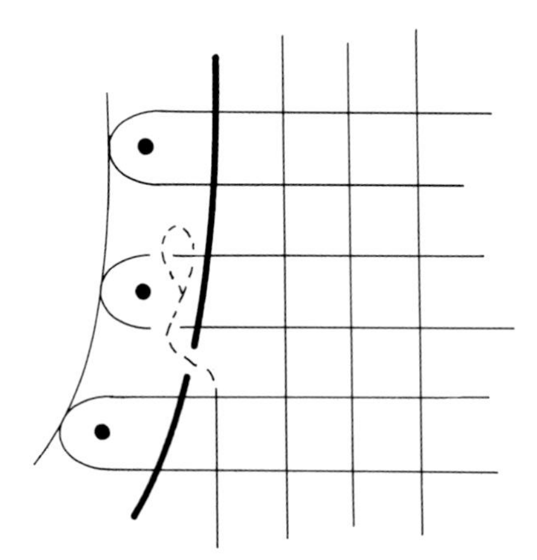

Diag. 32 *Adding a new pair in half stitch*

the work; hang a pair round it, and place each bobbin of the pair on either side of a bobbin whose thread lies on top of the runners (diags. 30–31).
In half stitch, new pairs are added as follows. Work to the edge stitch at the side at which a new pair needs to be added. Hang a new pair round the runners and put it aside (diag. 32). Make the edge stitch and continue the work. When reaching this side again, the new pair is included in the work. If the new pair is needed at a side where a sewing has to be made, sew it in the loop above the place where it is needed and then work it.

When taking out pairs in half stitch, lose the pair next to the gimp pair. Later on it must be sewn and tied.

If a pair has to be taken out at a side where sewings are being made, lose the last pair on that side. Later on this pair will be sewn into the next side loop.

SETTING UP AT A POINT

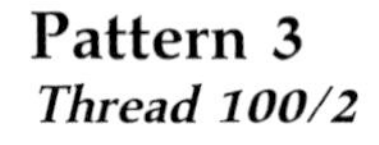

Pattern 3
Thread 100/2

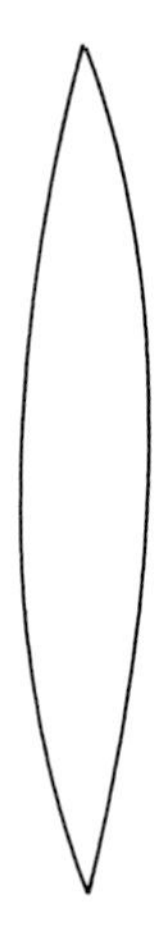

Set 1 pin in the point and hang 4 pairs on it.
Set 1 pin on either side of the side lines and hang 2 pairs on each of these (diag. 33).
Start the setting up movement from the centre towards the left and right, as in diags. 6 and 7 (diag. 34). Now add a double gimp pair (diag. 35).
If the point is very sharp, work a whole stitch with the two middle pairs to push the gimp pair against the edge pair (diag. 35).
Now study the pattern to decide on which side the first pin must be set and start the work on that side. Add as many new pairs as are needed straight away (diag. 36).

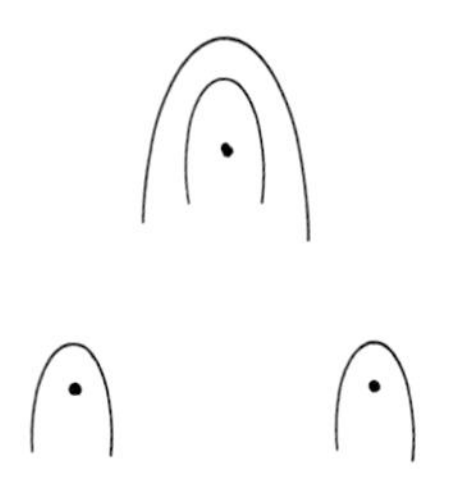

Diag. 33 *Setting up at a point*

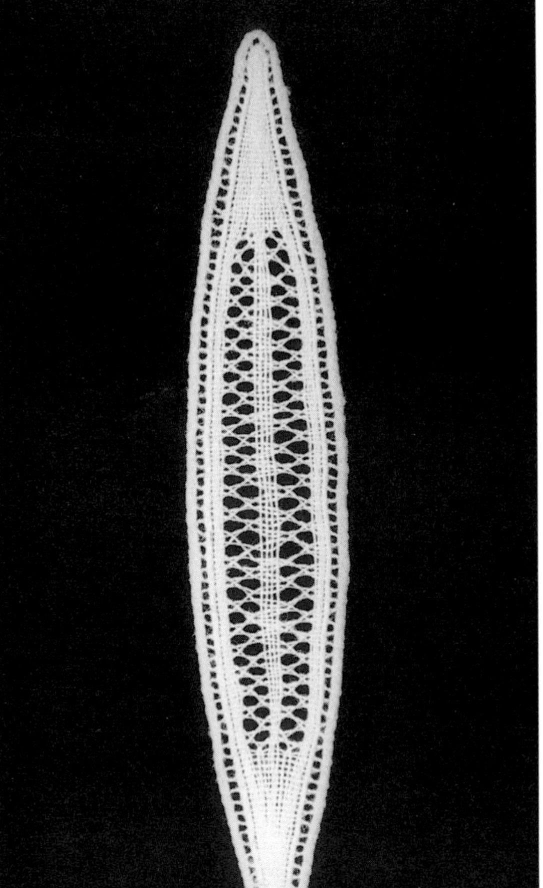
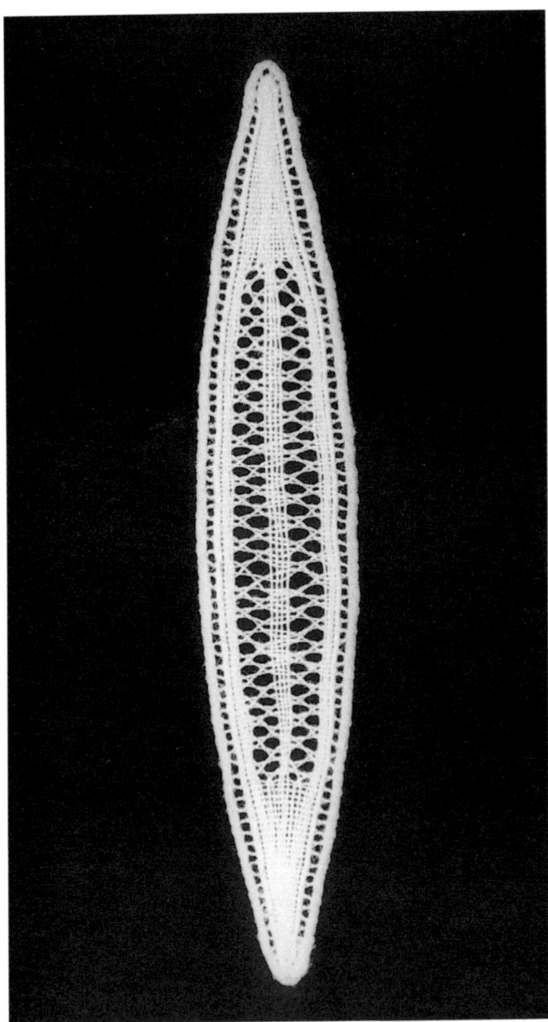

Setting up a point

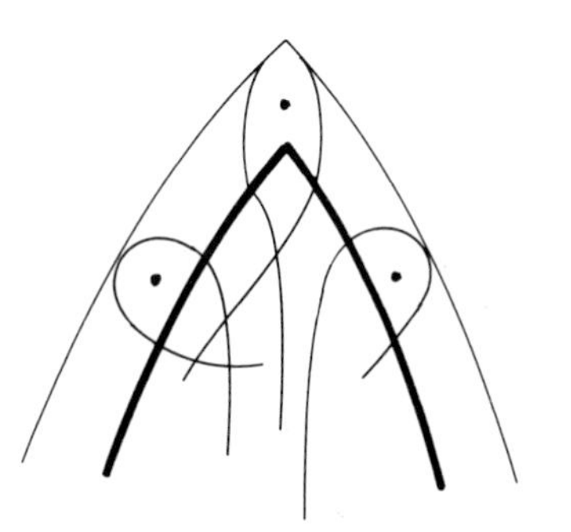

Diag. 35 *Whole stitch the 2 centre pairs, to push the gimp pair into the top*

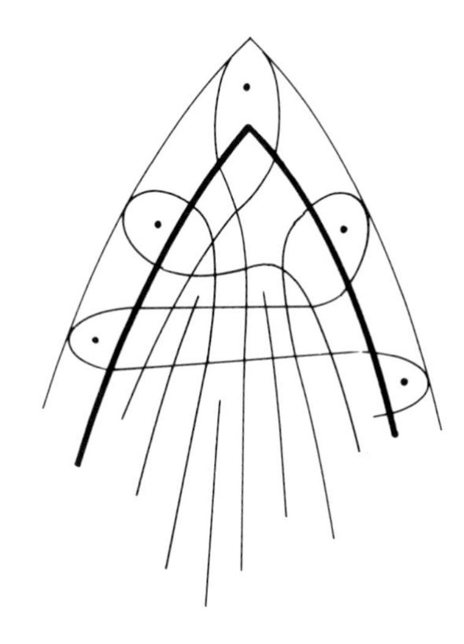

Diag. 36 *Adding new pairs straight away*

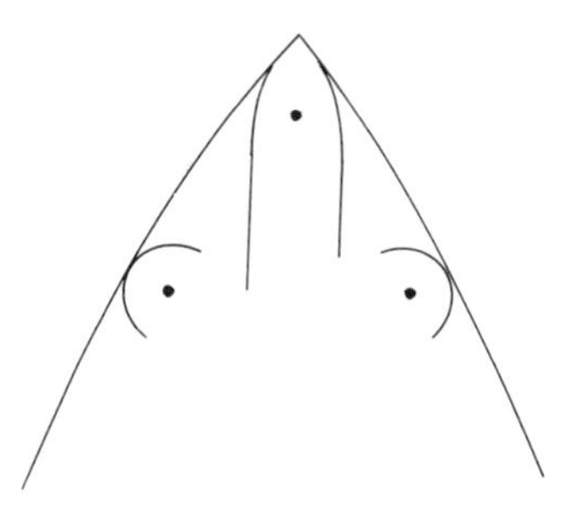

Diag. 34 *Joining the pairs*

When the pattern narrows, pairs have to be taken out. In whole stitch, take out 2 threads at a time, or any even number, always leaving one thread between two which are underneath the runners. Cut those threads later. For half stitch, see Round setting up, p.20.)

Not more than 5 or 6 pairs are left at the point, comprising 2 edge pairs, 2 gimp pairs, runners, and perhaps 1 pair of passives.
Take the passives out. Work the runners through one gimp pair and take them out. Now work a

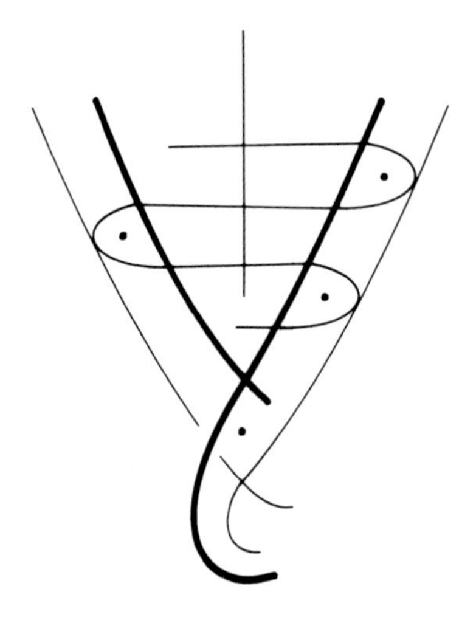

Diag. 37 *Finishing at the point, rolling the pairs on one side*

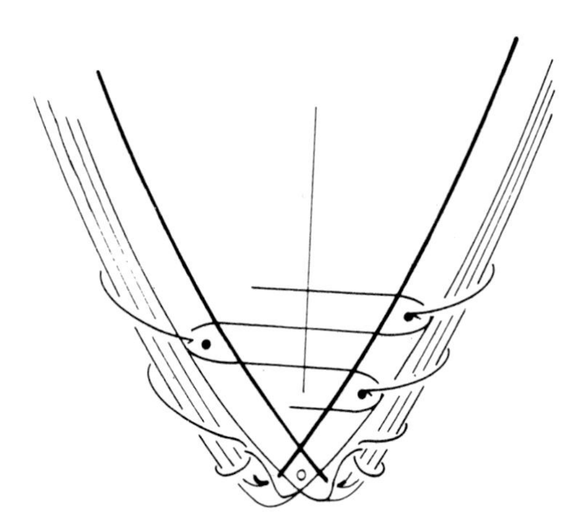

Diag. 38 *Finishing at the point rolling on 2 sides*

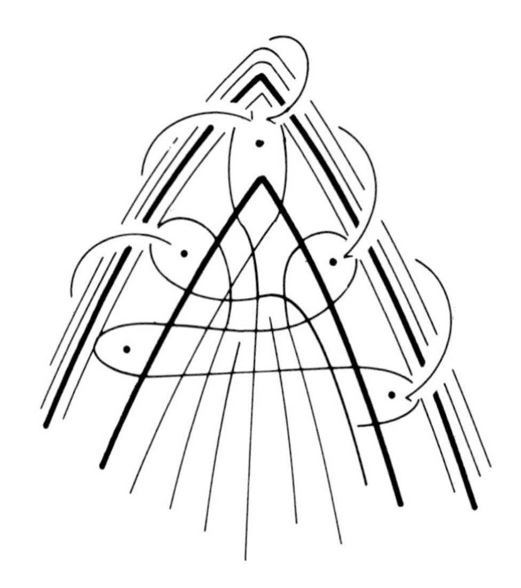

Diag. 39 *Two sewings have to be made in the top*

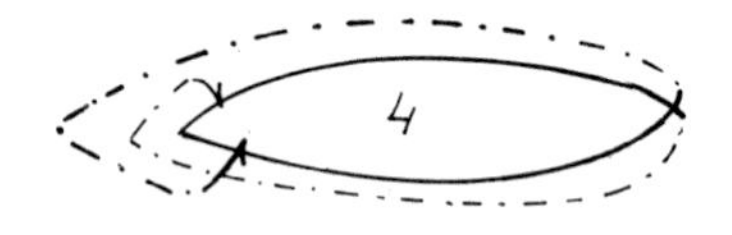

Diag. 40 *Finishing of the roll, which was started on 2 sides*

whole stitch with the 2 gimp pairs. Set the last pin in the point and work a whole stitch with the two edge pairs (diag. 37).

Decide how many pairs have to be rolled. Then roll on both sides, finishing in the point (diag. 38). Take out pairs that are not needed; if necessary, tie them and cut them off.
Two sewings have to be made in the point of the leaf to keep the point sharp (diag. 39). Finish the roll in the side loop of the pin-hole in which rolling began (diag. 19).
To finish the roll at the point see diag. 40.

ASYMMETRIC SETTING UP

Pattern 4

Thread 100/2

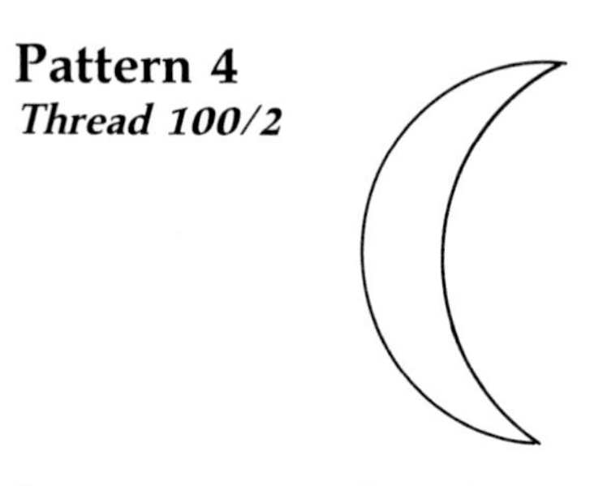

Set 3 pins, starting from the point, and join the pairs (diag. 41). Add a double gimp pair.

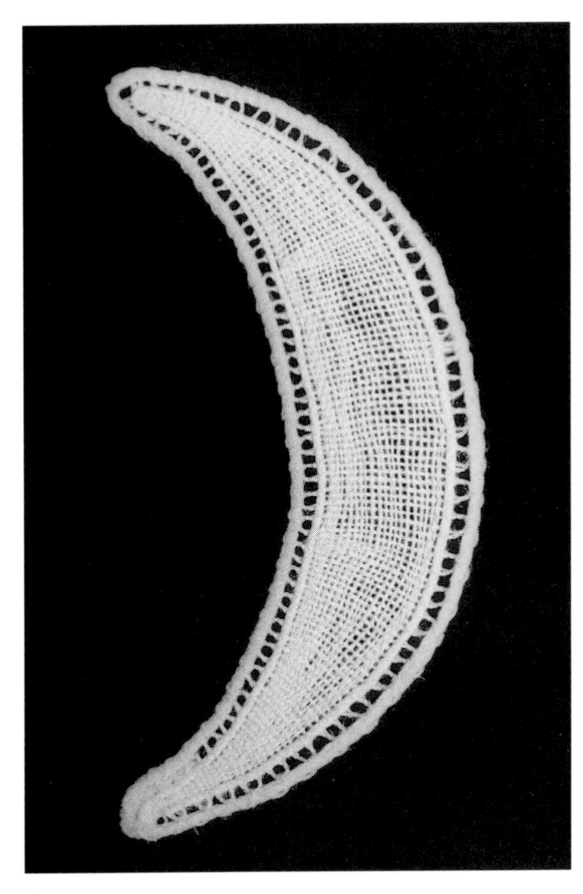

Asymmetric setting up

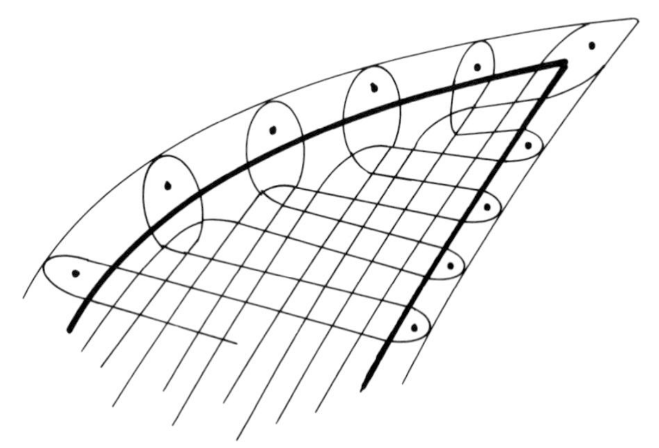

Diag. 43 *Decorative holes are produced by leaving the runners in front of the gimp pair and picking up a new pair of runners*

Work in whole stitch with the runners (2nd pair from the right) to the 2nd pin, but leave the runners before working the gimp pair (diag. 42). Using the last worked passives as the new runners work back to the right in whole stitch.

Edge stitch and pin. Work towards the left to the 3rd pin, leaving the runners in front of the gimp pair. Take the last worked pair of passives as the new runners and work back to the right. Repeat this (diag. 43).
If necessary, set new setting up pins (as diag. 63 on p.39). Whilst working this, decide where to leave the runners in order to pick up another pair to use as runners. This will produce decorative holes. Try to keep them evenly spaced.

Diag. 41 *Asymmetric setting up*

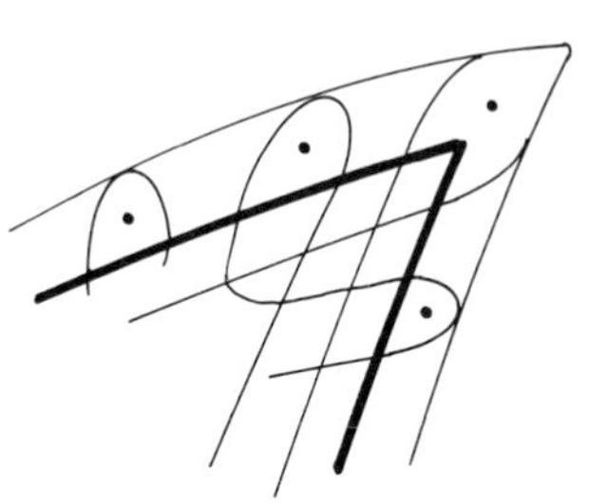

Diag. 42 *Joining of the pairs and adding double gimp pairs*

DOUBLE-SIDED SETTING UP

Rib

Set 2 pins and hang 8 pairs round pin 1 in such a manner that one bobbin of each pair is put to the front, and one to the back. The bobbins that are put to the back are fastened by a pin to keep them from moving.
Hang 4 pairs round pin 2 in the same manner (diag. 44). Make the edge stitch. After setting the 1st pin, work to the other side and leave the runners which may be twisted once. With the

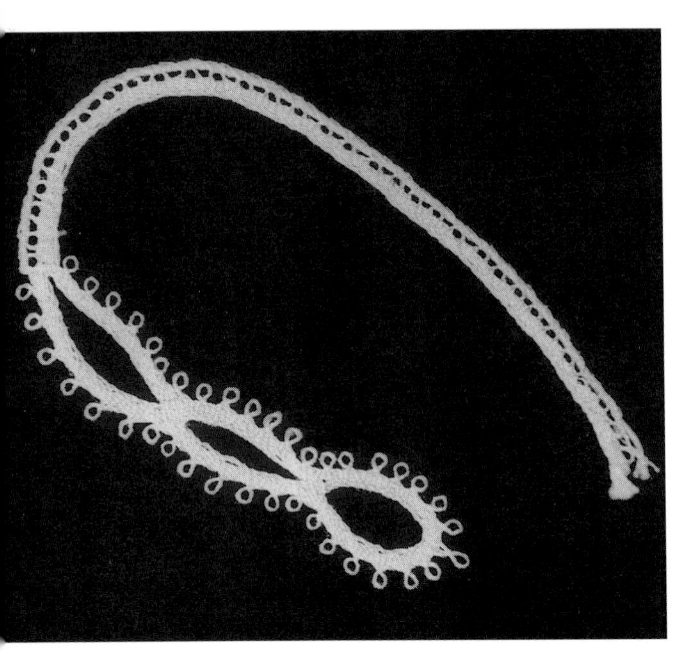

Double sided setting up for rib

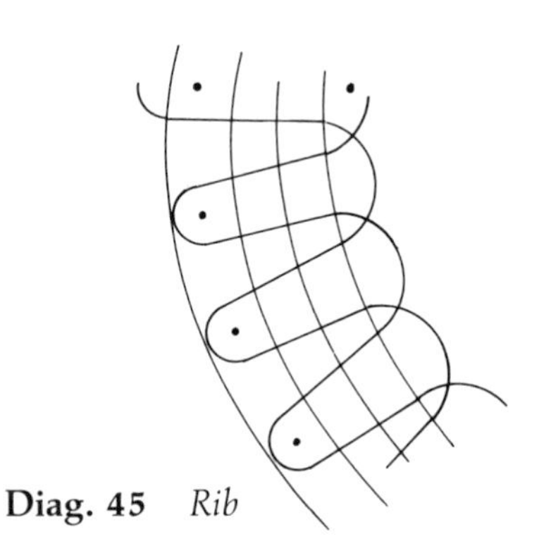

Diag. 45 *Rib*

2nd pair work back to make the edge stitch, and set the pin (diag. 45).

Continue to the place where both sides meet. Take out the setting up pins before working the other side of the rib. Where both sides meet, the passives only are worked in whole stitch. Continue the rib (diag. 46). When finished, the passives have to be sewn and tied off although some of them may be needed in the bundle.

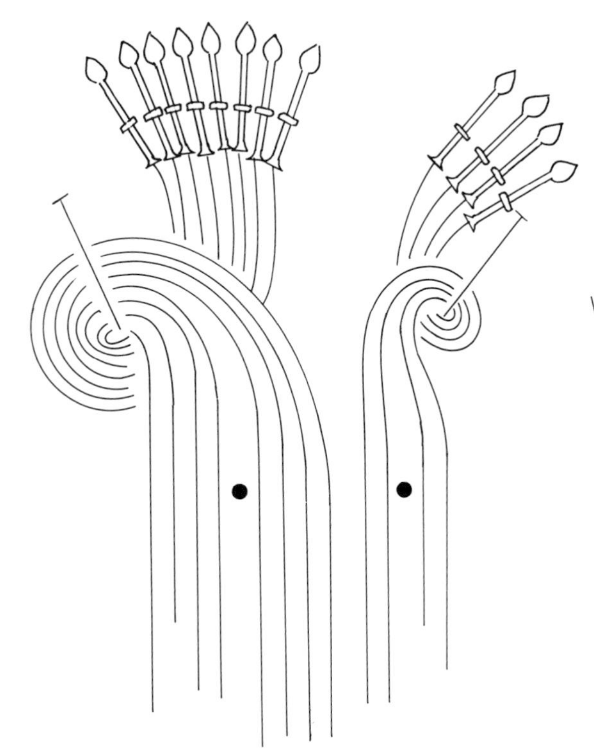

Diag. 44 *In double-sided setting up the pairs are twisted round the pins*

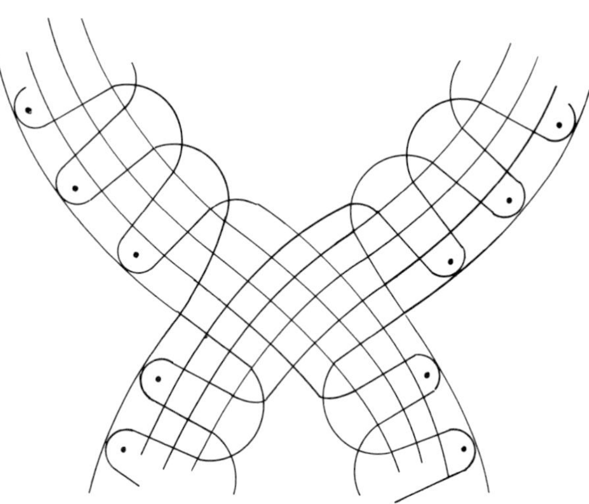

Diag. 46 *When 2 ribs meet, the passives are worked in whole stitch*

Changing sides of edge stitch in rib

The pins are usually set on the outside of a rib. It may be necessary to change the edge stitch from one side to the other. In order to do this, work as far as the edge stitch and leave the runners. Now work back through all the passives with the 1st passive and work an edge stitch on the other side (diag. 47).

Braid

To work a braid double-sided, more pins and pairs are needed. Two double gimp pairs must also be added.

Curves and bends

There are basically two ways of decreasing:
- decoratively
- 'decreasing 1,2,3' (meaning that 1, 2 or 3 pairs can be left unworked)

Decreasing decoratively is used mainly in the curves of braids or in decorative circles.

'Decreasing 1,2,3' is used mainly for very sharp curves (such as in the clover leaf, scrolls and circles) or when carrying pairs from one motif to another (for instructions see p.39).

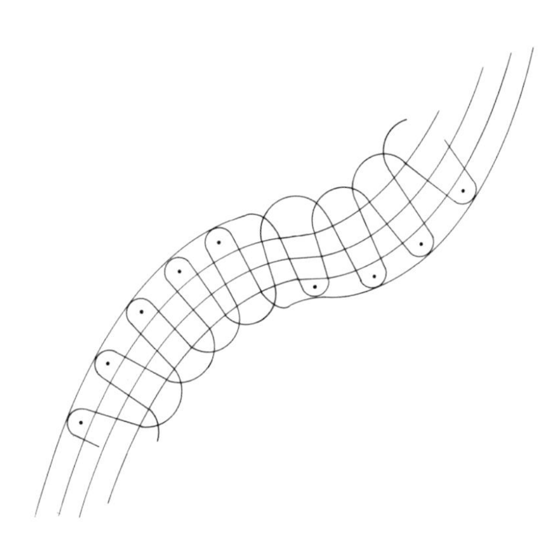

Diag. 47 *Changing the sides of the edge stitch in rib*

Decreasing decoratively
If the curve is only slight, set the pins a little further apart (diag. 48).
If the curve is sharp, leave the runners in front of the gimp pair on the inside of the work. Work back with the last used passives as runners (a support pin may be needed). Work an edge stitch in the next row. Repeat this where needed, but at regular intervals (diag. 49). Do not forget to take the support pin out after a few rows.

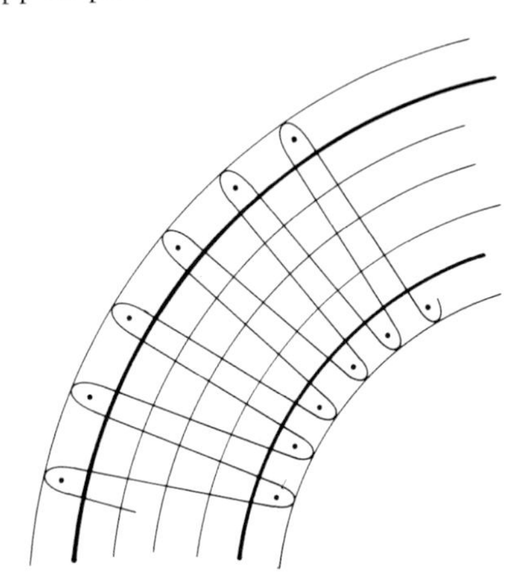

Diag. 48 *In a slight curve the pins are set wider apart*

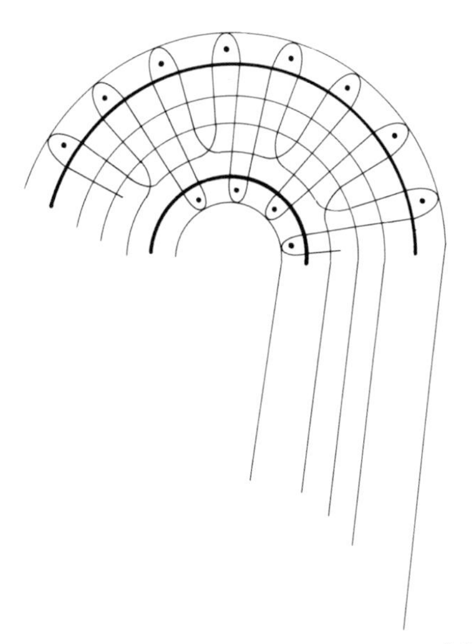

Diag. 49 *In a sharp curve the runners are left in front of the gimp pair. Last used passives will be used as runners*

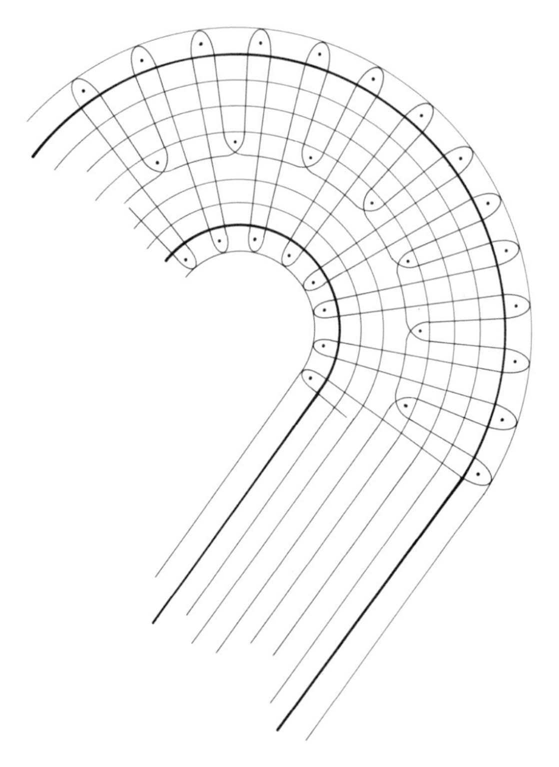

Diag. 50a *In a wide, curved braid, the runners are left in front of a certain number of pairs. Take the last used passives as runners*

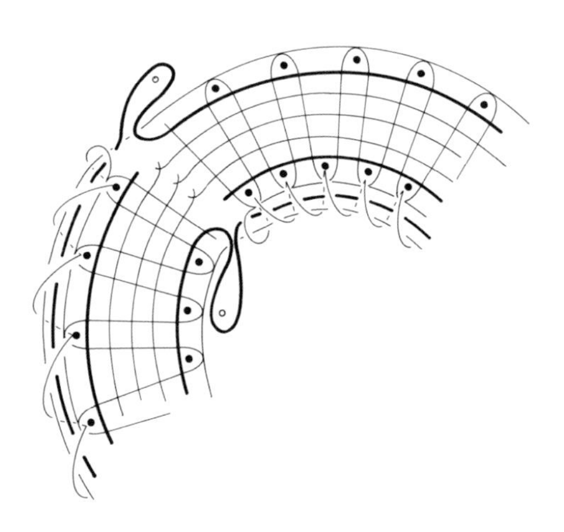

Diag. 50b *Closing and rolling of a braid set up double-sided*

If the braid is wider, leave the runners in front of a few pairs before the gimp pair. Set a support pin and continue in the same way as before. When a second support pin is set, take the first one out of the work. By doing this, tiny decorative holes are created (diag. 50a).

Pattern 5 – Elephant

Thread 140/2 **(for actual size see p.150)**

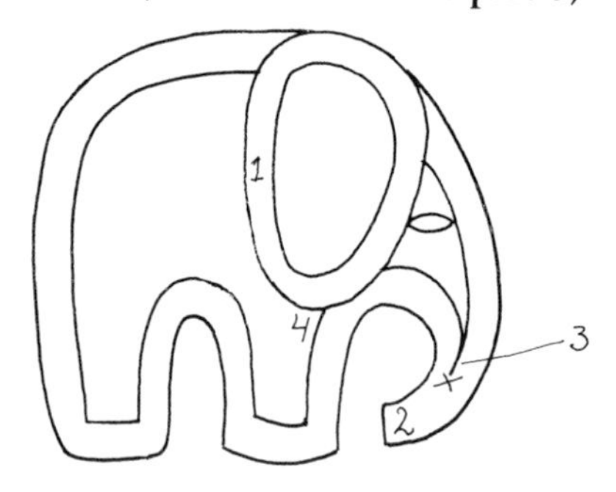

Start with the ear of the elephant (**1**). Use a double-sided setting up for the braid. When both ends meet, follow diagram 50b to close the ring and roll both sides of the braid. Take the gimp pairs round a support pin. Cut the loop off later. In this way, the gimp pairs will form a continuous line.

Use the straight setting up method at the end of the trunk (**2**) (diags. 6–9) and add double gimp pairs (diag. 12). Divide the braid in half at (*) (diag. 51). Add double gimp pairs and an edge pair on the inside of the braid (**3**). Follow diags. 48–50 to work the curves in the braid. When the ear is reached, sew some of the runners (diag. 52). Leave the gimp pair aside and roll back to the division of the trunk and leave these pairs there. Continue the braid with the rest of the pairs. Add a gimp pair and an edge pair on the other side of the ear (**4**) and finish the braid. Roll on both sides.

Return to the pairs left at the division of the trunk. Use 2 pairs of the bundle that was left, as an edge pair and a pair of runners to finish the braid. Roll.

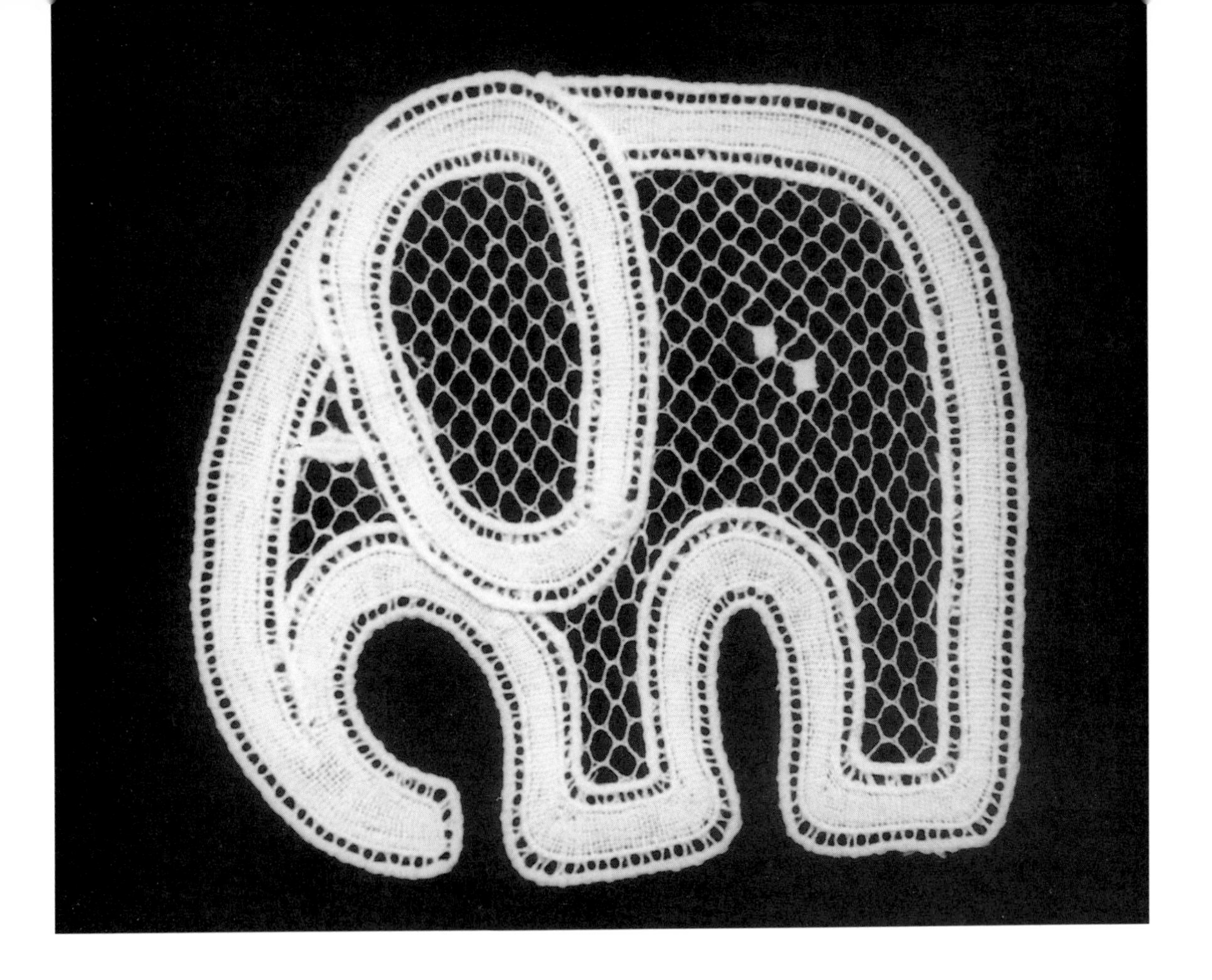

Work a leaf-shaped tally as an eye. The filling is point ground.

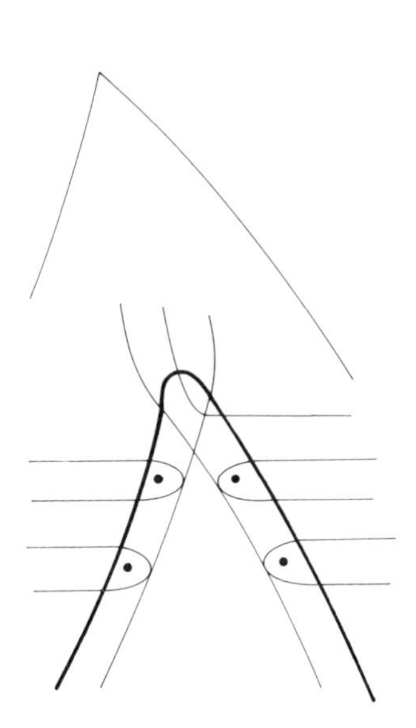

Diag. 51 *Division of a braid*

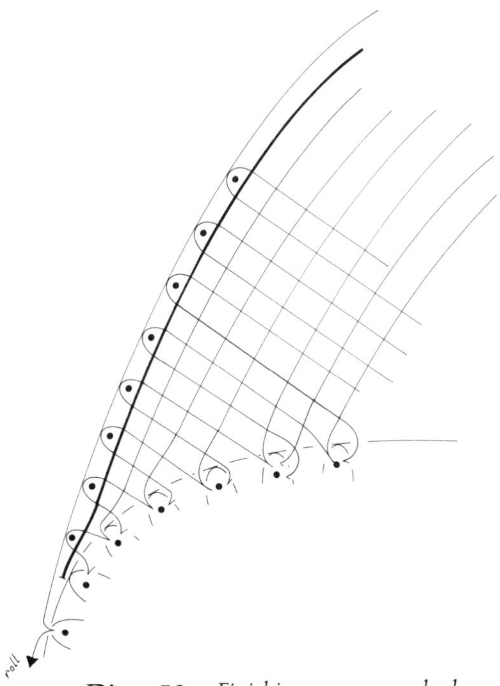

Diag. 52 *Finishing on a curved edge*

Pattern 6 – Mouse

Thread 140/2

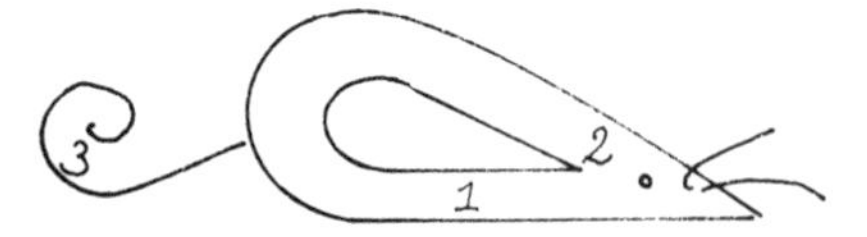

Set pins at (**1**) to start a double-sided setting up for the braid. Work both sides to (**2**) and join the two braids. Work a hole for the eye (diags. 53a & b) and finish at the point (diag. 37). Roll and work the tail, starting from (**3**). Add 2 pairs at the 1st pin-hole to roll the tail (diag. 54).

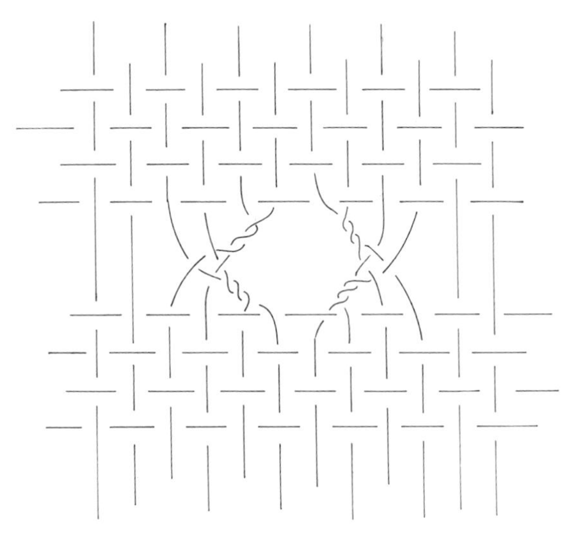

Diag. 53a *Mouse's eye shown in single threads*

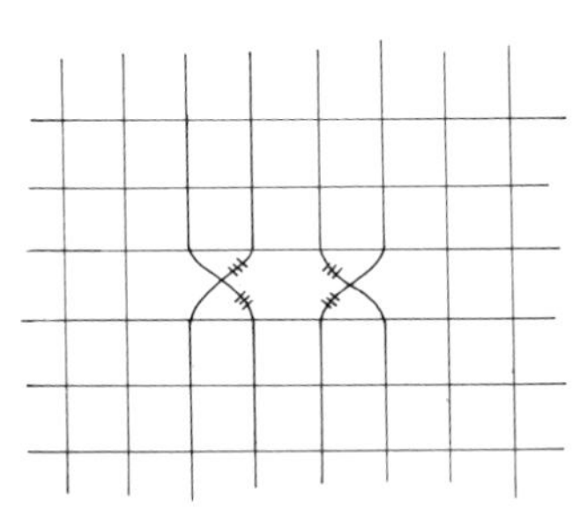

Diag. 53b *Mouse's eye shown in pairs*

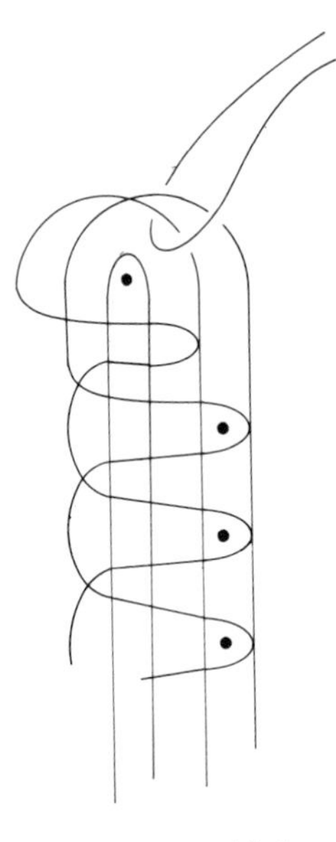

Diag. 54 *Two pairs are added at the first pin-hole to roll*

Pattern 7 – Baby bird I

Thread 120/2

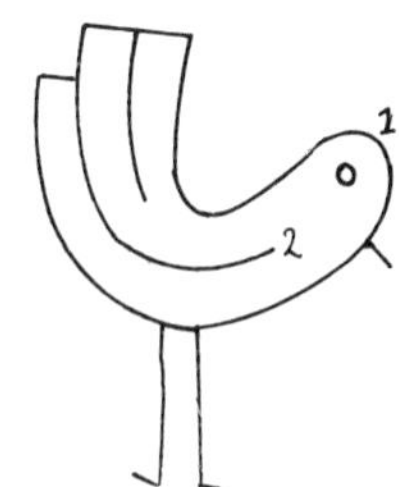

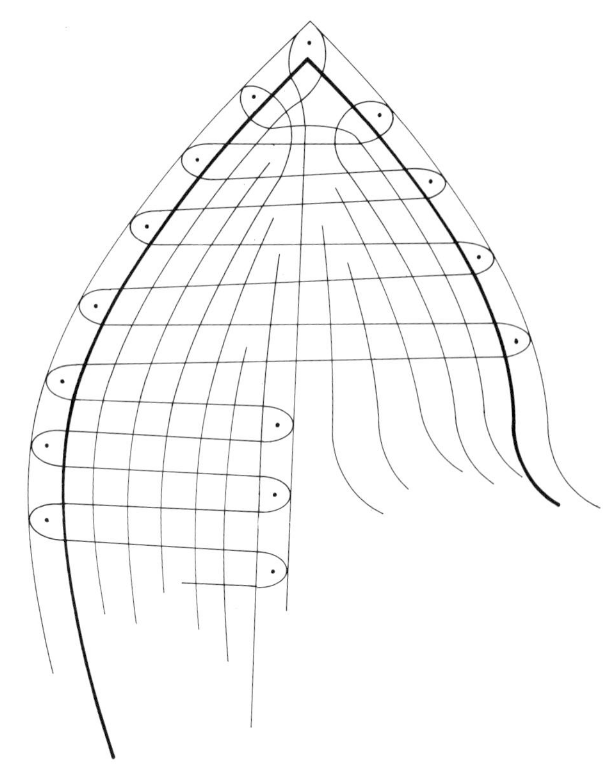

Commence with a round setting up at (**1**) as in diags. 28–30. Work an eye (diag. 53) and continue to (**2**). Work the top half first, leaving aside the pairs on the right-hand side. Using an edge pair as in diag. 55, work the curve (diag. 49) and finish with a straight edge as in diag. 17. Roll back (diag. 18) to (**2**).

Diag. 55 *One side of the leaf is worked first*

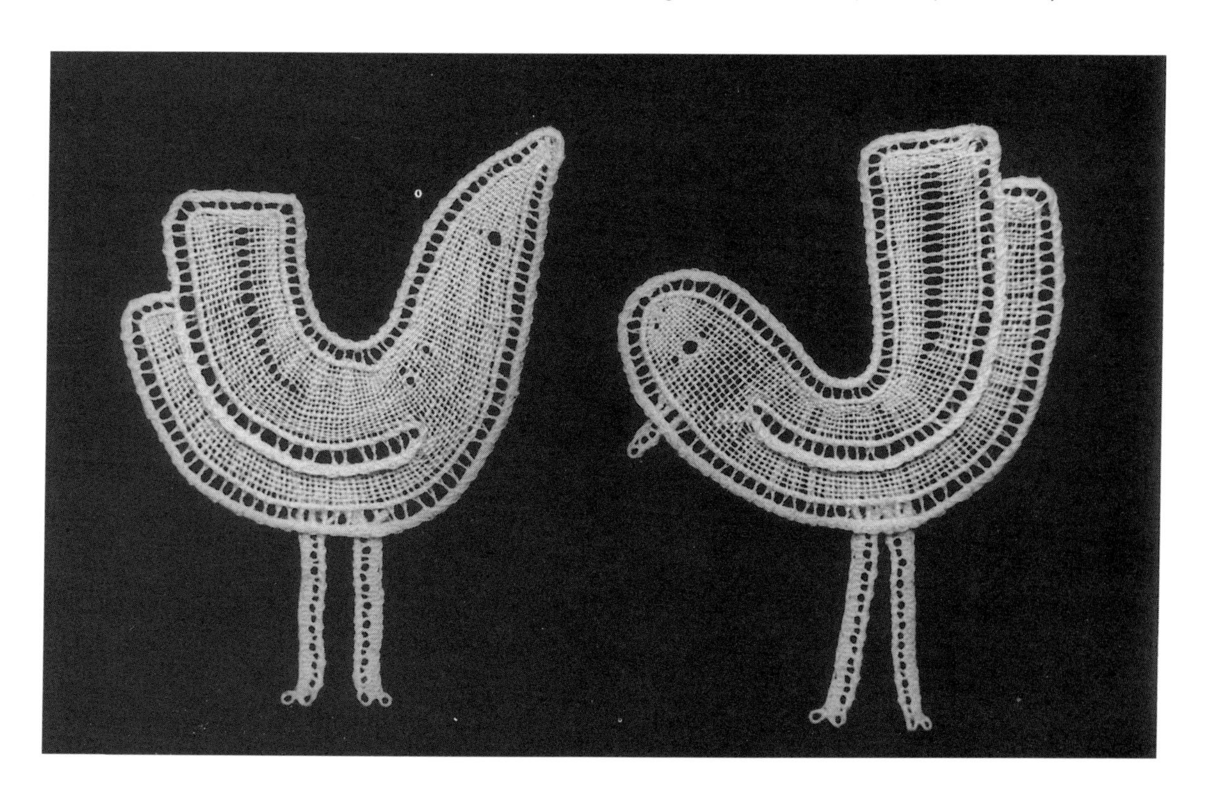

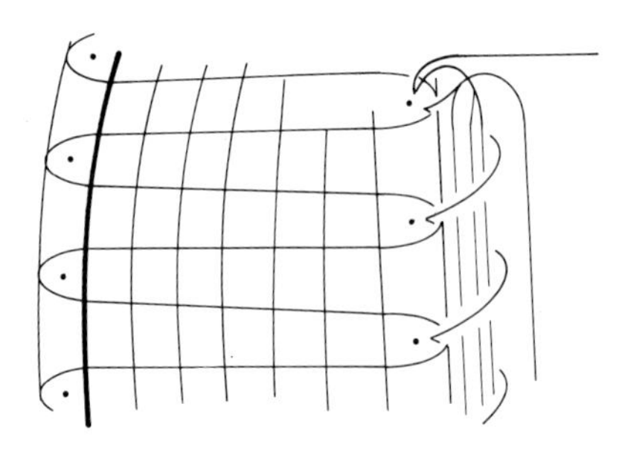

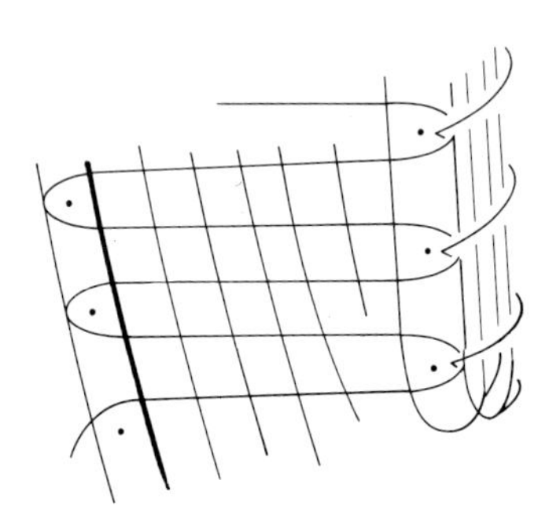

Diag. 56 *Roll along the edge with edge pair and next passives, making 2 sewings at the top*

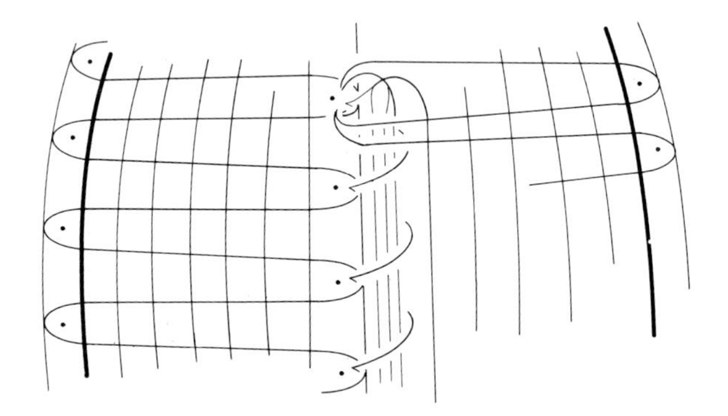

Diag. 57 *Pairs of the other side are picked up*

Pick up the pairs that were left here (diags. 56–57) and work the bottom half of the bird, finishing with a straight edge. Roll.

A rib is worked using only 4 pairs for the beak. Add 2 pairs on the first pin-hole to make a roll (diag. 54).
For the legs, set one pin. Hang 4 pairs round it and join the pairs in as for the straight setting up. Hang 2 pairs round the 2nd pin. Twist these pairs 7 times and work a whole stitch (diag. 58). There are now 6 pairs. Work in whole stitch with the 5th pair to the outside. Leave the runners before working the last pair. Take the last used passives and work these back in whole stitch through all the pairs. Leave the runners twisted once. Take the 5th pair back to the other side and work an edge stitch. Continue and sew into the body. Roll. The 2nd leg is now worked in the same way, but facing the other side.

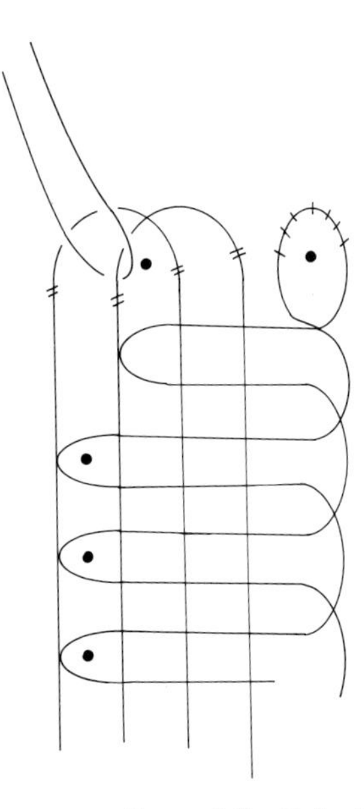

Diag. 58 *Legs of the Baby Birds*

Pattern 8 – Baby bird II
Thread 120/2

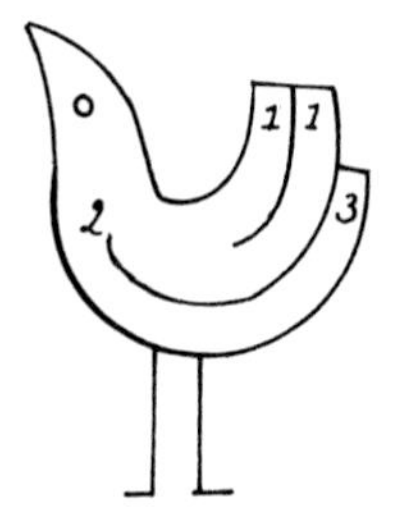

Work a straight setting up at (**1**) (diags. 6–9). Work the curve as in diag. 48. Continue to (**2**). Roll back (diag. 56) to (**3**) and use the pairs of the bundle to work the straight setting up. Add a gimp pair and work towards (**2**). Make sure the direction of the runners is the same as for the top half. At (**2**) the runners are sewn into the last pin-hole in the centre and used as passives. Continue both halves as one (diag. 59). The curve is worked as in diag. 50a. Work an eye (diag. 53). Take out pairs and finish at the point (diag. 37). Roll the bird. The legs are worked in the same way as in Pattern 7.

Diag. 59 *Runners are sewn into the the last pin-hole and used as passives*

Pattern 9 – Baby bird III
Thread 120/2

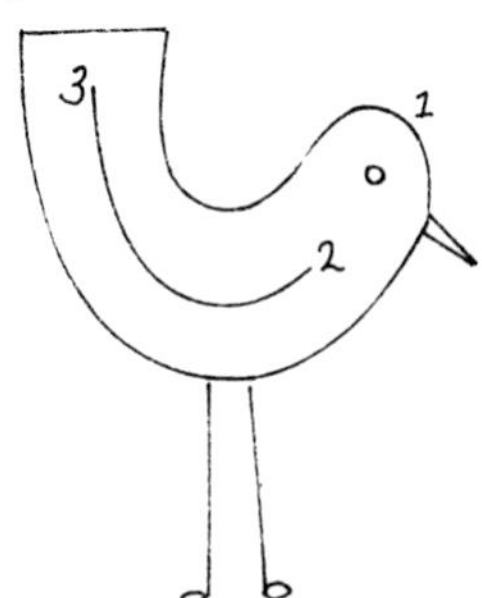

Start at (**1**) using a round setting up (diags. 28–30) and add pairs where necessary (diag. 31). Work as far as (**2**) and continue with the bottom half, taking up an edge pair (diag. 55). Continue to (**3**). Leave the runners on the outside and roll back to (**2**) (diag. 56). Pick up the pairs that were left (diag. 57) and work the top half. Work the curve as in diag. 49. Plaits could be added for decoration if desired (diag. 103). At (**3**) the runners are sewn into the centre pin-hole and used as passives. Work both sides and finish with a straight edge (diag. 17). Roll (diag. 18). For beak and legs, see Pattern 7.

Pattern 10– Baby bird IV
Thread 120/2

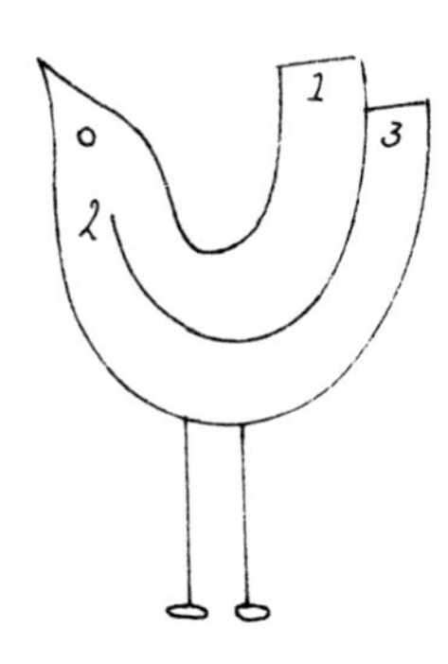

Start with a straight setting up (diags. 6–9) at (**1**). Work the curve as in diag. 49 and continue to (**2**). Roll back to (**3**) and use the pairs to work a straight setting up. Add a gimp pair. Work the bottom half, making sewings along the edge.

Sew the runners into the last centre pin-hole and use this pair as passives. Continue both sides, taking out pairs as necessary. Work the eye (diag. 53) and finish at the point (diag. 37). Roll the bird. For the legs, see Pattern 7.

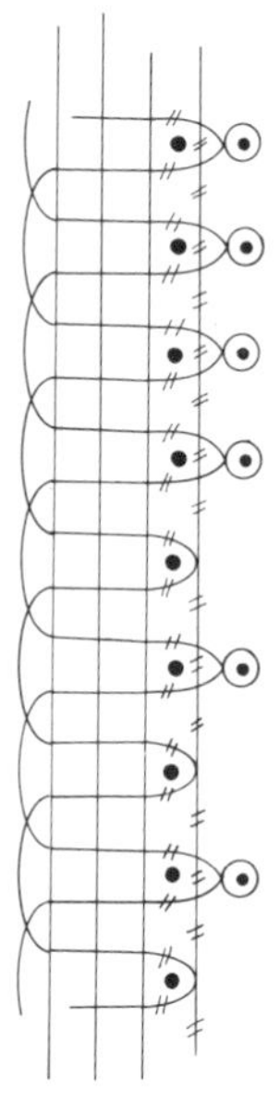

Diag. 60 *Rib with picots*

Pattern 11 – Baby bird V

Thread 120/2

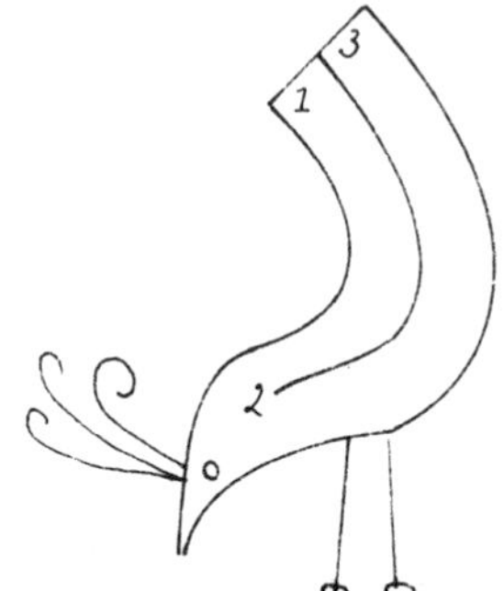

Work the straight setting up at (**1**) (diags. 6–9). Decorative holes could be made in the curve if desired, following diagram 85 (p.48). Continue to (**2**); roll back to (**3**) and work a straight setting up to commence the bottom half. At (**2**) the runners are sewn into the last centre pin-hole (diag. 59).

Work both sides. Take out pairs as necessary, work the eye (diag. 53), and finish at the point (diag. 37). The feathers are ribs with picots (diag. 60).

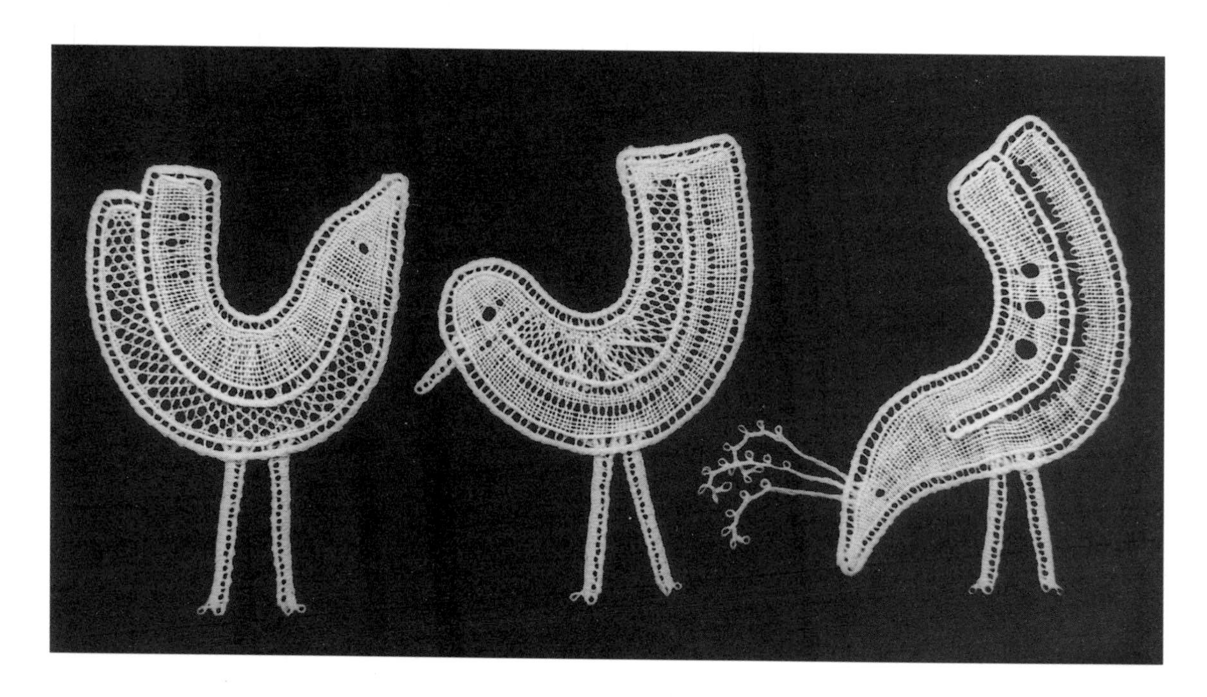

Pattern 12 – Pram

Thread 120/2

(for actual size see p.150)

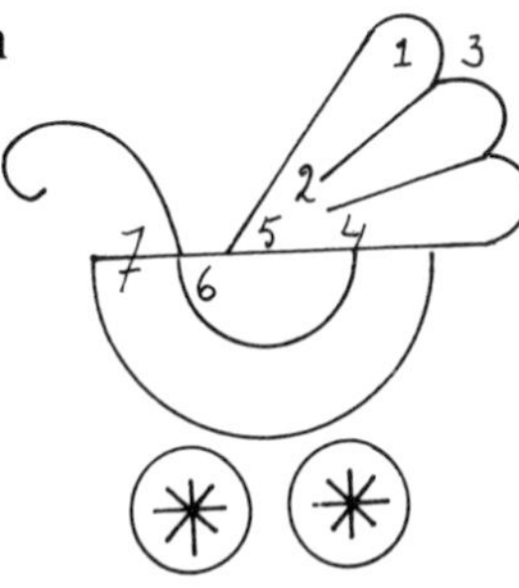

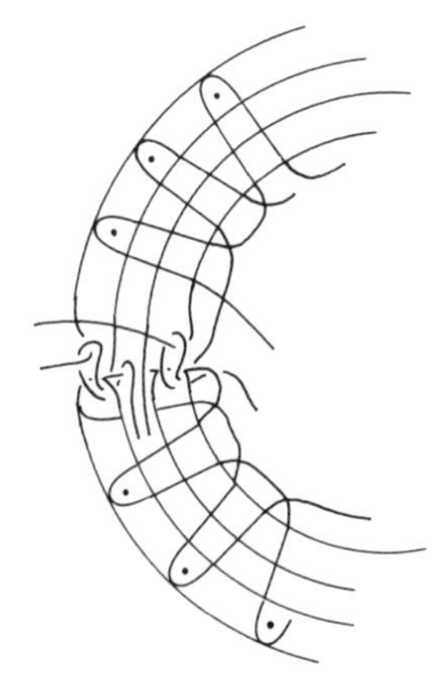

Diag. 61 *Closing a rib*

Start with a round setting up at (**1**) (diags. 28–30) and work as far as (**2**). Roll back with the runners and the gimp pair (diag. 56) to (**3**). Make 2 sewings in the last pin-hole. Set 2 pins in the curve and hang 2 pairs round each pin. Work the narrow setting up (diags. 25–27), starting with an edge pair from the bundle. Work the gimp pair in whole stitch and leave it next to the edge pair. Work to (**4**), sew the runners in the last pin-hole (diag. 59); leave them there as passives. Again, using the edge pair and runners at (**4**), roll back. Work this part in the same manner as the second. Check the work at (**2**) and (**4**) is level. When the runners have been sewn in at (**4**) (diag. 59), take the runner from the other side and finish at point (**5**) (diag. 37), taking out pairs (see round setting up). Use pairs from the bundle together with pairs that were taken out to work the rib to (**6**); roll. Start with a straight setting up (**7**) using pairs from the bundle (diags. 6–9) and add one gimp pair. Sew into the rib at regular distances apart. Roll.

Work ribs for the wheels (see Flower and diag. 61); roll and work another rib for the handle; roll.

Pattern 13 – Surfer
Thread 120/2

(for actual size see p.150)

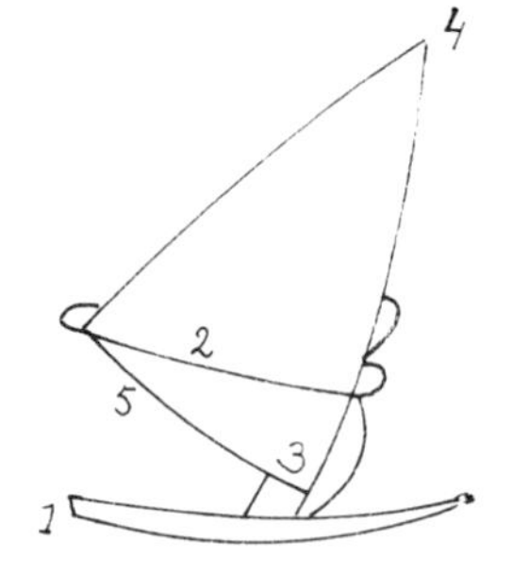

Set up at (**1**) and work a narrow braid starting with 2 pins. Roll. Set up at (**2**) and make a double-sided rib (diag. 44), working towards both edges. Leave the pairs hanging.

Set up at (**3**) and work a rib to (**4**). Roll back. Use the pairs to start a straight setting up at (**5**) (diags. 6–9). Pairs have to be taken out towards the point (see Round setting up). Finish at the point (diag. 37). Roll. Now the rib (**3**) can be finished. For the surfer, sew in a few pairs. Finish and roll.

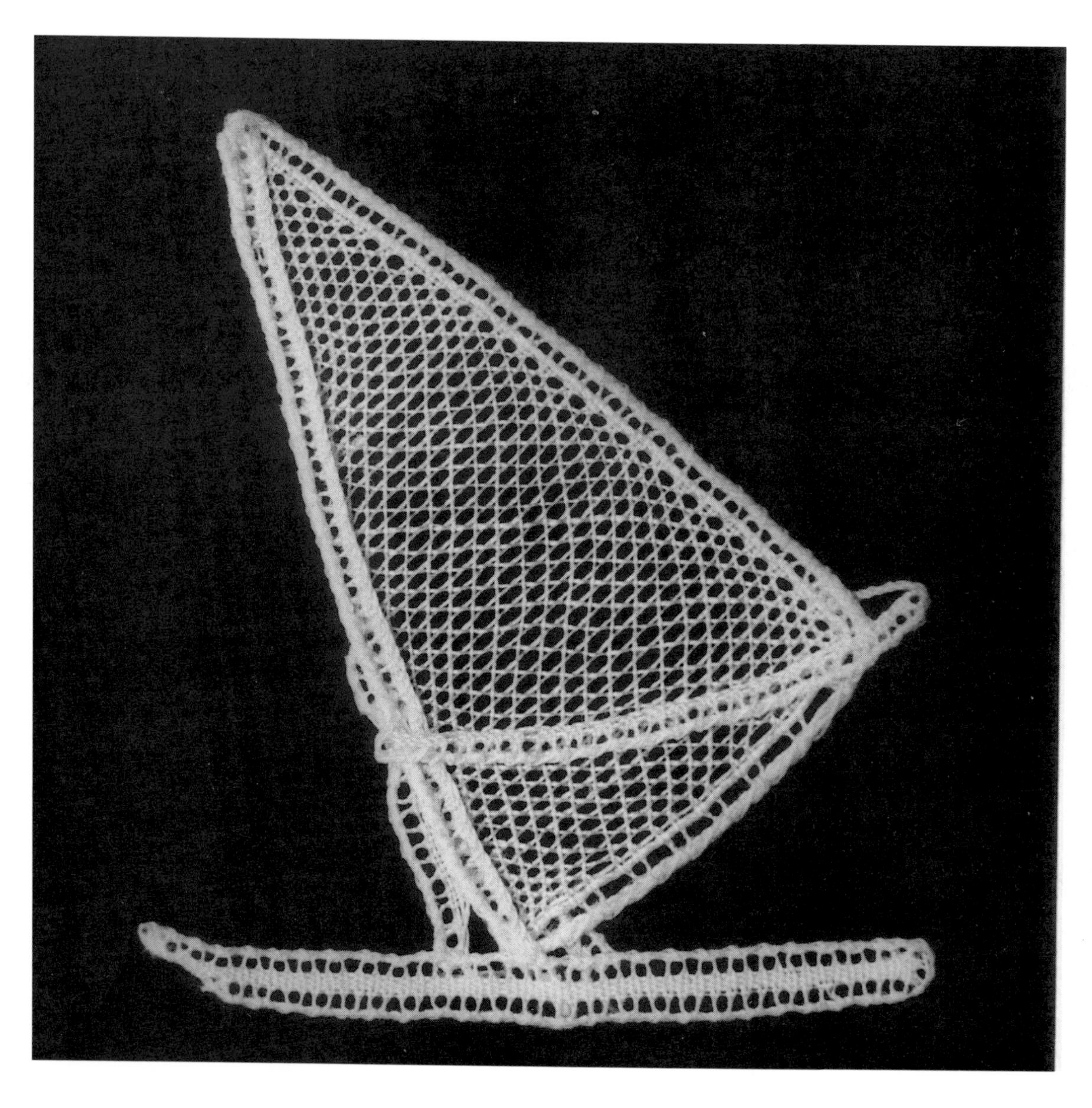

2. Flowers

Pattern 14 – Flower Centre
Thread 100/2

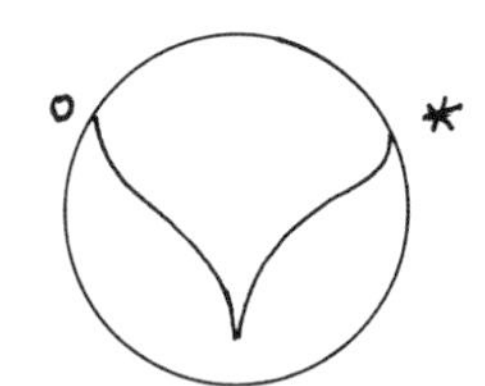

Set 2 pins at (*) to start the rib. At (**0**) add as many pairs as needed when the rib widens. Work the edge stitch at the outside. On the inside there are various choices of stitch, including straight edge stitch, twisting twice round a pin, and a picot edge. Take out pairs where necessary and add them again on the other side. It might be necessary to work the curve as in diag. 49 or 50. Make sure you finish with the same number of pairs with which you started. Close the ring (diag. 61).

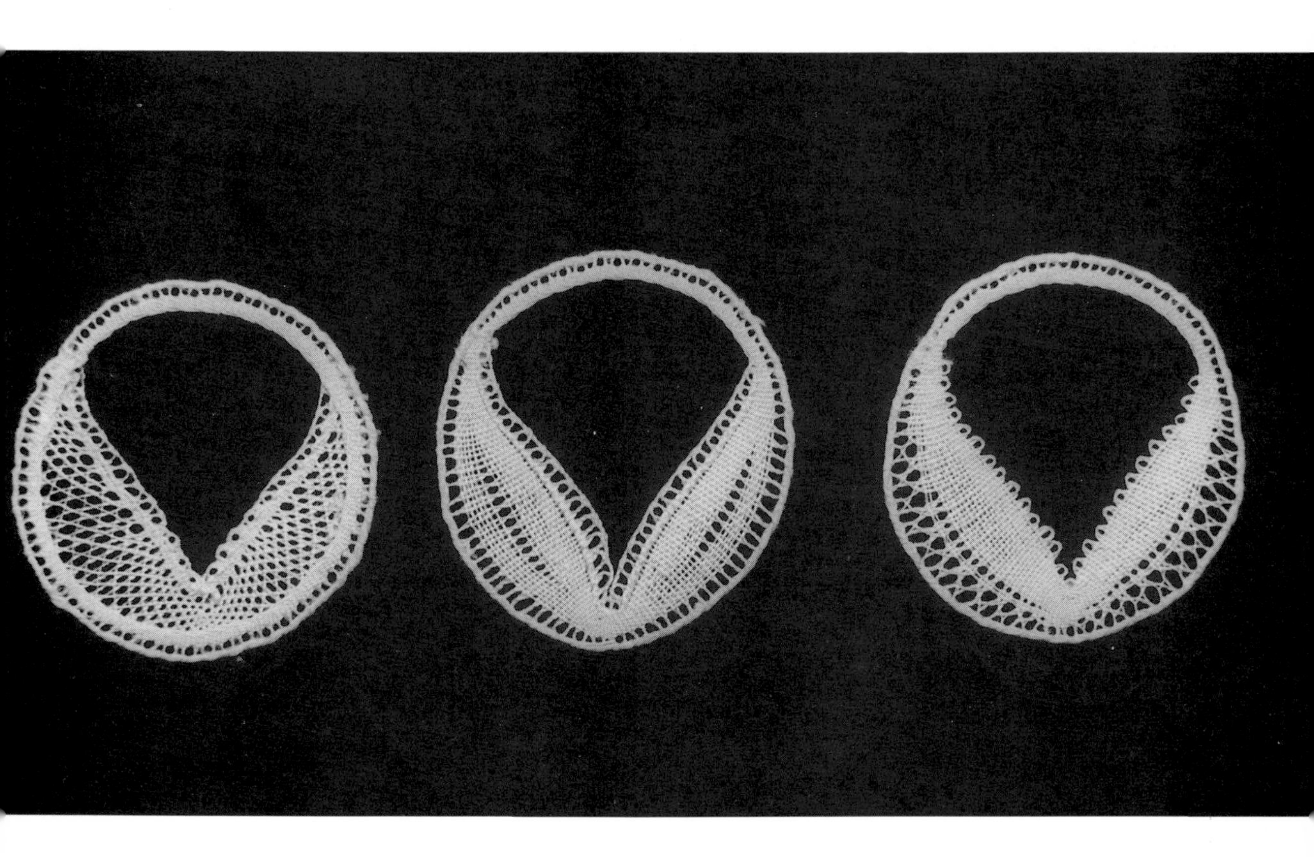

Pattern 15 – Flower

Thread 120/2

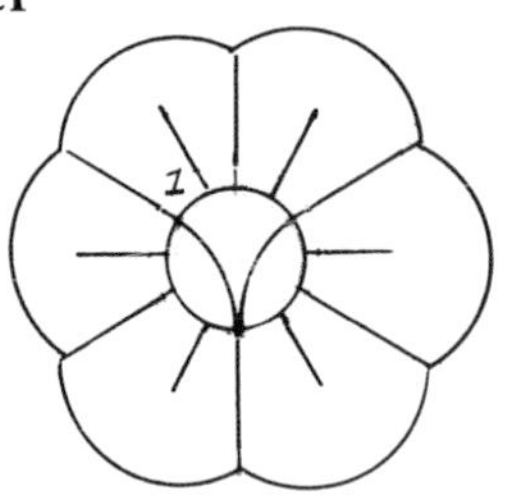

Work centre first (the rib). Set up with 2 pins using 6 pairs in the same way as the braids. The pins of the rib are set in the inner circle. After setting the 1st pin, work to the right. Leave the runners on this side (this pair may be twisted once). Work back with the 2nd pair on the right to the left and edge stitch; pin. Continue in this way until the ring can be closed as follows. Leaving the runners on the right-hand side, sew the 5th pair (from the left) through the 2nd pin-hole and take the 4th pair through the loop. With the 4th pair from the left, whole stitch through all pairs to the left without making the edge stitch. Twist the runners twice and leave them to make the edge pair of the petal. Sew the 3rd pair through the 1st pin-hole and the 2nd pair through the loop. The ring is now closed (diag. 61).

CARRYING PAIRS ACROSS FROM RIB TO PETAL (TRANSFERRING)

Add a gimp pair between the 1st and 2nd pairs on the left-hand side. Work from right to left in half stitch if the flower is worked in half stitch (whole stitch if the flower is to be worked in whole stitch) as far as the gimp pair. This is

always worked in whole stitch. Make an edge stitch and set the 1st pin on the horizontal line.

Decreasing 1,2,3 (see also p.27)
Work back to right and leave the runners there – 1st passive pair (1).
Work back to left, edge stitch and set 2nd pin.
Work back to right, leave the runners there – 2nd passive pair (2).
Work back to left, edge stitch and set 3rd pin.
Work back to right and leave the runners there – 3rd passive pair (3).
Looking at diagram 62 the pairs are – from right to left:

1st, 2nd and 3rd passives (1, 2 and 3)
runners (r)
passive pair (pp)
gimp pair (gp)
edge pair (ep), with 3 pins on the horizontal line.

If needed, more pairs have to be added now. Set as many pins as you need next to the 3 pins on the horizontal line. Hang 2 pairs round each pin. Work a whole stitch with the edge pair and the right-hand pair on the new pin, and twist both pairs twice. Put the left-hand pair round the pin and continue setting up from right to left (diag. 63).

The gimp pair is always next to the edge pair. Work this pair across in whole stitch. Next to the gimp pair is the passive pair, not yet used. Now work this pair in half stitch (whole stitch for a whole stitch flower). Work these runners in half stitch (or whole stitch) to the edge. Make the edge stitch and set the pin in the curve.

Check whether there are enough pairs in the work. If necessary, add a pair on the 1st or 2nd pin next to the rib. Work in half stitch back to the rib and make the first sewing. Take the thread that runs across the work through the pin-hole. Then put the other bobbin of this pair through the loop. Twist once and work back to the edge. Make at least 2 sewings in each hole and 3 where necessary. Take care that the spread is even.

When the pin has been set between two petals, put the runners aside and work in whole stitch

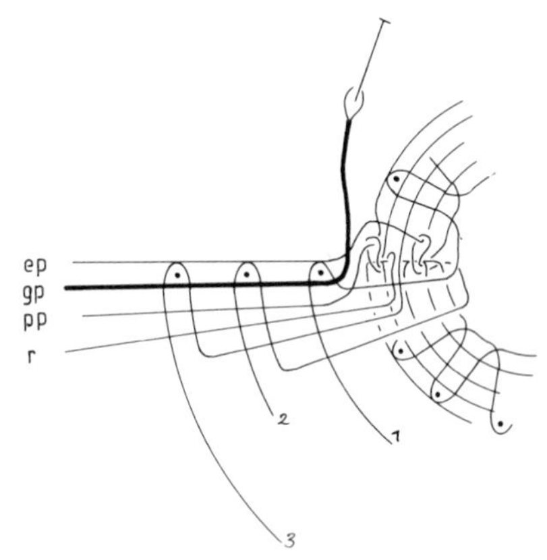

Diag. 62 *Carrying pairs across from rib to petal*

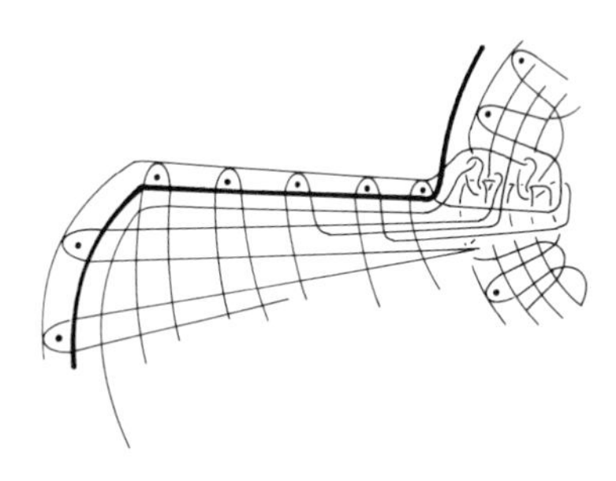

Diag. 63 *New pairs are added on new setting up pins*

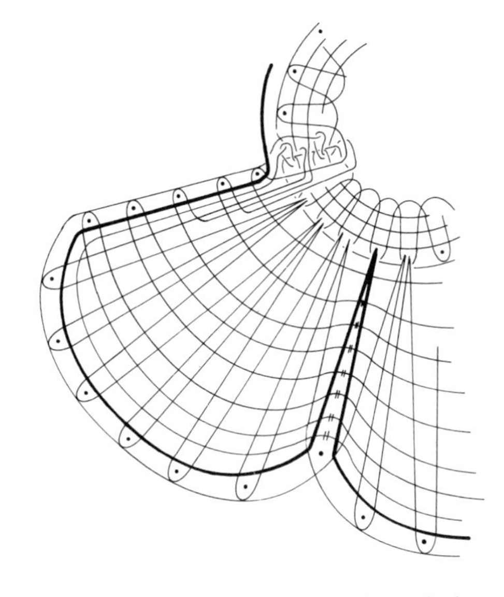

Diag. 64 *At the division of each petal, the passives are twisted twice*

with the gimp pair to the rib. Take the fine thread through the pin-hole and the other thread through the loop. Twist once. All the passives are then twisted twice before the gimp pair works back to its original position. Pick up the runners and continue (diag. 64).
Work each petal in this way.

FINISHING

When the last pin has been set, leave the runners on the outside. Work the gimp pair to the rib and leave it there. All the passives may be twisted once. Start sewing from the inside to the outside, one pair at a time. An even spread is very important. Tie each pair with a reef knot (diag. 65). After tying, the pairs that will be used for rolling have to be bundled. If the gimp pair is used as well, put this pair round a pin into the bundle (diag. 66).

Finish the roll, put the bundle across the work and sew into the side loop of the first pin-hole. Tie one thread of the bundle with the thread that was used for rolling (diag. 67). Do not cut off any pairs before you have made sure that they cannot be transferred to another part of the pattern.

VARIATIONS

Flower with decorative picots

This flower may be worked either in half stitch or whole stitch. The rib in each petal has an uneven number of pins. Work a picot at the centre pin (diag. 68). Transfer the pairs from the rib to the petal. Work the petal as far as the picot and leave the runners on the inside. Return to the outside with the last used passives as runners. Repeat this until the number of sewings required after the picot is the same as the number already worked before. Each petal is worked in this way (diag. 69).

Flower with half stitch plait as a vein

Mark the position of the vein. Work the runners to here. Set a support pin and work a half stitch plait together with the next passives up to the rib. As the plait has to be sewn first, the other passives need to be laid back. Take one pair of the plait through the pin-hole, and pass the other through the loop. Replace the passives that were laid back. One pair of the plait is to be used as passives and the other pair will be the runners. Continue the petal (diags. 70–71).

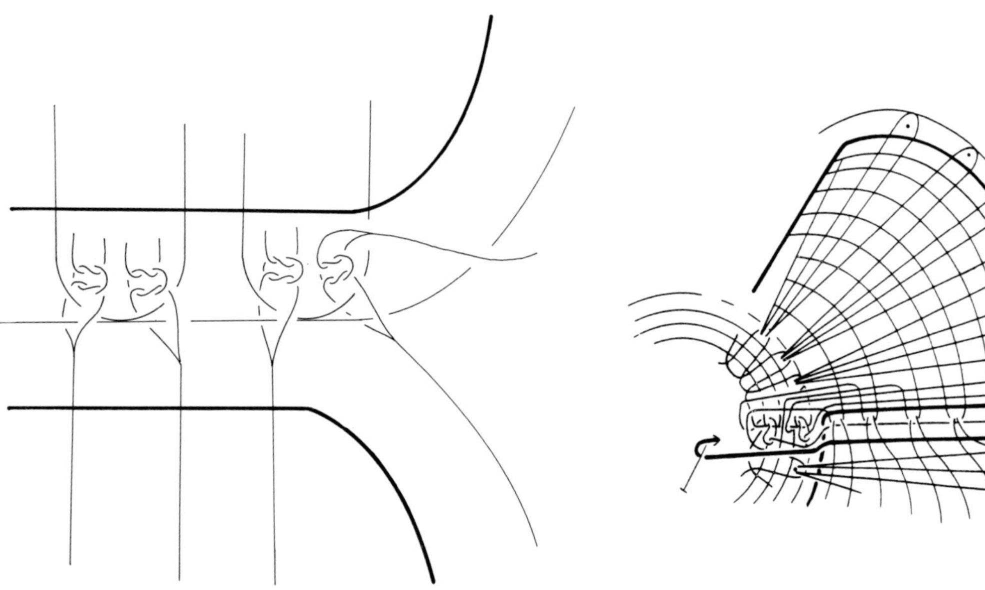

Diag. 65 *Reef knot, to tie the pairs*

Diag. 66 *Gimp pair is taken into the bundle*

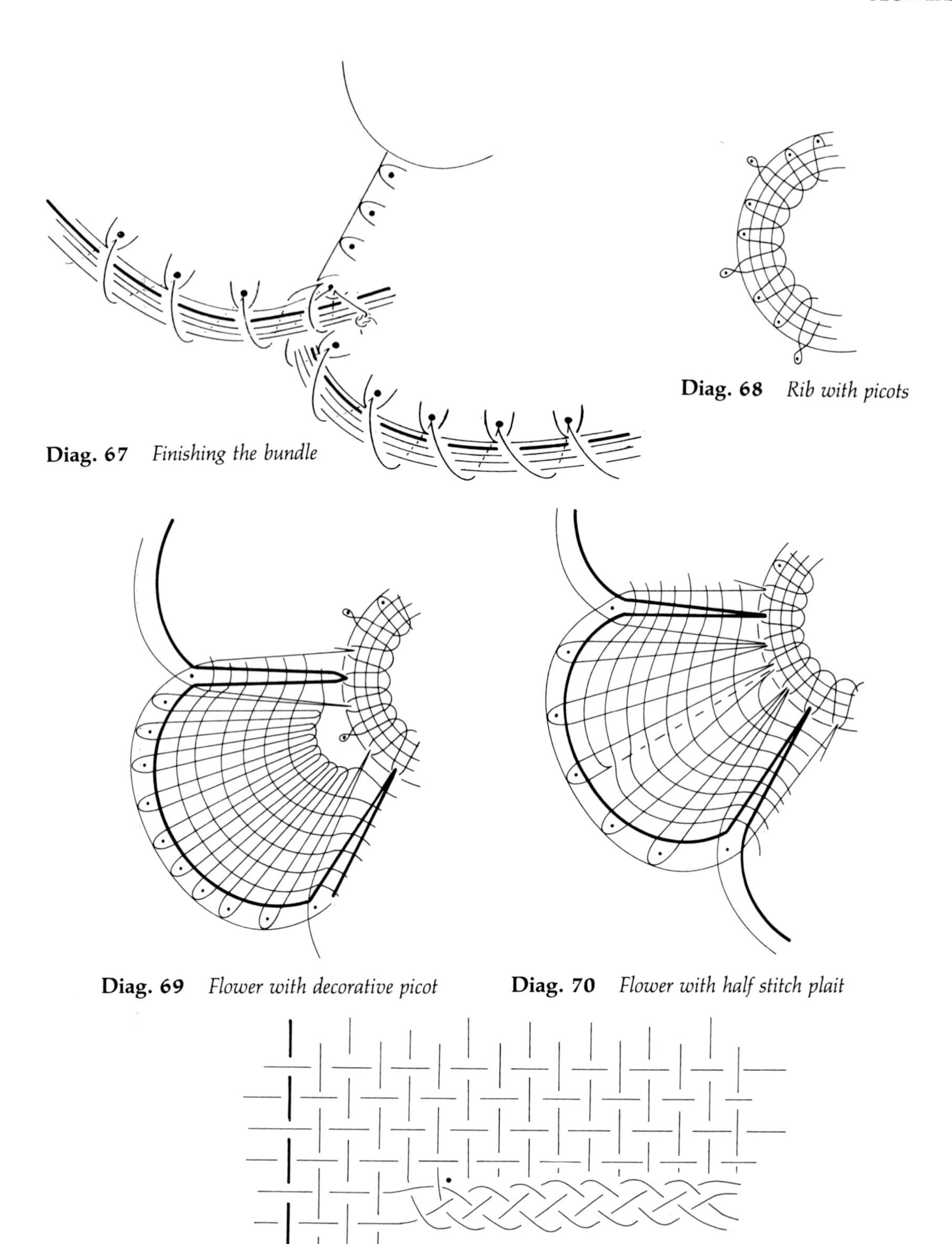

Diag. 67 *Finishing the bundle*

Diag. 68 *Rib with picots*

Diag. 69 *Flower with decorative picot*

Diag. 70 *Flower with half stitch plait*

Diag. 71 *Half stitch plait in petal, shown in single threads*

Flower in whole stitch with open vein – 1

Mark the position of the vein. When the work reaches this point, twist the passives (diags. 72–73) and continue working.

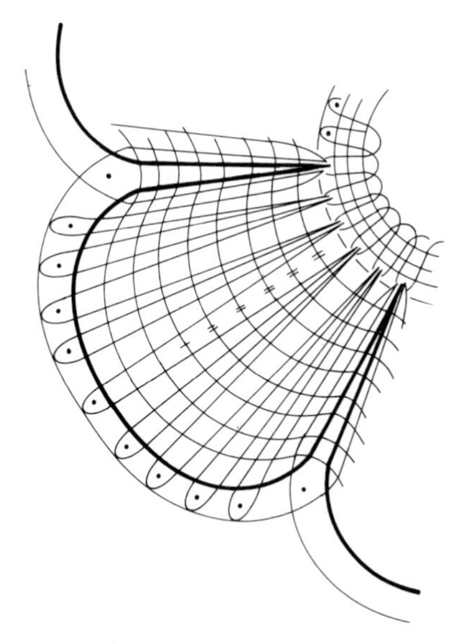

Diag. 72 *Flower showing twisted passives*

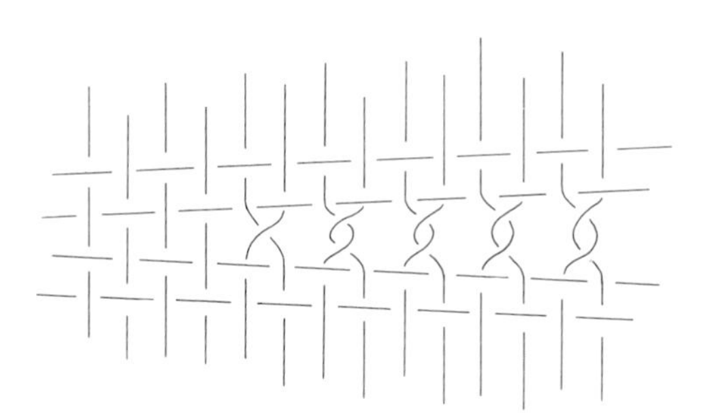

Diag. 73 *Twisted passives, shown in single threads*

Flower in whole stitch with open vein – 2

Mark the position of the vein. When the work reaches this point, starting with the pairs next to the rib, set a pin between the 1st and 2nd passive pairs. Twist both pairs twice; whole stitch; twist twice and set another pin between them. Repeat this as required. At the outside of the petal, the runners will work through the pairs that are not used in this way. Set a pin; twist the runners twice; work back to the outside; edge stitch (diags. 74–75). Continue the petal.

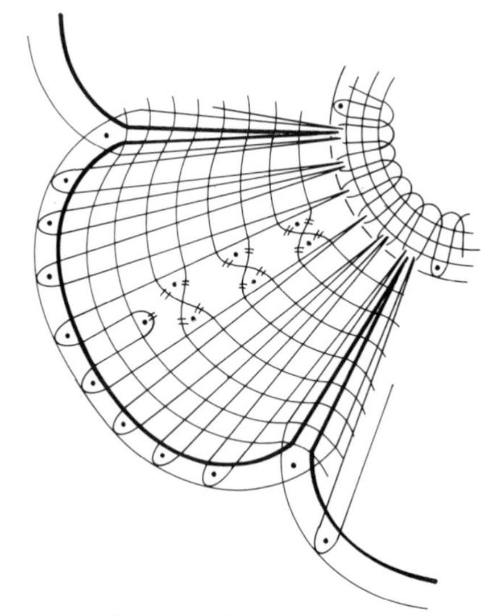

Diag. 74 *Flower with open vein and whole stitch in passives*

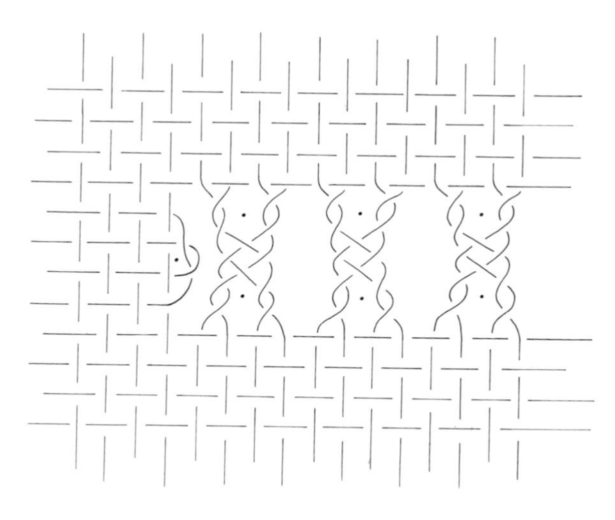

Diag. 75 *Open vein shown in single threads*

Flower with hole – 1

Mark the position of the hole. At this place, twist the runners and passives twice to form the hole (diags. 76–77).

Flower with hole – 2

Mark the position of the hole. Four pairs of passives are used for the hole. Twist the two centre pairs once. Work a whole stitch with the 2 left-hand pairs and another with the 2 right-hand pairs. Twist the 2 centre pairs once more (diags. 78–79). Continue the petal.

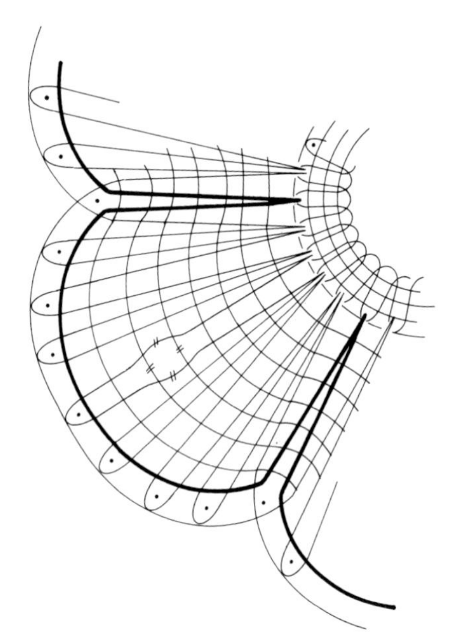

Diag. 76 *Flower with decorative hole*

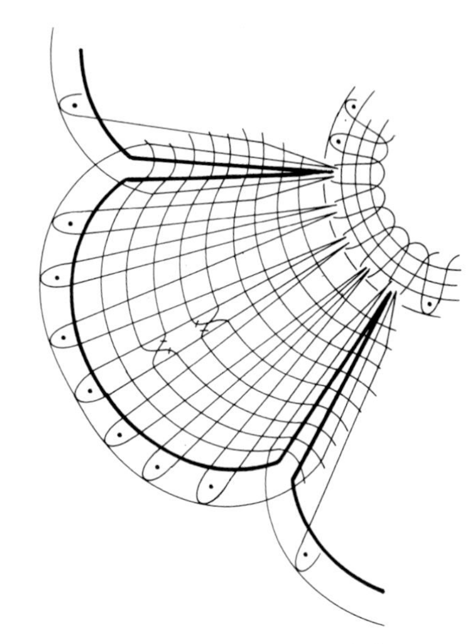

Diag. 78 *Flower with decorative hole*

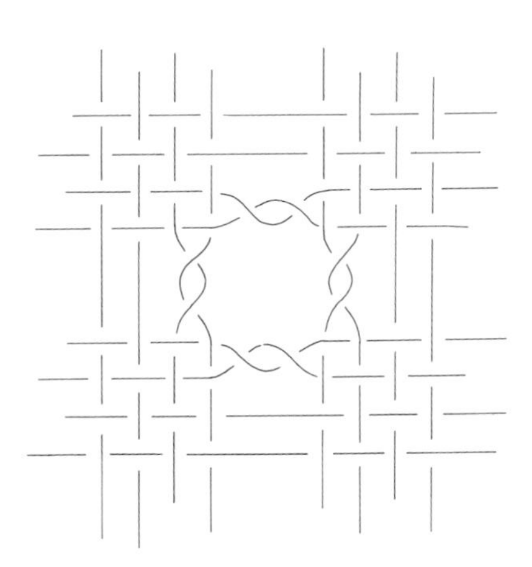

Diag. 77 *Decorative hole shown in single threads*

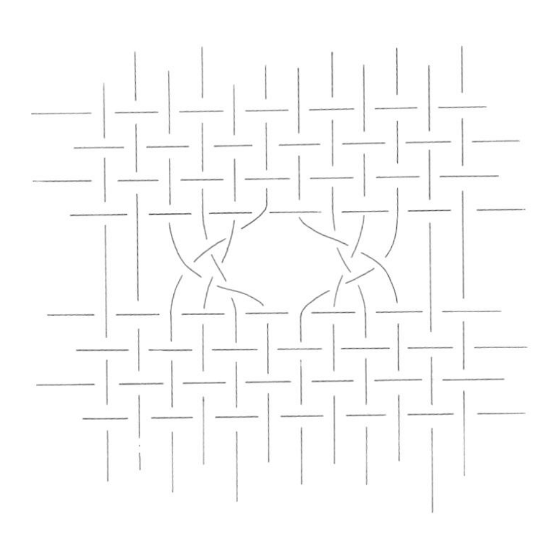

Diag. 79 *Decorative hole shown in single threads*

Pattern 16 – Flower with picots
Thread 180/2

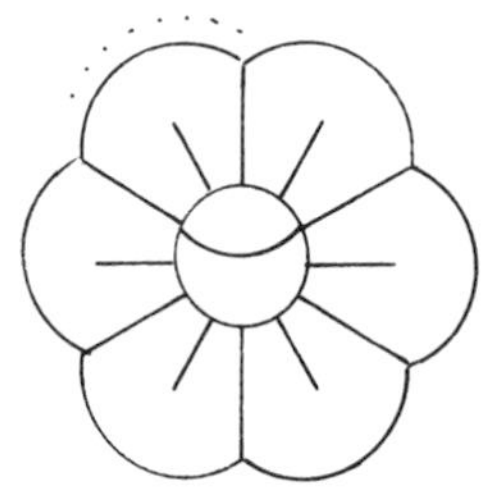

Work the centre of the flower first in the same way as a berry (see Pattern 55, p.91), but instead of sewing into a rib, twist the runners twice round the pin. Roll the centre and transfer the pairs to the petals. The 3 outside pairs are worked in whole stitch and the others in half stitch. Before changing into whole stitch one extra twist is made, which gives an attractive effect.

Work and finish the flower in the usual way. Roll and use the pairs to work a rib round the flower, of which the outside stitch is a half stitch with a picot edge (see diag. 80).

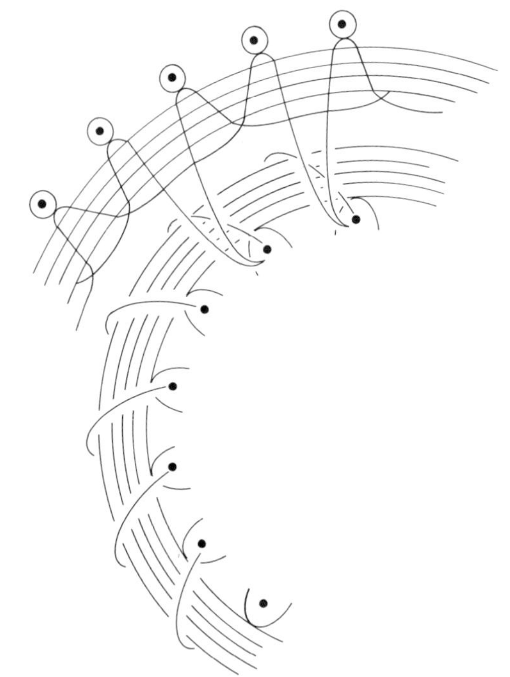

Diag. 80 *Adding a rib to a rolled edge*

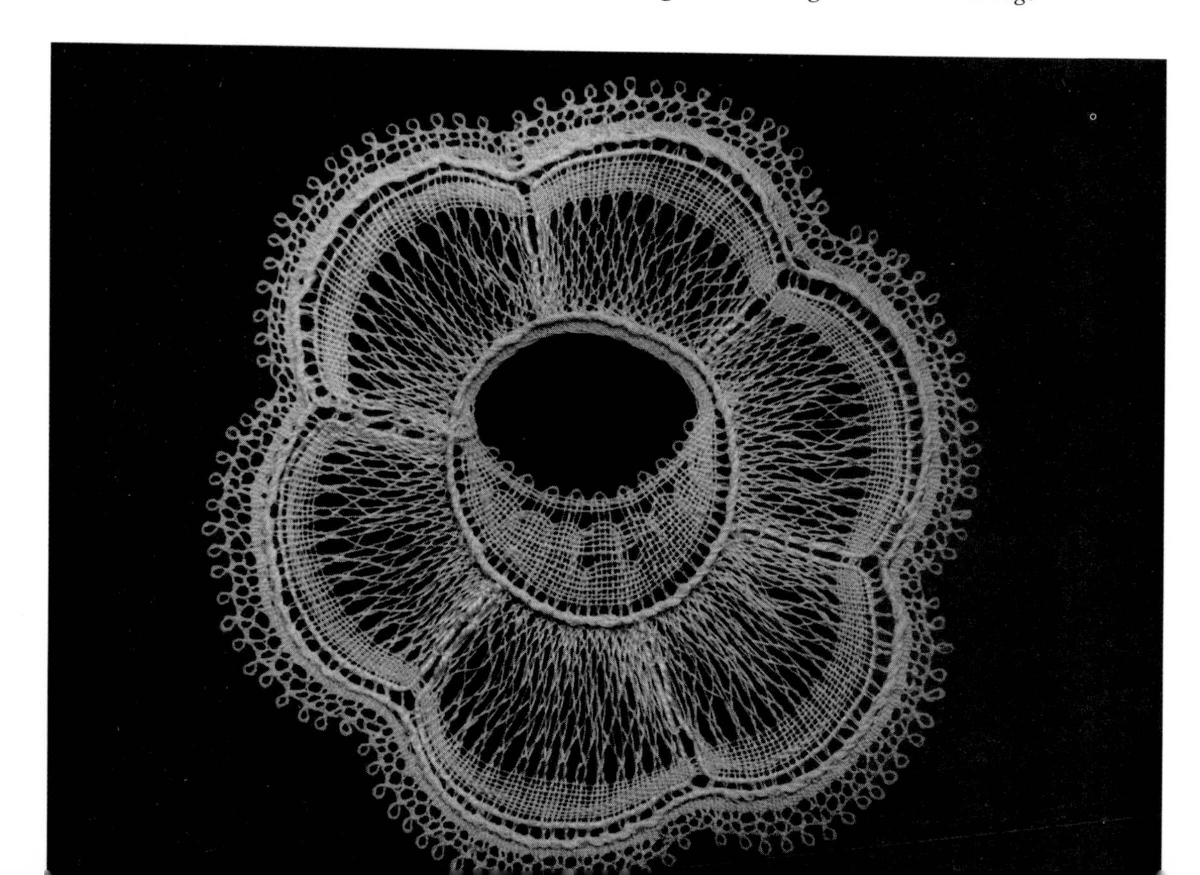

Pattern 17 – Butterfly flower

Thread 180/2

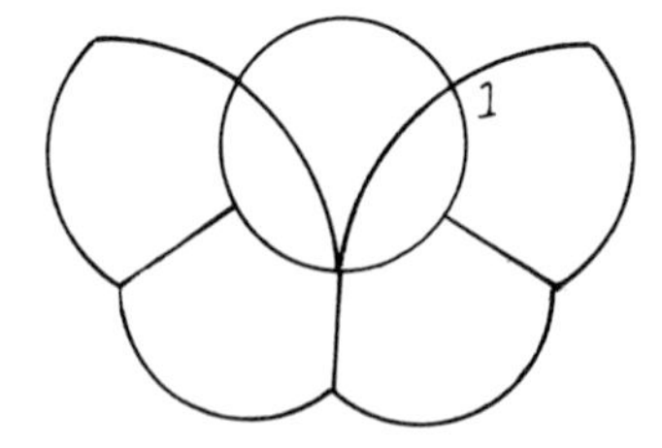

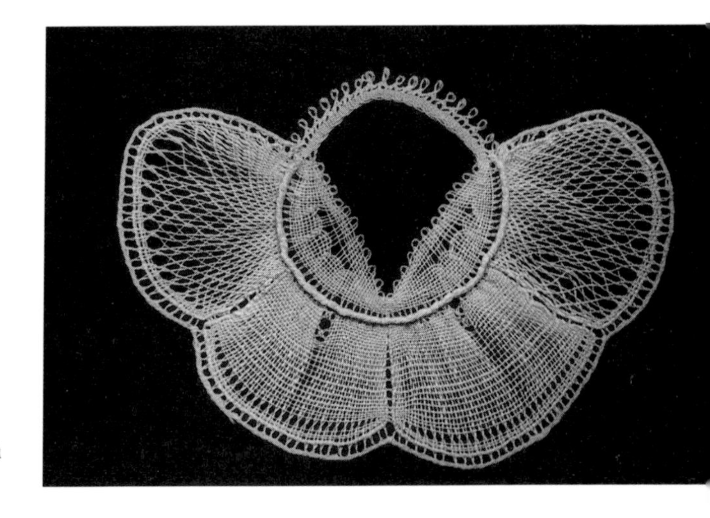

Start with the centre, using the flower centre described in Pattern 14. As picots are to be worked at the top of the centre, only the bottom part will be rolled.

Transfer the pairs to the petals as described in Pattern 15. All 6 pairs needed for the rib will probably not have been used to roll and, therefore, more pairs will now need to be added. The first petal is worked in half stitch. The 2nd and 3rd petals are worked in whole stitch, so extra pairs must be added (diag. 81) as soon as the 2nd petal is started, and must be taken out at the end of the 3rd (diag. 82). The 4th petal is worked in half stitch. To finish with an edge stitch all round this petal, several sewings must be made into the rib; and pairs must be taken out to decrease the number of pairs, enabling you to finish at point (**1**) (diag. 83).

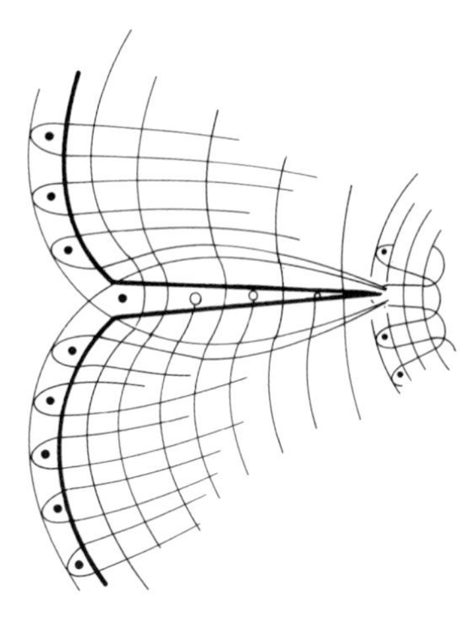

Diag. 81 *Adding pairs in a whole stitch petal*

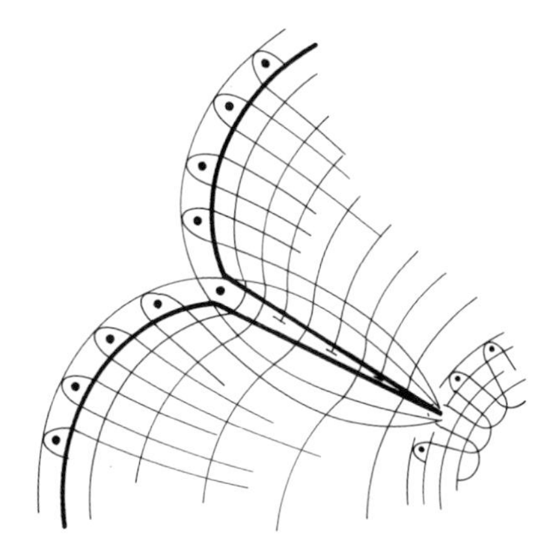

Diag. 82 *Taking out pairs in a whole stitch petal*

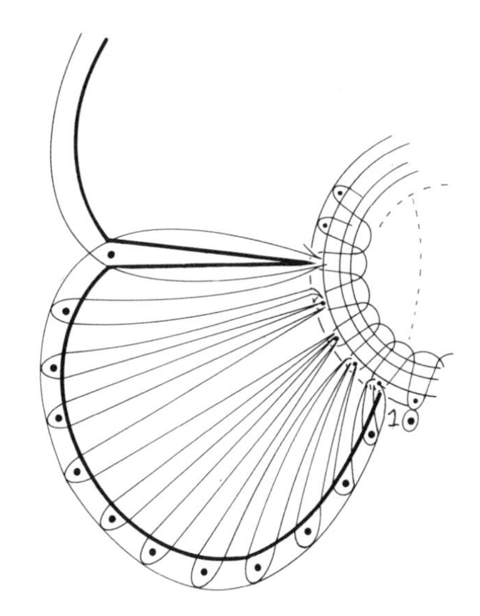

Diag. 83 *Finishing a half stitch petal at the point*

Pattern 18 – Clover flower
Thread 120/2

The petals of this flower are worked by a different method, which is described in chapter 8, 'Waves', p.123. The curve is worked without sewings into the top of the vein. By turning the pillow with the direction of the work, the hole will remain small.

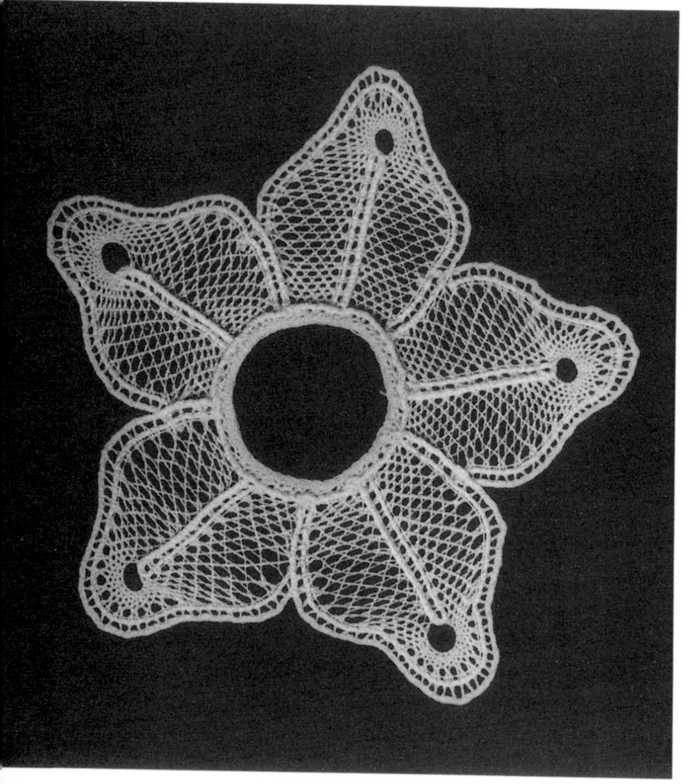

Pattern 19 – Blossom
Thread 140/2

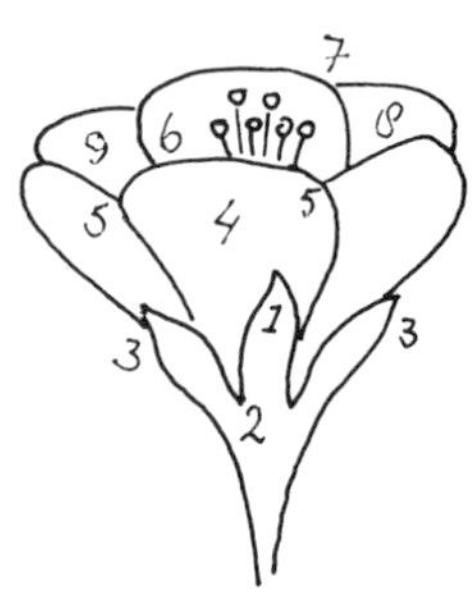

Set up at a point (**1**) (diags. 33–35) and work as far as (**2**). Leave the pairs hanging. Set up at (**3**). Make side sewings when necessary and work level with the first section. Repeat with the 3rd leaf. Take pairs out, including the gimp pairs, but not the ones at the sides. Finish at a point (diag. 37) and roll.

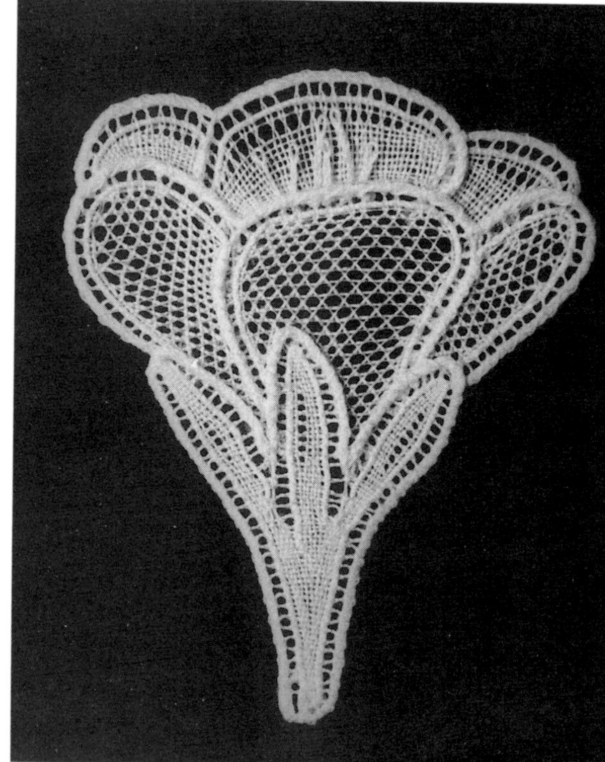

Set pins to work the centre petal (**4**). When finishing this into leaf (**1**), one side has to be sewn in first, then the other side. Roll both sides to (**5**) and use the pairs to set up the petal (**5**), using the narrow setting up method as for the flower (diag. 63). Finish and sew into (**3**). Roll all three petals.

Now work the stamens. Hang 2 pairs around a pin; twist each pair 7 times and work a plait. Sew into (**4**). Now work the petal behind the stamens from (**6**) along to the other side. Roll up to (**7**) and use the pairs to work (**8**). Roll these two petals. Use the pairs of the bundle to work petal (**9**). Roll.

Pattern 20 – Waterlily

Thread 160/2

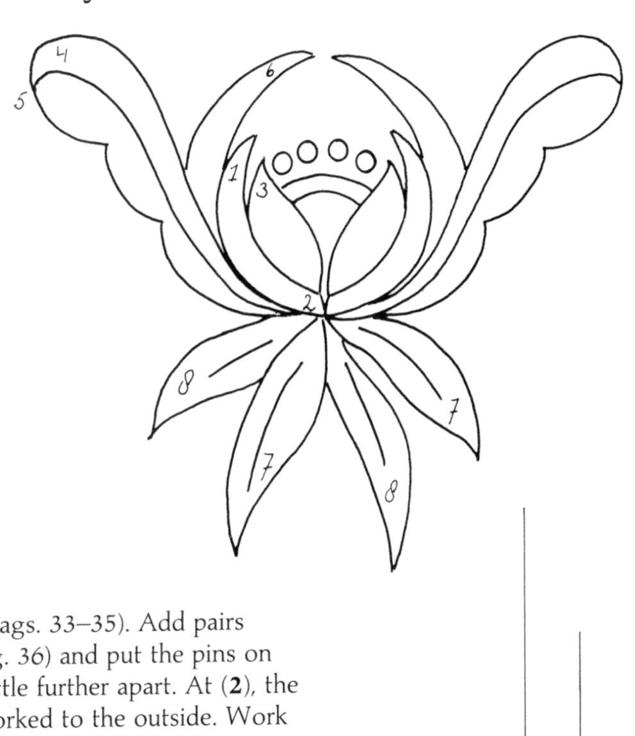

Set up at point (**1**) (diags. 33–35). Add pairs where necessary (diag. 36) and put the pins on the outside curve a little further apart. At (**2**), the inside gimp pair is worked to the outside. Work gimp pairs as catchpins (diag. 84). Twist all passives twice. Bring the inside gimp pairs through these passives back to their original place. Work the opposite leaf in the same way and finish at the point (diag. 37). Roll these 2 leaves.

Set up at the point of leaf (**3**) and add pairs where necessary. When the leaf becomes narrower, pairs have to be taken out (see round setting up). The leaves (**4**) are set up asymetrically, as in Pattern 4. Work holes (diag.

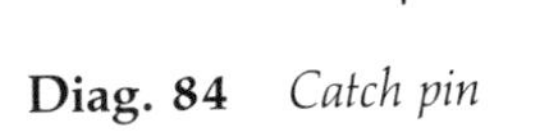

Diag. 84 *Catch pin*

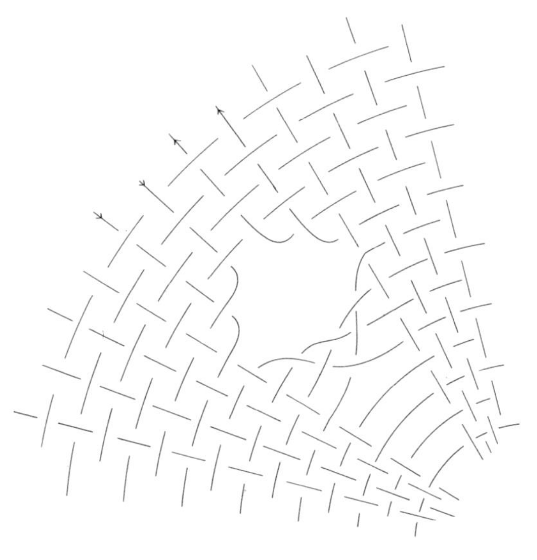

Diag. 85 *Decorative hole as worked in Waterlily*

85) to keep the line flowing. Take pairs out where necessary and roll the leaves. Add passive pairs, a gimp pair and an edge pair to work the other half of this leaf (**5**) in half stitch. Take out pairs where necessary (see Round setting up). Set up at the point of leaf (**6**). Roll the top side with picots (diag. 24). Work leaves (**7**) and (**8**) as you wish.

Pattern 21 – Chinese flower

Thread 180/2

(for actual size see p.150)

The inner flower is worked in the same way as the basic flower (Pattern 15). Once this flower has been rolled, the pairs are to be transferred to the outer flower. (For decoration of this, see diagrams 74–75.) The small leaves of this pattern are started with a rib as the stem, adding pairs where the leaf starts. A gimp pair is also added at this point. One half of the leaf is worked to the end of the vein. Leave all the pairs except 2 and roll back with these (diag. 56) to where the leaf commenced. Add pairs to work the other half of the leaf towards the tip. The 2 pairs that were used to roll will be the edge pair and the pair of runners. Sew into the vein. The runners are sewn in at the top of the vein and continued as passives (diag. 59). The runners of the other side are picked up and the leaf can be continued.

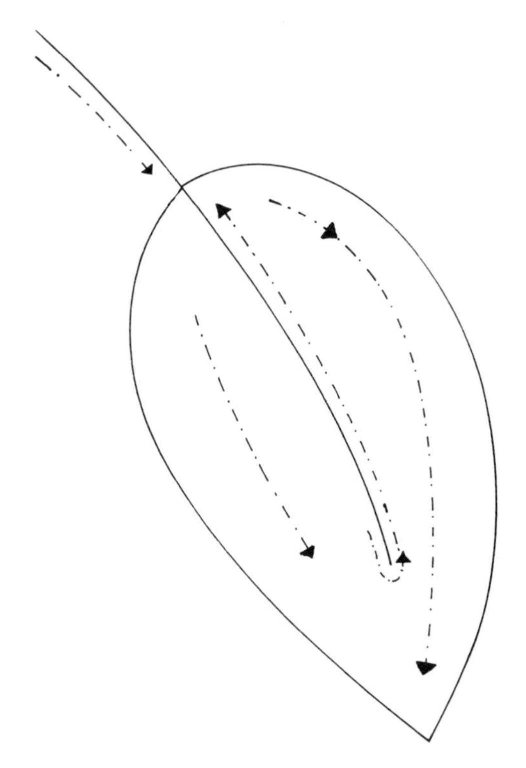

Diag. 86 *Working order of leaves in Chinese flower*

Finish at the point (diag. 38) and roll on both sides, but continue the rollings on one side only from the leaf into the stem and finish at the flower. On the other side, the roll is sewn into a side loop at the bottom of the leaf (see diags. 86–87). Work each leaf with a different decorative stitch.

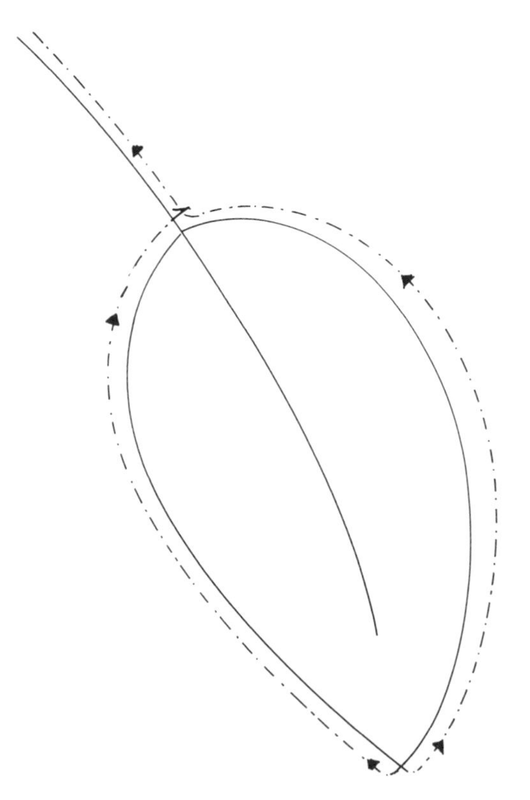

Diag. 87 *Rolling of leaves in Chinese flower*

Pattern 22 – Brooch
Thread 160/2

Work the flower first and then the leaves, starting from their points (diags. 33–36). The leaves are worked according to diagrams 55 and 56. The second half of each leaf is sewn only a few times at regular intervals. Finish the leaf at the flower. Roll with a few picots.

If this pattern is to be used as a corner for a handkerchief, be careful where the picots are added.

Pattern 23 – Pansy
Thread 180/2

As the pairs used in the flower can also be used for the stem, start the rib on the same side as the stem (*). Finish the roll by putting the bundle across the work and sewing it into the side loop of the first pin-hole (diag. 67). Tie one thread of the bundle with the thread that has been used already for rolling (diag. 88). Refer to diag. 89 to

transfer the pairs from the flower to the stem. By plaiting the pairs, they can be sewn into the edge and used for the stem.

The pointed leaf is started at the top (diags. 33–36), working the runners straight across the leaf. For the vein, see diag. 102. To finish the leaf, see diag. 94. See next chapter for the clover leaf, which is started at the stem and worked as in diags. 92–94.

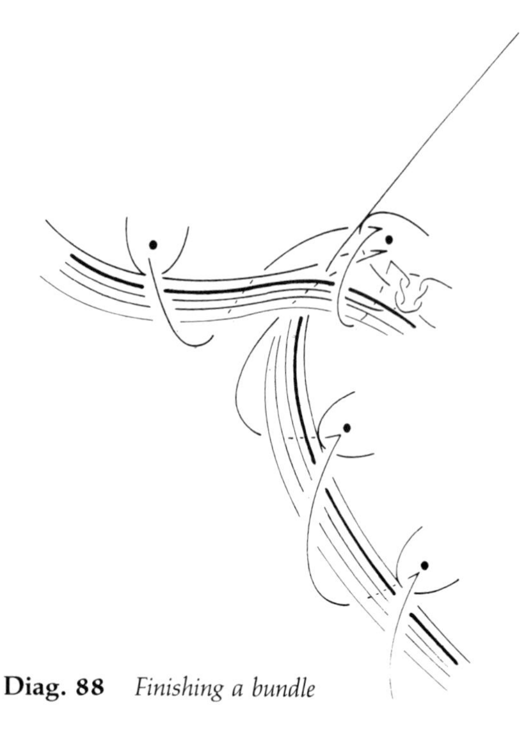

Diag. 88 *Finishing a bundle*

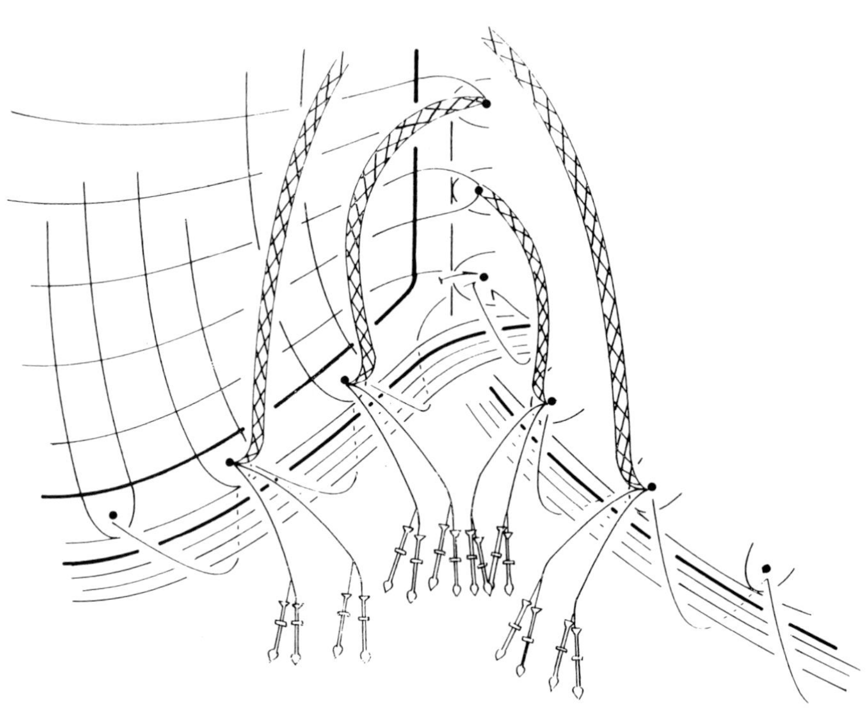

Diag. 89 *Transferring pairs to use for the stem*

3. Leaves

CLOVER LEAF

Pattern 24
Thread 120/2

Start with the stem (straight setting up). Add a double gimp pair after the straight edge has been formed. The stem is worked in whole stitch as far as (**1**) (diag. 90). Lay the gimp pair aside (diag. 91).
Work the corner to (**2**) as in diag. 91. The pin in the outside corner has to be set after the inner corner pin. Decrease 1,2,3 (see p.54) until the outside and the vein can be worked together (diag. 91).

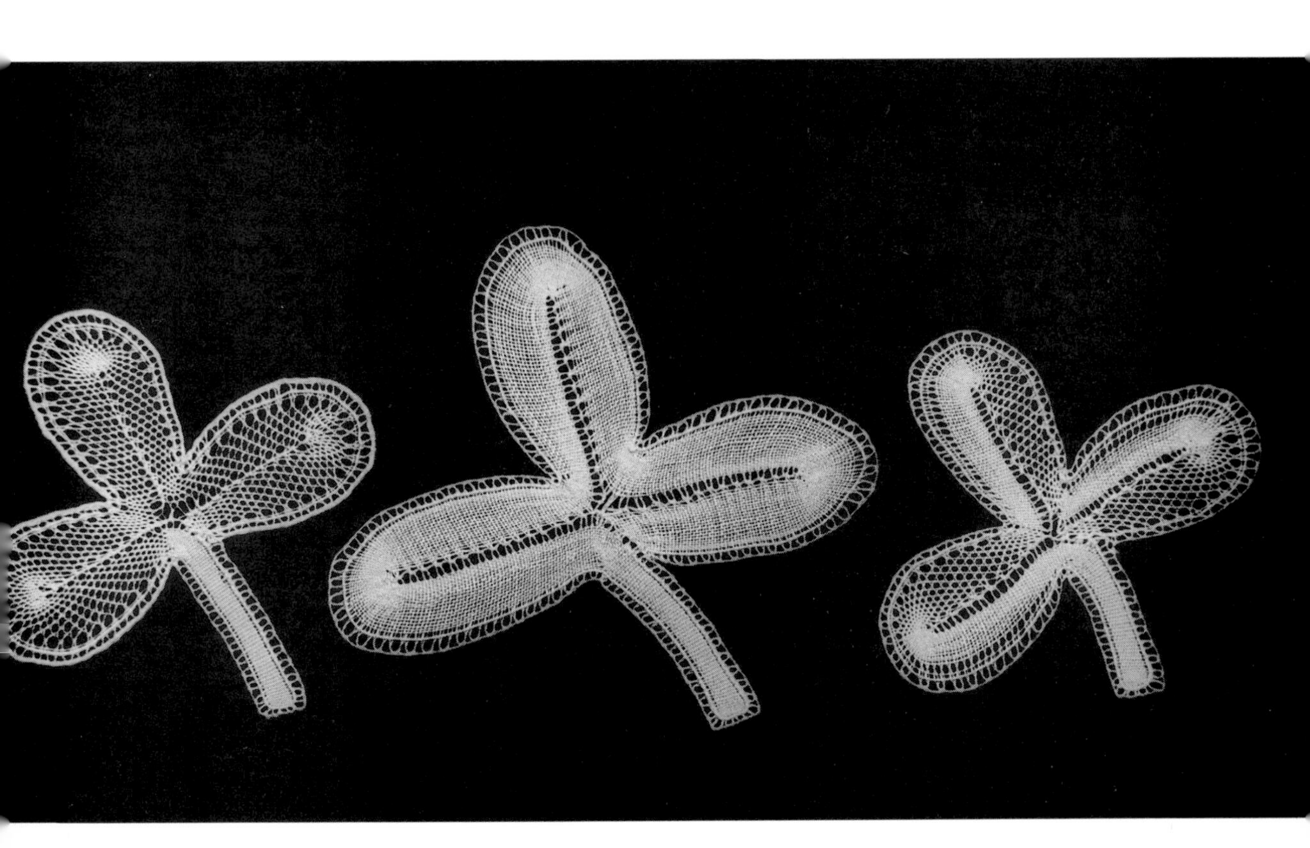

Diag. 90 *Working order for Clover leaf*

Add new pairs in the middle of the work where needed so as not to disturb the line of the threads on the outside (diag. 92).

Work a straight edge stitch along the vein. On the curved line the pins have to be set a little further apart. The last pin is set at the end of the vein. Work the runners to the outside. Untwist the edge pair of the vein.
Now work the runners through every pair back to the middle. Leave the runners, take the last used passives as new runners, and continue working round the curve of the leaf, making sewings where needed, and decreasing 1,2,3.

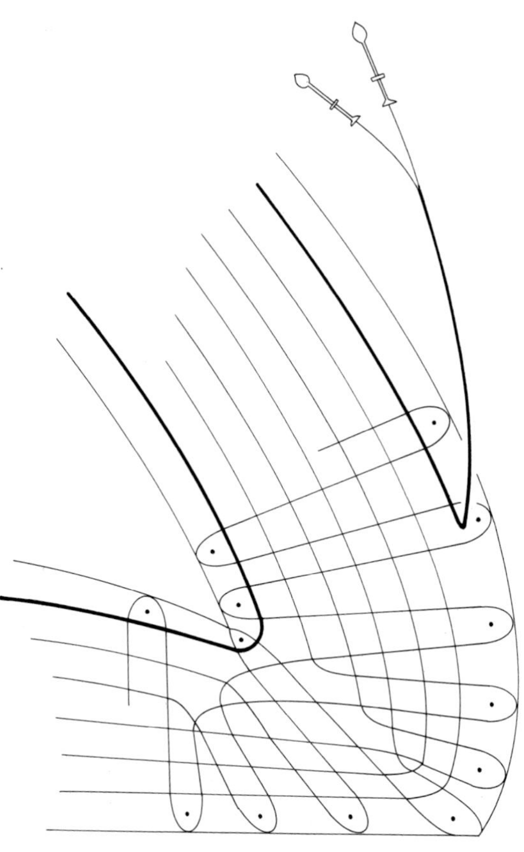

Diag. 91 *Decreasing 1,2,3 from stem into the 1st leaf*

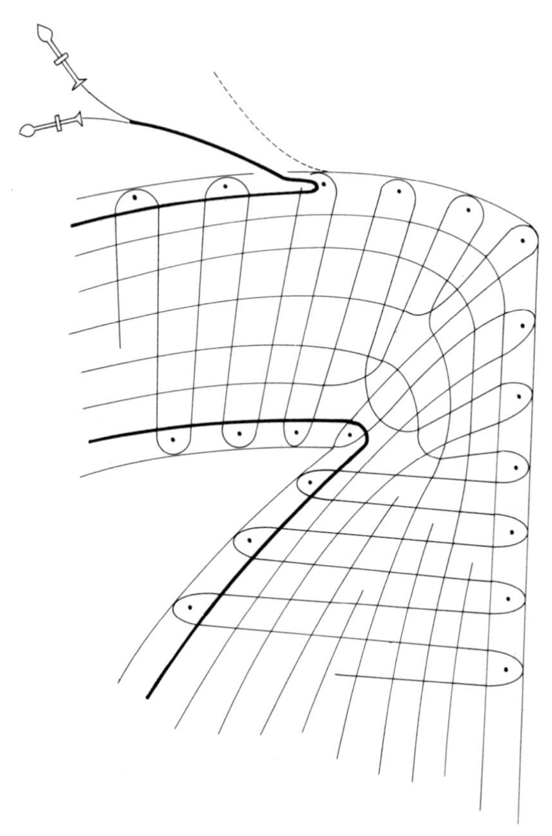

Diag. 92 *Adding new pairs in Clover leaf*

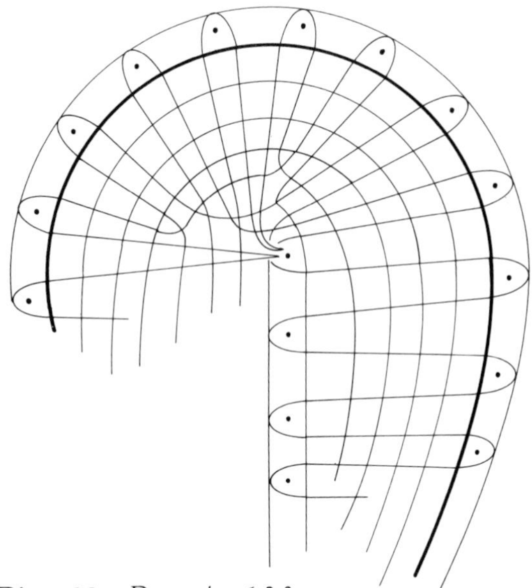

Diag. 93 *Decreasing 1,2,3 to work the top of the Clover leaf*

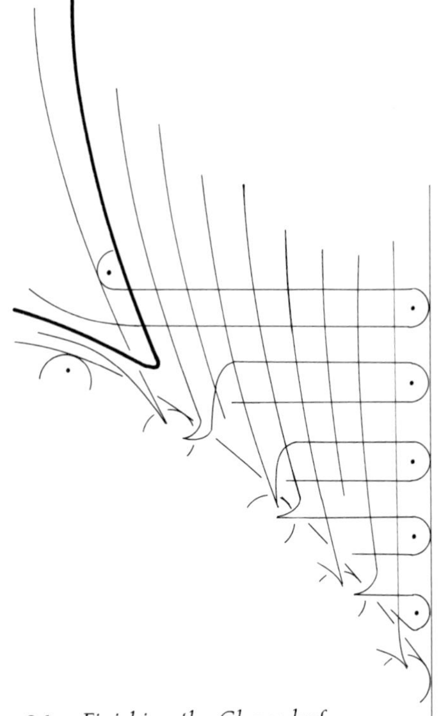

Diag. 94 *Finishing the Clover leaf*

Make sewings along the vein when the curve has been worked (diag. 93). Take pairs out as the leaf becomes narrower. The commencement of the 2nd leaf is worked in the same way as changing from the stem into the 1st leaf. The 3rd leaf is also worked in this manner.

FINISHING

Work the runners to the outside and leave them (to take into the bundle). Put aside the gimp pair or keep it to use for the bundle. Sew the edge pair and take it into the bundle. Sew the first passives and use these as runners to work to the middle and back. Now put this pair aside; sew another pair of passives and use this pair as new runners. Continue in this way until the leaf is completed (diag. 94).

VARIATIONS

Whole stitch and half stitch

Change into half stitch on the highest point of the curve.

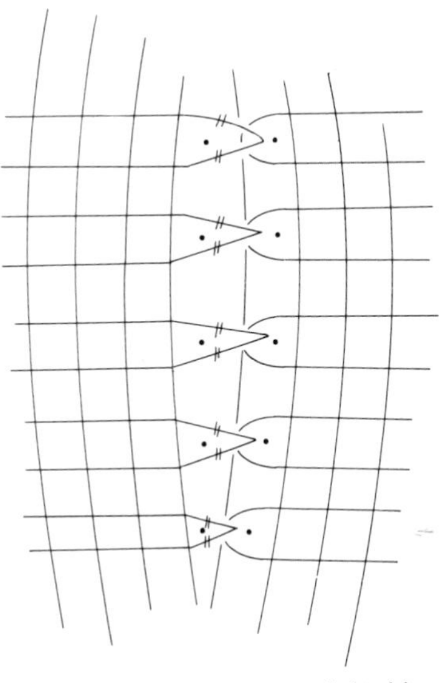

Diag. 95 *Open vein and double pin*

Open vein and double pin

At the side of the vein, twist twice, make a sewing, twist twice (diag. 95).

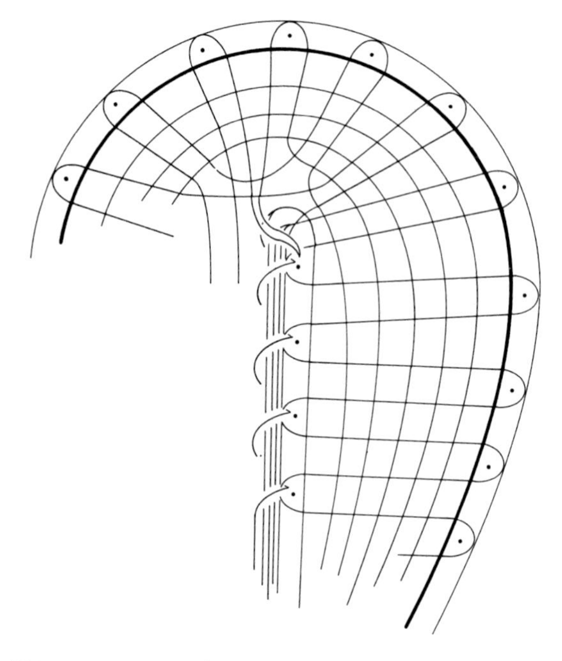

Diag. 96 *Raised vein in Clover leaf*

Raised Vein

Work the leaf to the end of the vein and set the last pin. Work back to the outside. Untwist the edge pair of the vein. Work through all the pairs back to the middle. Work back to the outside with the edge pair of the vein as runners. Take the 2 pairs of the vein into a bundle and roll back to the starting point of the vein. Leave these pairs here for use in the 2nd leaf (diag. 96).

Note that a clover leaf started in the centre should be worked as in diag. 97. See also Pattern 26.

Clover leaf with half circles in whole stitch

Work the leaf (see pattern 33) to the end of the vein and set the last pin. Work back to the outside. Untwist the edge pair of the vein and work the runners through all the pairs to the centre and leave them. Take the last used passives to the outside and make an edge stitch. Now work through the gimp pair and one or two passives only and leave the runners here. Take the pair on the inside of the work and work them to the outside. Make an edge stitch. Work through the gimp pair and the same number of passives as before and leave them. Repeat this until on the other side sewings have to be made along the vein (diag. 98). Take care not to make too big a hole. It is important that the passives lie evenly round the circle. Turn the pillow with the work to achieve this.

Clover leaf with half circles in half stitch

Work the leaf to the end of the vein and set the last pin. Work back to the outside and untwist the edge pair of the vein. Work the runners through all the pairs and leave them. Take the last used passives to the outside. Work back to the middle. Work the last used passives to the outside. Repeat this until sewings have to be made on the other side along the vein (diag. 99).

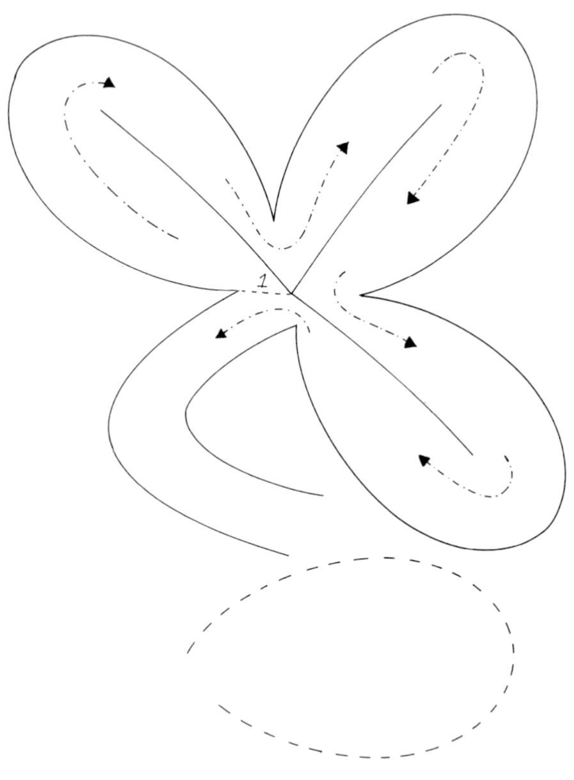

Diag. 97 *Working order for Clover Leaf Roundel*

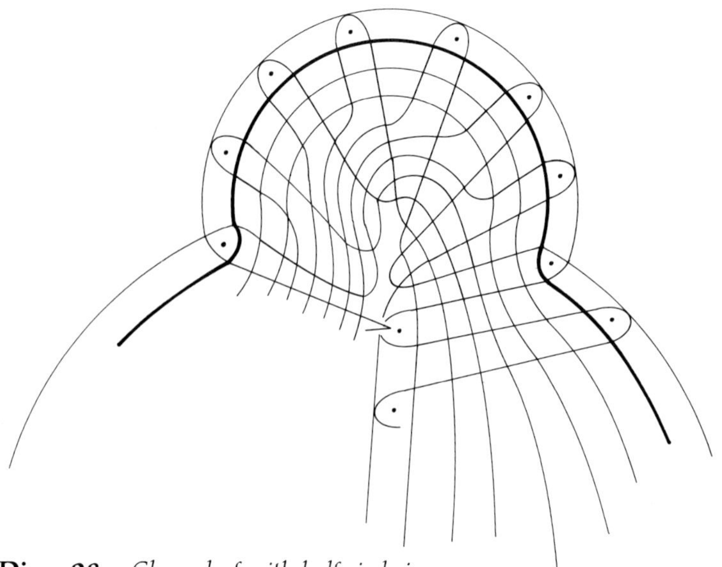

Diag. 98 *Clover leaf with half circle in whole stitch*

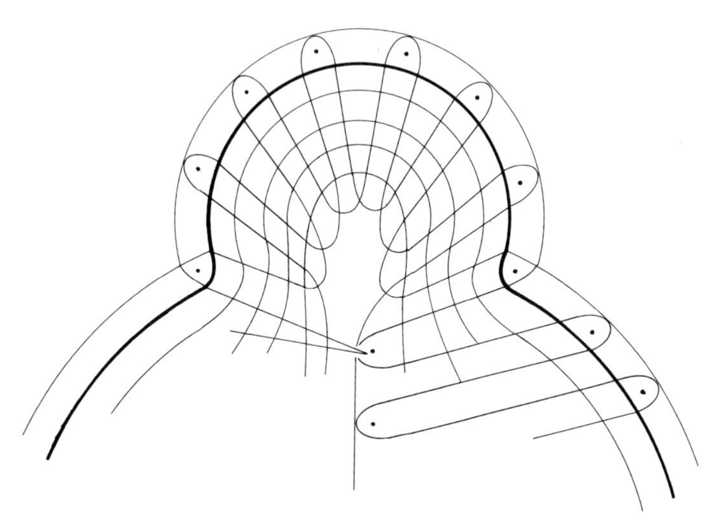

Diag. 99 *Clover leaf with half circle in half stitch*

DECORATIVE POSSIBILITIES

Twisted Vein

Mark the starting point of the vein. One passive pair is needed to work it (diag. 100). The runners are twisted once to emphasize the vein. Work to the starting point of the vein. Twist the next pair of passives and pass the twisted runners between the 2 threads. Alternatively, 2 passive pairs may be used (diag. 101) or 2 gimp threads added (or 2 extra pairs) (diag. 102) and used in the same way.

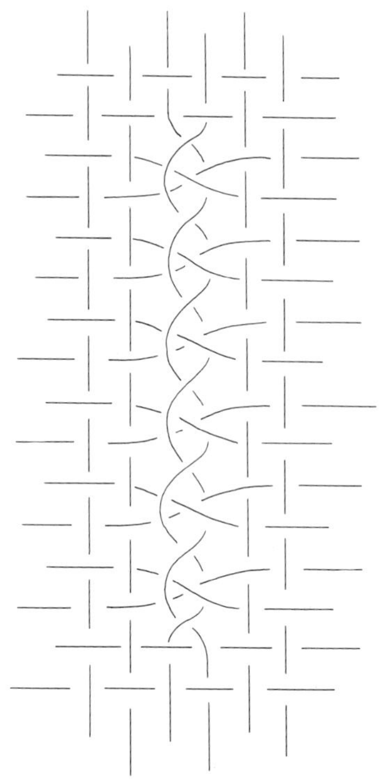

Diag. 100 *Twisted vein with 1 passive pair*

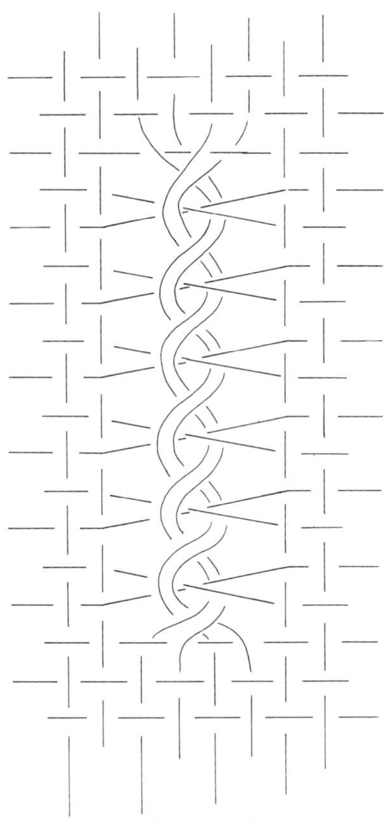

Diag. 101 *Twisted vein with 2 passive pairs*

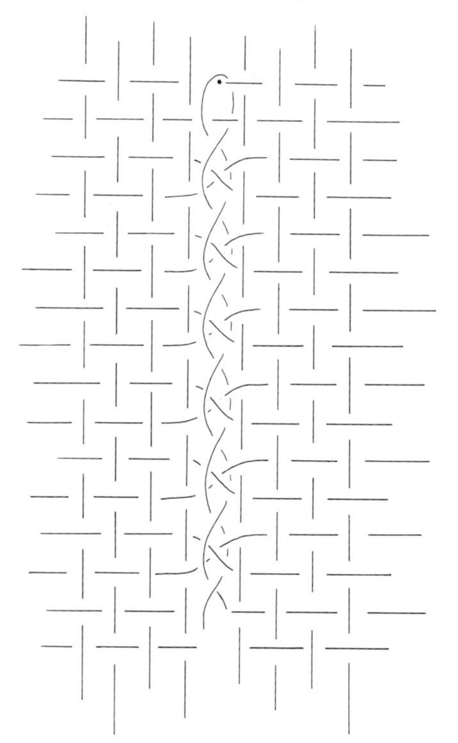

Diag. 102 *Twisted vein with 2 gimp threads or 2 extra pairs*

Raised vein

Mark the direction of the threads on the pattern so that when working the leaves both halves are in line. Work the leaf up to the vein. Now decide which side of the leaf has to be worked first and put aside the pairs ready to work the other side (diag. 55). Work the 1st half up to the end of the vein (straight edge stitch on the vein side). Work the runners to the outside and leave them there. Take the edge pair of the vein and the passives next to this pair into a bundle, and roll back to the starting point of the vein. Make a top sewing with one pair of the bundle and use this pair as the runners to work to the outside (diag. 56). The other pair of the bundle is used as passives (diag. 57). The 1st top sewing is made in the bottom loop of the same pin-hole. At the end of the vein the runners are sewn into the vein and used as passives (diag. 59). Continue the leaf.

Plaited raised vein

Work to the point where the side vein starts and set a pin at the top. Hang 2 pairs round this pin. Work these pairs once so that they are secured in the work and make a half stitch plait with them to the point where they have to be sewn (diags. 103–104) and leave. Continue the leaf to this point. Pass the runners through the pairs of the plait and make the edge stitch. Now put the pairs of the plait aside until they can be tied without risk of them coming adrift. In the case of the leaf widening, and thus requiring more pairs, one pair of the plait may be used as passives, the other pair being tied. On the other side of the leaf, the plait can be sewn straight away.

Diag. 103 *Securing the half stitch plait on the runners*

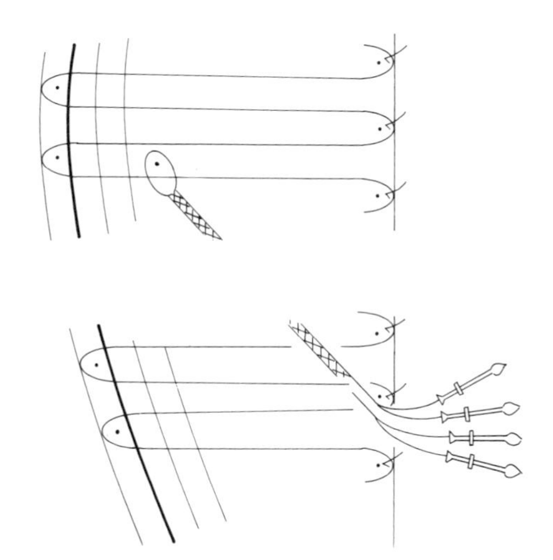

Diag. 104 *Half stitch plait being worked aside*

Pattern 25 – Starfish

Thread 180/2

Always commence with the section that is foremost. Start at (**1**), working downwards and finishing at the point; roll on both sides. When the top is reached again, leave pairs of one roll. Add pairs to the other one and come back down to (**2**). Finish at the point and roll. When (**5**) is reached, the pairs of the roll at (**3**) should be hanging there.

Start (**8**) with a scroll (see Chapter 4). Then work (**9**). Follow the numbers. Always try to carry pairs from one section to the next, especially since everything happens in the centre.
It is a good idea to enlarge this pattern and use a thicker thread as it is difficult to work a small pattern where all the parts meet in the centre.

Pattern 26 – Clover leaf roundel
Thread 180/2

The stems finish between two clover leaves, which is why the pattern is started in the centre of the clover leaf (**1**) (diag. 97) and finished in the stem. Before the stem can be finished, the clover leaf next to it has to be worked and rolled. The same happens with the stems of the 2nd and 3rd clover leaves. The braid is set up double-sided (diag. 44) but use more pins to work the full width. The ring is closed as in diag. 50b. For the circles refer to Chapter 5.

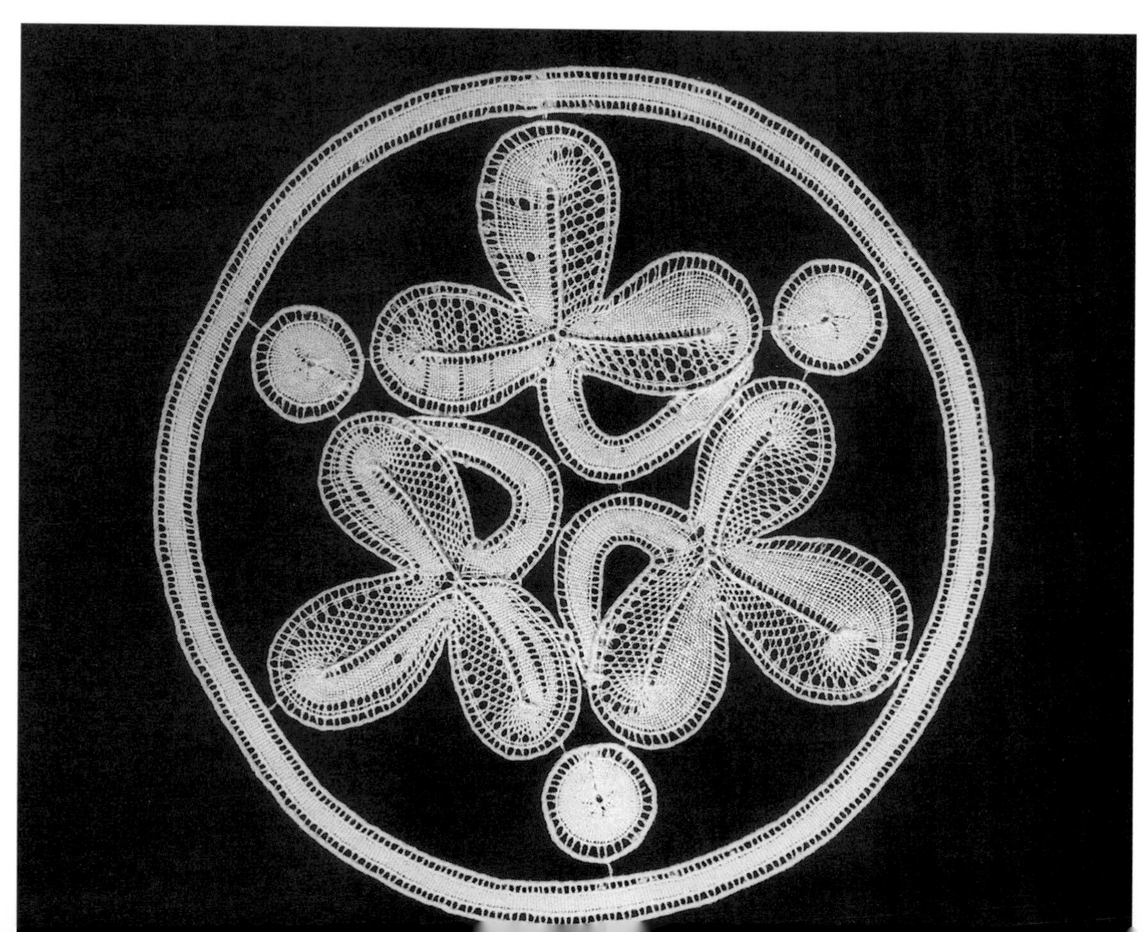

Pattern 27 – Tulips
Thread 160/2

Set up at the point of the centre leaf; add pairs and work the leaf as in diags. 55–57. Finish at the point and roll. Set up at the points of leaves (**2**) and (**3**) (diags. 33–35). After a few rows make top sewings with the runners into the centre leaf, adding pairs. When finished, the leaf has to be rolled. Work the pointed leaf (**4**) as in diags. 38–40.

The tulips at the side are worked in a different way (diag. 105). Start with a rib on one pin (**5**) and add pairs (diag. 106). When the top is reached (**6**), fill the tulip (although the top is pointed) working as shown in diag. 140 (p.103) as far as (**5**). On side (**A**) the work can be continued, adding pairs where necessary. Roll the rib as shown in the diagram picking up the pairs on side (**B**). When finished, continue rolling.

Set up at the point of leaf (**7**). Use the decoration shown in diag. 107. At the bottom of the tulip leave the edge pair and gimp pair at the side (sew, tie and cut off), and sew the runners. On the other side of the tulip a new edge pair and gimp pair are needed. When the point is reached make side sewings and finish at the point. Roll inside and outside. Leaf (**8**) can now be worked (diags. 55–57) starting at the points. For

Diag. 105 *Working order for Tulips*

Diag. 106 *Working order for centre leaf of side tulip*

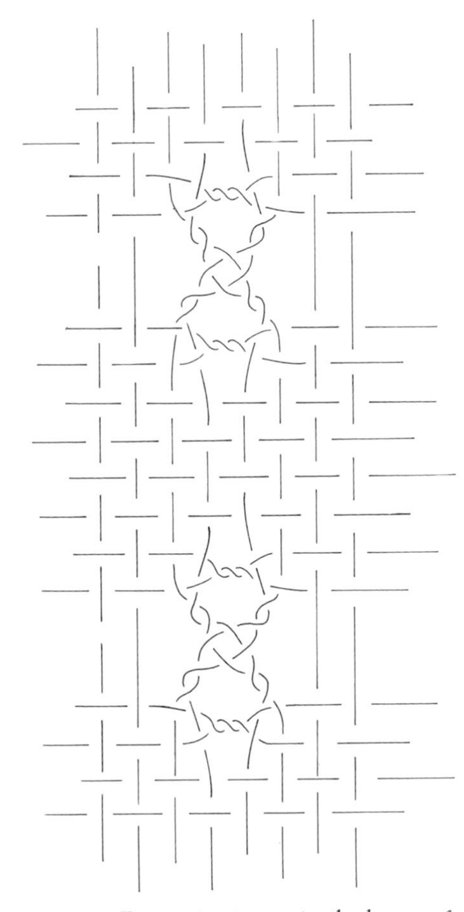

Diag. 107 *Decoration to use in the leaves of the Tulips*

finishing, see diag. 52. Leaf (**9**) is worked in the same way, using any of the decorations shown in the diagrams.

4. Scrolls

Pattern 28

Thread 120/2

Set up with 2 or 3 pins. Take a double gimp pair and work this through all the passives after joining the pairs and working the straight edge (diag. 108). Work the the scroll decreasing 1,2,3.

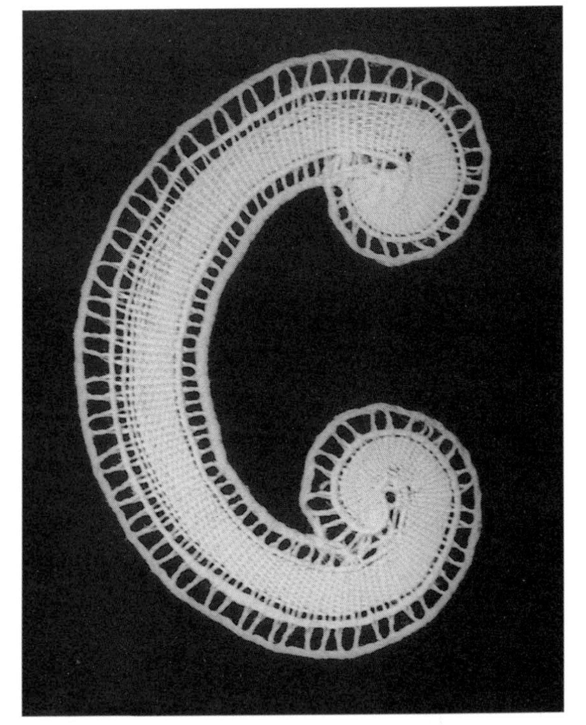

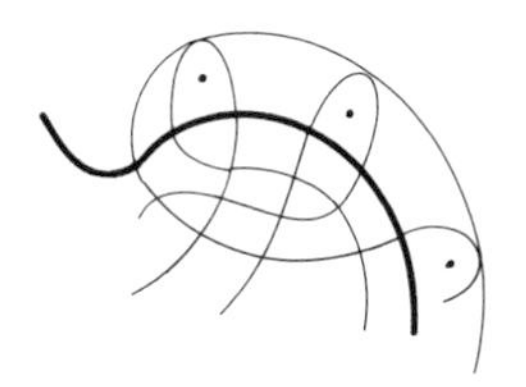

Diag. 108 *Setting up for the scroll*

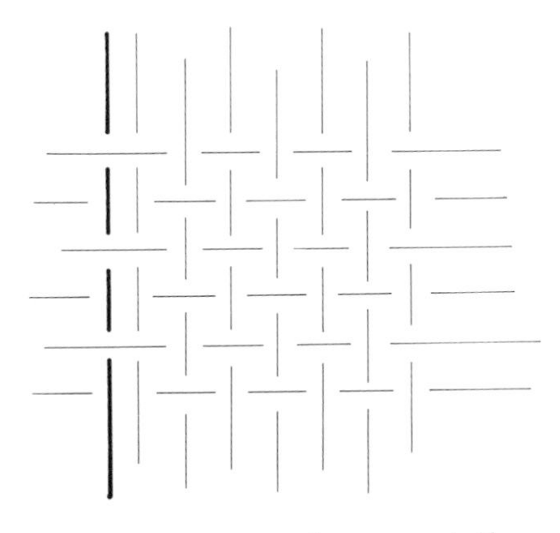

Diag. 109 *Passing the gimp pair through the runners*

Do not work the gimp pair in whole stitch, but put through the runners using it as if it were a single thread (diag. 109). Before taking the first sewing, leave the runners in front of the gimp pair. Untwist the edge pair; put the gimp pair through this pair (diag. 109) and use the edge pair as the runners (diag. 110). On the outside of the curve spread the pins a little further apart. Add pairs where needed. Hang new pairs round a support pin which is set outside the work (diag. 110).

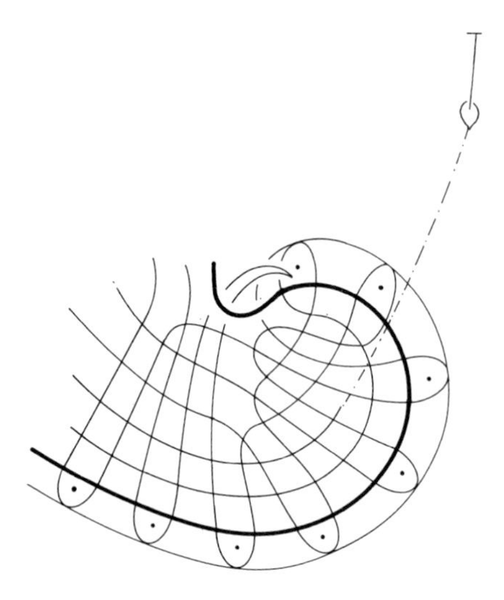

Diag. 110 *Sewings are made into the centre pin-hole and new pairs are added*

When adding pairs make sure that the flow of the line of the passive threads is not interrupted. It will probably be necessary to add them towards the inside in order to push the other pairs outwards near the edge stitch. Include the new pairs in the work for a few rows before taking the support pin out and easing the threads gently into place.

Add an edge pair when the scroll changes into a braid (diag. 111). Work the braid in the usual way. If it changes into another scroll do not forget to space the pins on the outside curve, otherwise the curve of the scroll will be thick and lumpy. Work the sharp curve as before, decreasing 1,2,3, and put aside pairs where necessary. When the scroll is nearly complete, work the runners through all the passives and leave them there, using the edge pair from the centre as runners (do not work the gimp pair) to the outer edge. Work back to the centre; put the gimp pair through the runners; make a sewing and put them aside. Take the next passives and use them as runners. Repeat this as many times as is necessary (diag. 112).

Alternative method: Put away the runners; take the next passives and pass the gimp pair through them; make a sewing and work back to the outer edge (diag. 124). When the scroll is filled, put the gimp pair aside and sew the passives into opposite pin-holes. Be careful to keep the shape of the scroll flowing. Bundle the edge pair, runners, and possibly the gimp pair, and roll along the work.

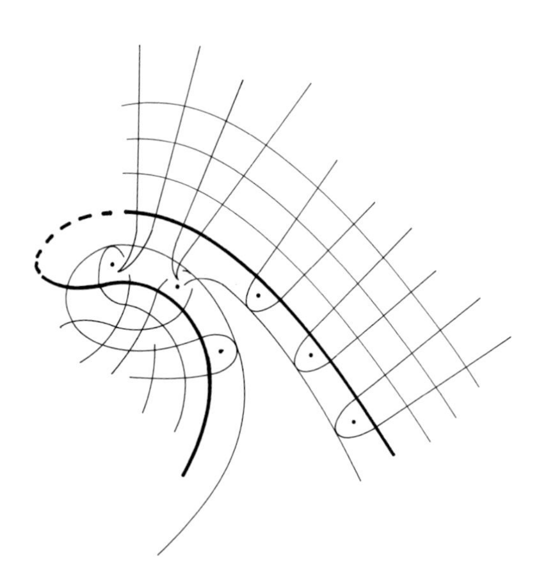

Diag. 111 *The scroll changes into a braid*

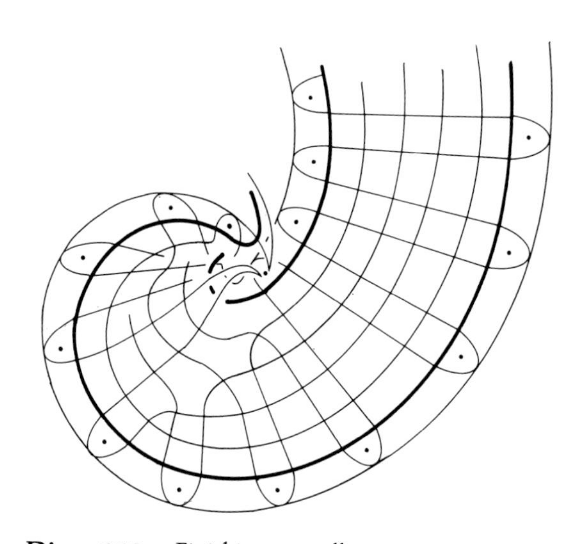

Diag. 112 *Finishing a scroll*

Pattern 29 – Keyring with partly hidden flower motif

Thread 180/2

and

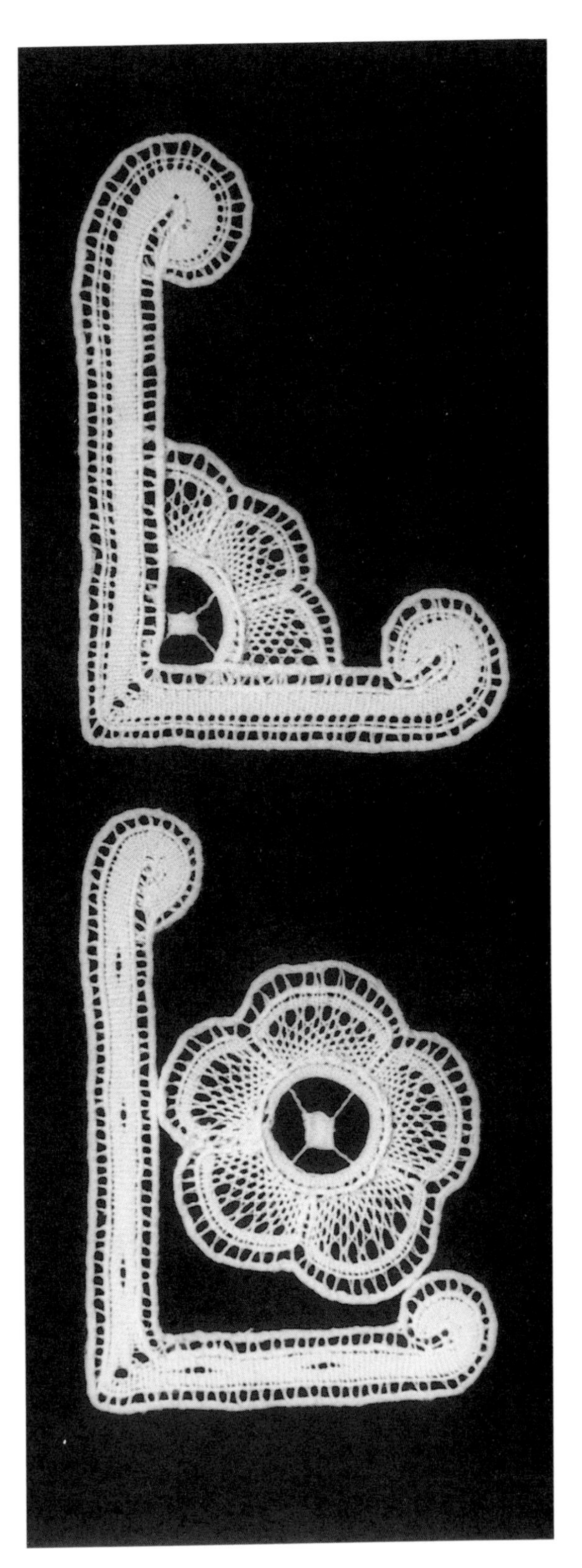

Pattern 30 – Keyring with flower motif

Thread 180/2

These patterns are worked according to the basic instructions for the scroll. Once the scrolls are rolled, the flower is worked.

Pattern 31 – Valentine

Thread 140/2

Start with the scrolls (**1**) (diags. 108–110) adding pairs if necessary. Change into the braid (diag. 111) and finish with another scroll (diag. 112). Now study the pattern carefully and make sure that every time a scroll is worked the braid can be sewn into one already finished. The pointed leaves (**2**) are started and finished at their points (diags. 33–36) and rolled (diag. 37).
The pointed details (**3**) are also set up at their outer tips; sew into the braids and roll.
Start the flower with a rib with picots (diag. 68), referring to diag. 69 in order to work the petals.

Pattern 32 – Elegant swan

Thread 140/2

(for actual size see p.150)

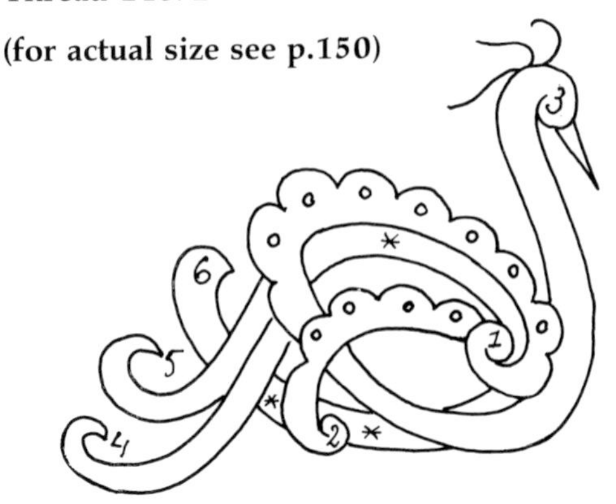

Start at scroll (**1**) (diags. 108–111). The centre of the scallop is worked in half stitch. This can be seen clearly in the photograph. When the braid is half completed, put the pairs aside and sew in pairs to roll as far as possible. Leave these pairs also. Set up at scroll (**2**). Work the braid in the same way as the previous one; sew into scroll (**1**) and roll.
Now the 1st braid can be finished and sewn into the 2nd one. Finish rolling the first braid.

Start scroll (**3**). Sew the neck into the braid (**2**). Leave those pairs and use them to roll back. Add the joining braids (*****). Roll. Set up at the points of the feathers (**4**,**5**, and **6**). Work a curve decoratively as in diag. 49 and roll.

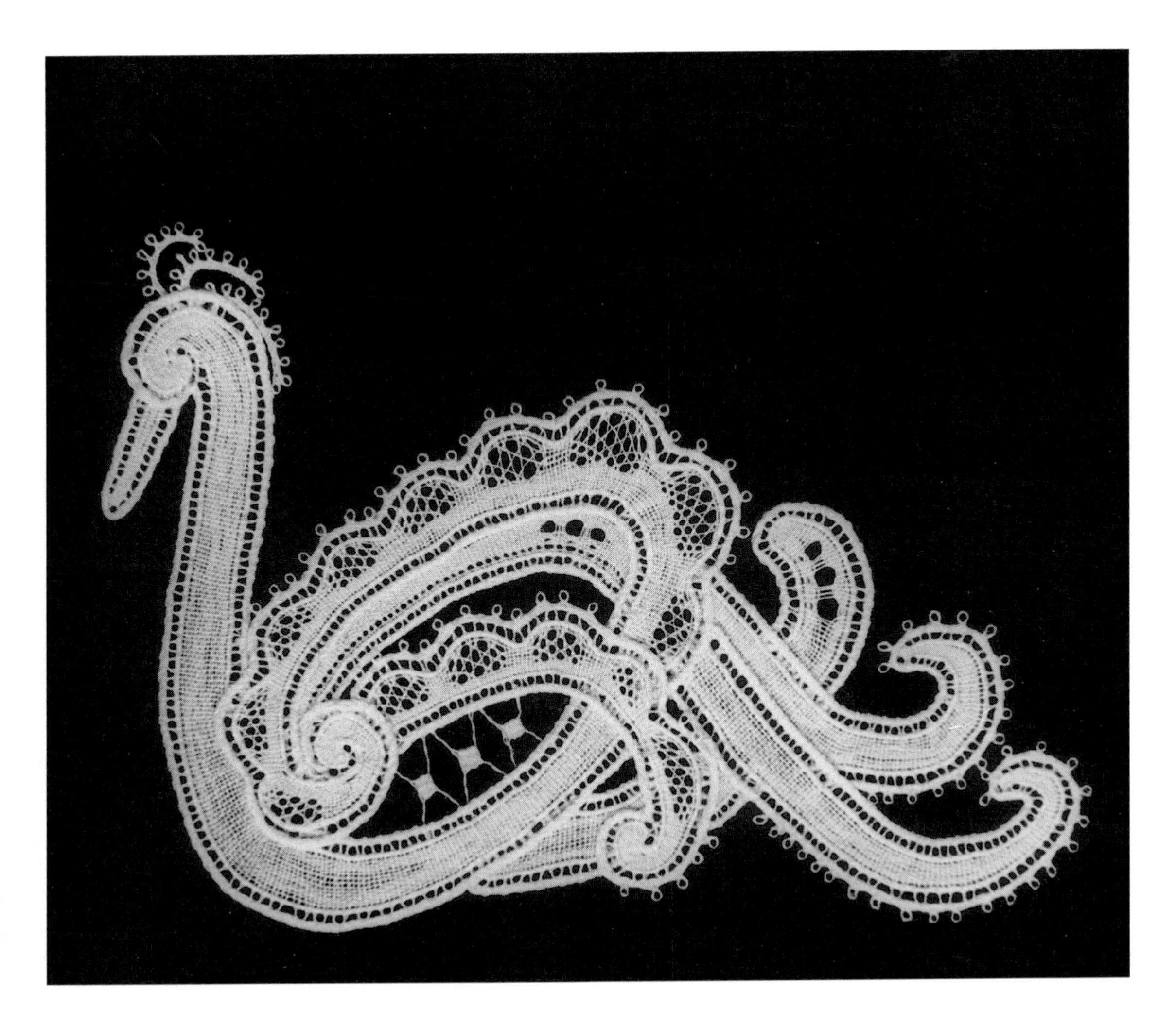

Pattern 33 – Winter aconite
Thread 180/2

Start this motif with the scroll (**1**) (diags. 108–110), changing into the braid (diag. 111). Work it according to the instructions for the clover leaf. Once the last pin of the vein is set, roll with 2 pairs (diag. 96) and work the top of the leaf, as in diag. 98. Continue the leaf, making top sewings along the vein. Work the other one in the same way and roll along the motif.

Hang in new pairs at (**2**) and add as many pairs as required. To work round the corner, follow diag. 50. Finish this detail as in diag. 94. Roll with picots (diag. 24). Then work the rib (**3**) and roll. Add pairs at (**4**) for 2 ribs. These ribs are worked at the same time and cross (diag. 46).

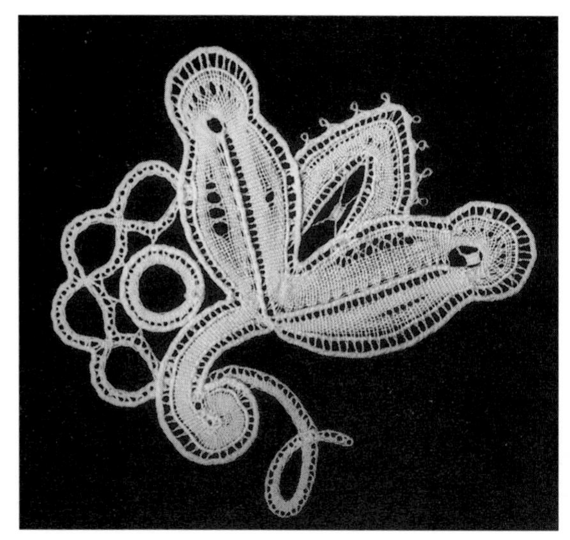

ROLLED SCROLLS

Pattern 34
Thread 80/2

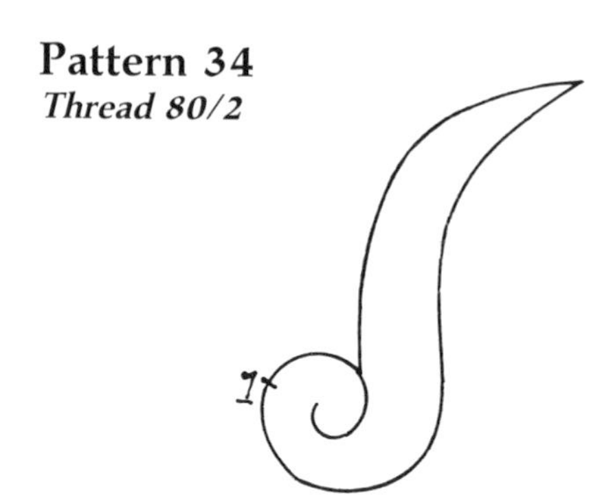

Set up with 2 or 3 pins (diag. 108). Add a double gimp pair after joining the pairs. One half of the double gimp pair is used in the outer edge of the scroll. The other half is used to roll along the scroll from the centre, together with the edge pair of the centre and, if required, the passives next to the gimp pair (diag. 113). Work the scroll as far as (**1**). Bundle the pairs and roll along the edge (diag. 113). As the pairs in the bundle were reserved for this purpose, it will be necessary to add new pairs on the inside of the curve as well as on its outside (diag. 114). Take good care that your threads create a flowing line.
As soon as the scroll changes into the braid, a gimp pair and an edge pair will have to be added (diag. 115).

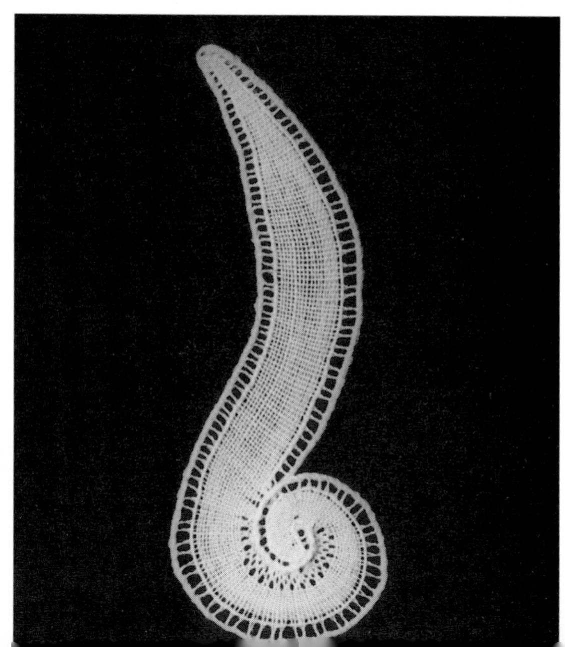

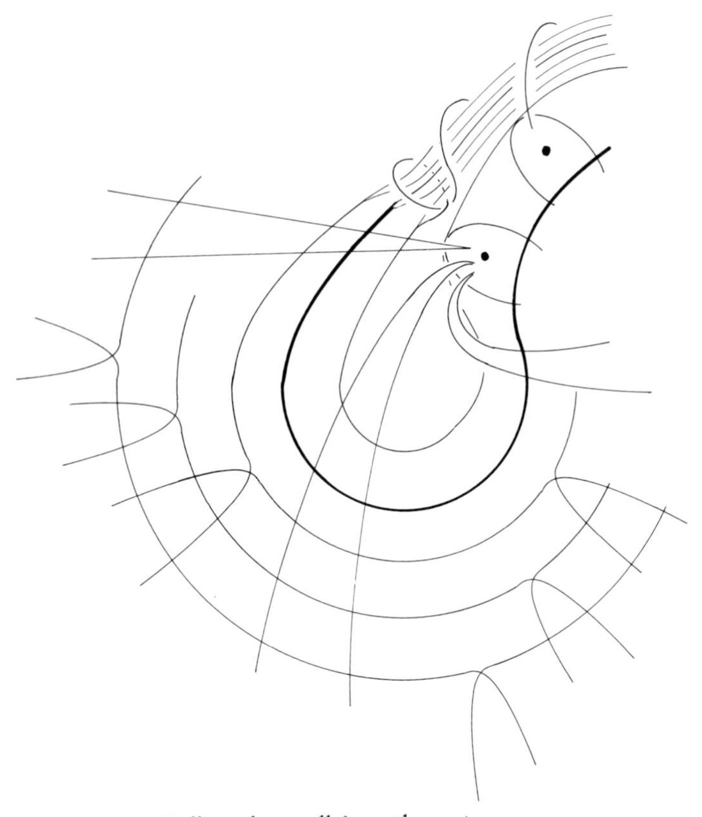

Diag. 113 *Rolling the scroll from the centre*

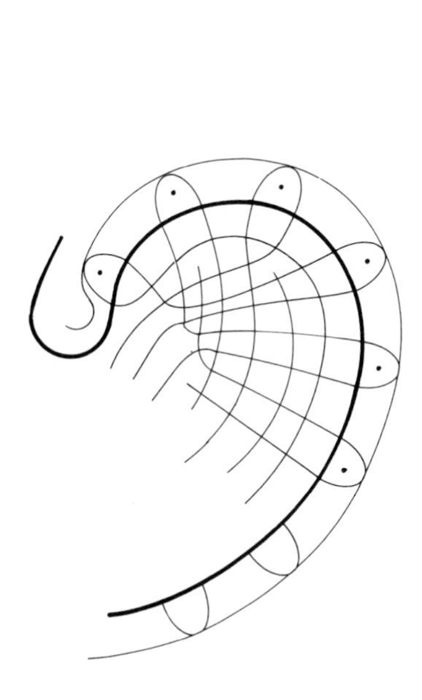

Diag. 114 *Adding new pairs*

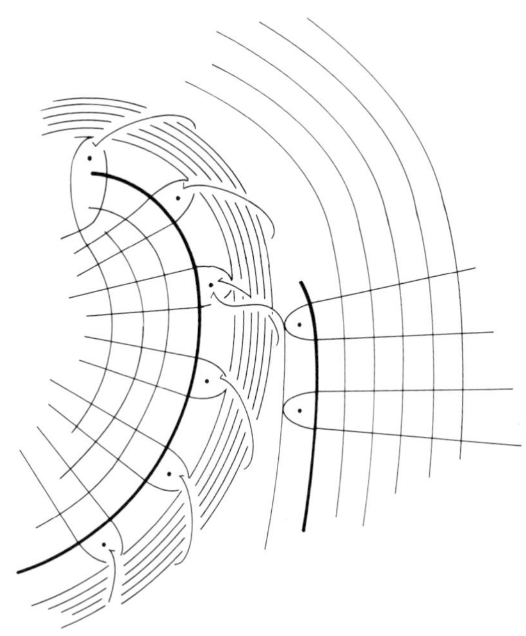

Diag. 115 *The rolled scroll changes into a braid*

Pattern 35 – Flower bouquet
Thread 140/2

Start with the small flower (**1**) and continue with the big flower (**2**); roll. Use some of the pairs to work the stem to the small flower. Work flower (**3**) and roll. Work the braid between the 2 flowers.
Work a rolled scroll (**4**), setting up with 2 pins (diags. 113–115) and add pairs where necessary. Sew the braid into the flower. The leaves can now be worked choosing from the various decorative possibilities (diags. 100–104). Make sure, when rolling the tops of the leaves, that they remain pointed (diag. 39).

The twigs with picots (**6**) use double-sided setting up at the top with 4 pairs on one pin. Where both sides cross, only the passives are worked in whole stitch (diag. 46). When both sides become the stem, work whole stitches with the passives and put aside the 2 pairs on the side of the edge pair. Work the stem and sew into the leaf. Use the 2 pairs that were put aside to roll the stem. The 2 small ribs (**7**) are set up on one pin. Add 2 pairs at the first edge stitch to roll the rib before the curve prevents it from being rolled.

REVERSE SIDE

Pattern 36
Thread 160/2

This is used, for example, as the reverse or underside of a twisted leaf-shape. The heavy drawn line is the continuous line. This has to be taken into account when rolling. Leave the bundle where indicated (**1**). The pairs to work the reverse side are sewn in at (**2**). Add a few pairs at the side where sewings are made (see Round setting up, p.20). Finish at the curve in the same way as finishing at a point (see diag. 37). Take out both gimp pairs. Finish both edge pairs in a side loop, as in diag. 19. Pick up the bundle from where it was left and roll.

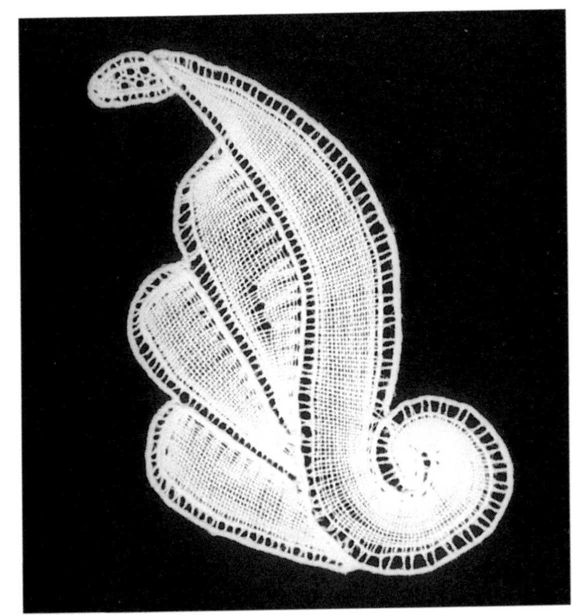

Pattern 37 – Lapel pin
Thread 140/2

Set up at (**1**) and work a rolled scroll (diags. 108–110 and 113–114). Be careful when working the curved braid (diag. 115). Study the pattern to see which scroll is foremost and work that one first. Finish with the small leaves and roll.

Pattern 38 – Snail house

Thread 80/2

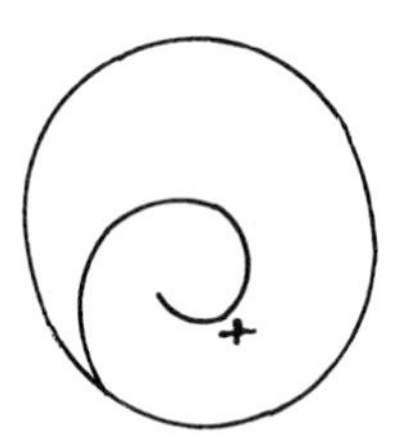

Set 3 pins for the rolled scroll (diag. 108). Starting at (*), make one half stitch before taking a sewing. After a few rows make 2 half stitches before the sewing. Then work 3, until there are only a few whole stitches left. Where the pattern narrows, put the runners aside, sew the last used passive pairs and use those as new runners (diag. 52) until all pairs are sewn.

The 2nd motif is worked in whole stitch, as in diag. 50a.

Pattern 39 – Duckling

Thread 160/2

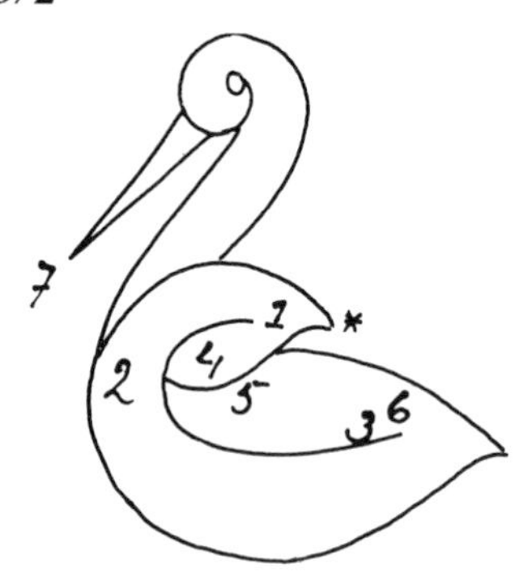

Refer to diag. 116 to work this pattern.
Set up at point (*) (diags. 33–36) and work to the division. Leave the pairs on the inside and continue working the top of the wing (**2**) (diag. 55) until the end of the vein (**3**), and roll back with 2 pairs (diag. 56). If more than 2 pairs are wanted, add them by setting a pin outside the work, and hanging a new pair or pairs round this pin. Do not take more than 2 pairs out of the work. At the end of the vein (**3**), one of the pairs is used as runners (diag. 56). If more than 2 pairs were used for the roll, these are cut off later. Work the underside of the wing (**4**). Finish at the point and roll (**5**) back to (*). Leave the bundle to be used later.

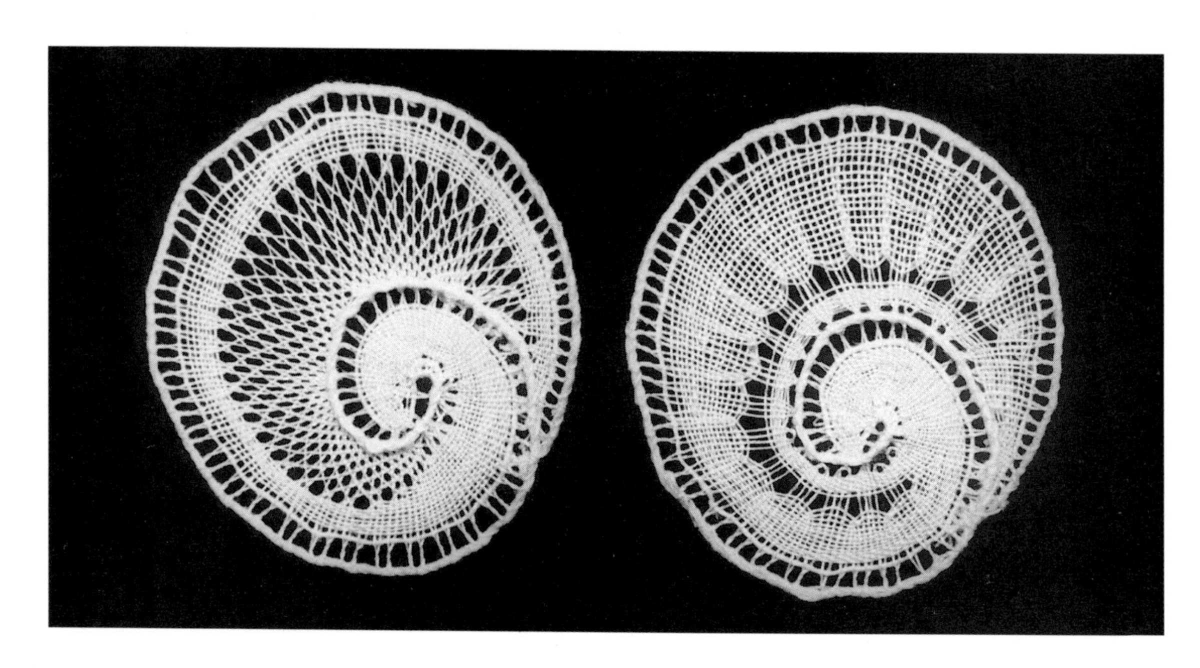

Diag. 116 *Working order for Duckling*

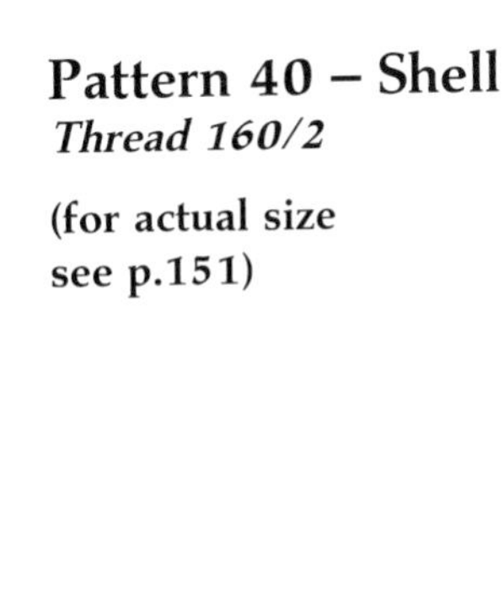

Pattern 40 – Shell

Thread 160/2

(for actual size **see p.151)**

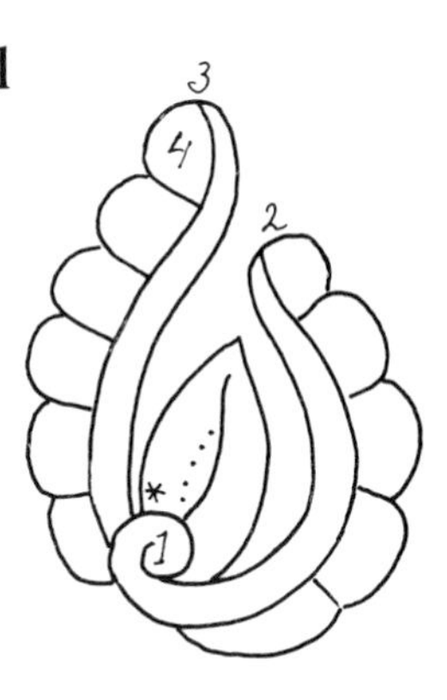

Now pick up the pairs left at (**3**). Work round the curve and finish the other side (**6**) (diag. 52). Pick up the bundle and roll the whole body.
The head is started as a rolled scroll (diags. 108–110 and 113–114). Change into a braid for the neck (diag. 115) and sew into the body (diag. 52).

Start the beak with a single pin (**7**) (diag. 143). On the top side twist the runners 4 times round the pin.

Set up a rolled scroll at (**1**) (diags. 108–110 and 113–115). Finish at the point (diag. 37) and roll. Now transfer the pairs that were taken out when reaching the point and the gimp pair to the petal shapes (**2**). Work them like the petals of a flower. Finish at the point and roll them.

Set up at point (**3**) (diags. 33–35). Add pairs and sew them into the scroll at the end. Roll, making sure the tip retains its point (diag. 39). Add pairs for the petal shapes (**4**) and work them in the same way as those on the other side. Roll.

The centre leaf shape is set up at its tip and worked as in diags. 55–56. Work some sewings as in diag. 57. Put pins on the dotted line and twist the runners 3 or 4 times around each pin. Sew into the scroll. Roll.

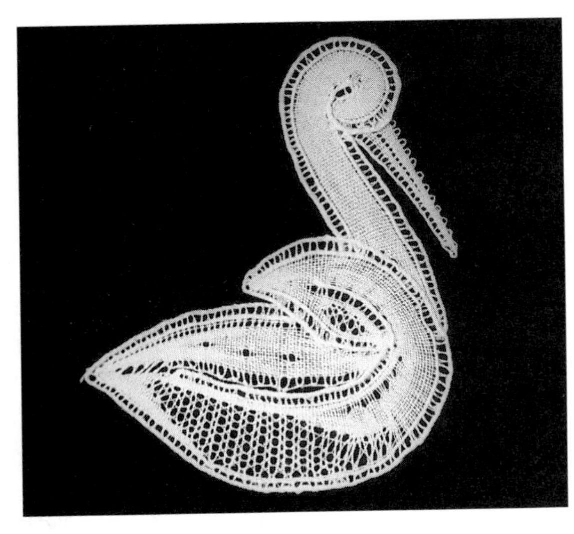

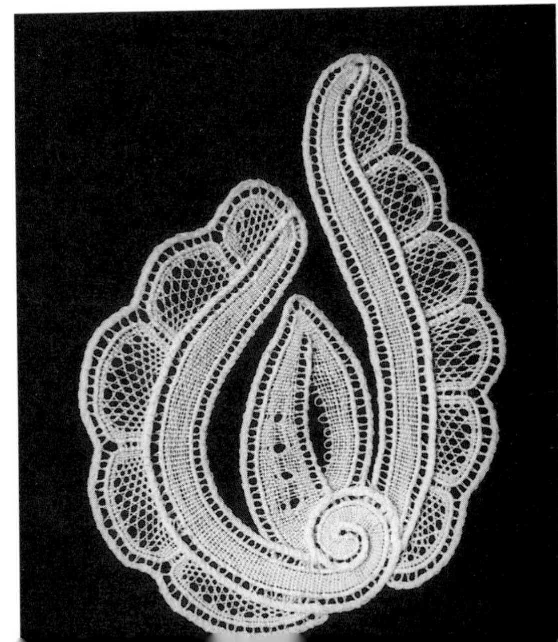

Pattern 41 – Grannie's bonnet

Thread 100/2

Start this pattern with one of the rolled scrolls (diags. 108–110 and 113–114). When the point is reached, finish the bundle at the top, tie and cut off (diag. 37). Start with the leaf that is foremost, setting up at the tip (diags. 33–36). Where indicated (diag. 117) divide the pairs and work tallies. Finish this leaf at its point (diag. 37). Roll. Work the leaves in the indicated order. Instead of making sewings all the way down, twist the runners round the pin and make sewings at regular intervals. This gives a shadowy effect.

When all the leaves have been worked, the circle must be worked. For this refer to Chapter 5 (diags. 122–124). Join the circle to the scrolls when rolling (diag. 21). The braid is worked with picots (diag. 60). The filling is whole stitch, twist, pin, whole stitch, twist etc (see Chapter 10). If leaf (**4**) is worked in half stitch, it should give an illusion of movement.

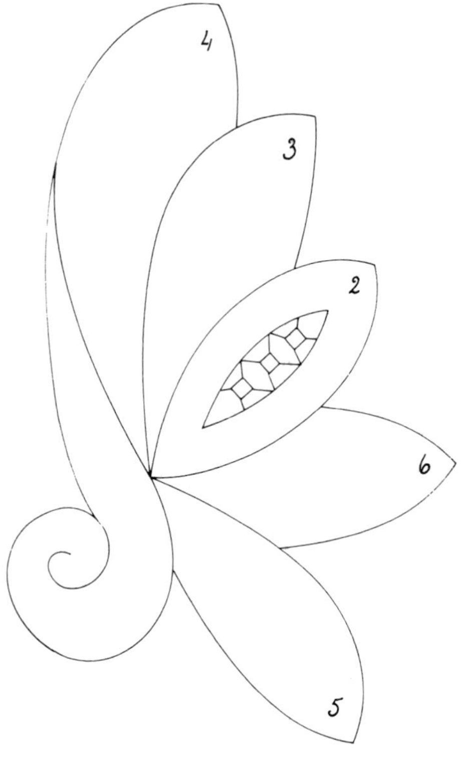

Diag. 117 *Working order for Grannie's Bonnet*

Pattern 42 – Buta (also known as Paisley)

Thread 160/2

Set up at (**1**) and work a rolled scroll (diags. 108–110 and 113–114). Work the curves as in diag. 50a. Towards the point, take out pairs so that only 2 pairs are left to roll along the inner side of the scroll; an edge pair and a gimp pair to make the edge. Add pairs along the edge to work the half stitch filling. When the side is reached, add as many pairs as necessary.

Pick up the edge pair and gimp pair and continue the filling (see Round setting up).

(**5**) is a rolled scroll. The ribs in between these scrolls are set up on both sides.

As this pattern was used as an edge for a scarf, picots were added on one side when rolling.

Pattern 43 – Modesty

Thread 100/2

Set 3 pins for a rolled scroll at (**1**) (diags. 108–110 and 113–114). Work the braid to (**3**). Leave the pairs hanging and start the 2nd rolled scroll at (**2**) in the same way. When point (**3**) is reached, with this braid work a whole stitch with both edge pairs, as well as with the gimp pairs. The 2 thin threads of the gimp pairs are used as passives. One of the 2 runners is worked to the centre and left with the 2 thick threads from the gimp pairs. The braid is continued with the other pair of runners. The 2 edge pairs and the thick threads can be used to roll both sides, starting from the centre, back to the scroll. At the bottom, the braid separates (diag. 118). Finish the braids in a scroll (diag. 112).

Set up with a scroll at (**4**) and finish with a scroll. Roll. Work the ribs (**5**), roll them and the circles (**6**). Hang in pairs for the lattice filling, twist them, work a whole stitch on the crossing, with a pin in the centre, and twist both pairs again as many times as needed. Work the joining braids.

The leaves are worked in different ways. For leaf

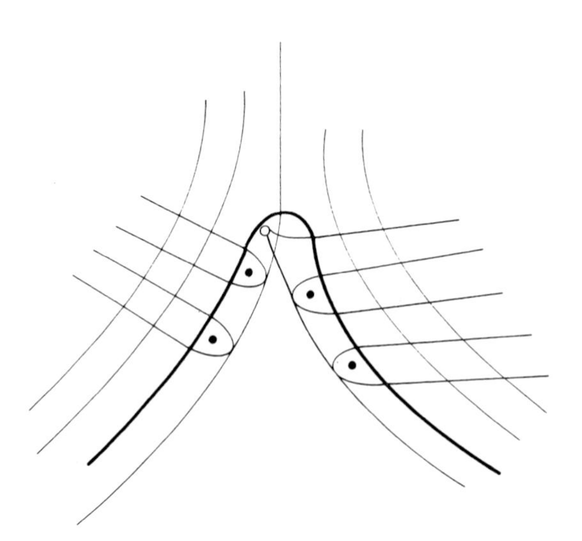

Diag. 118 *Division of braid in Modesty*

(**7**), see diag. 102. In leaf (**8**), the runners are twisted. For leaf (**9**), see diag. 119. Diag. 120 shows another variation.

As this pattern can be used either as an inset for a blouse or for the end of a shawl, roll with picots either on the top or at the sides.

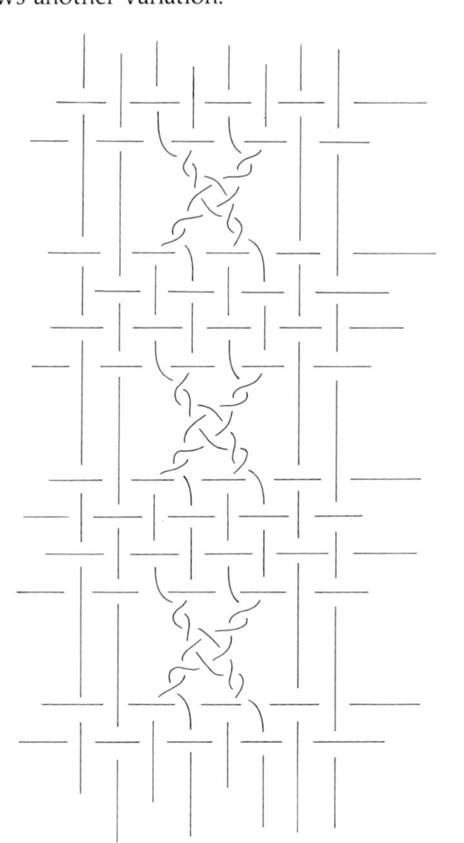

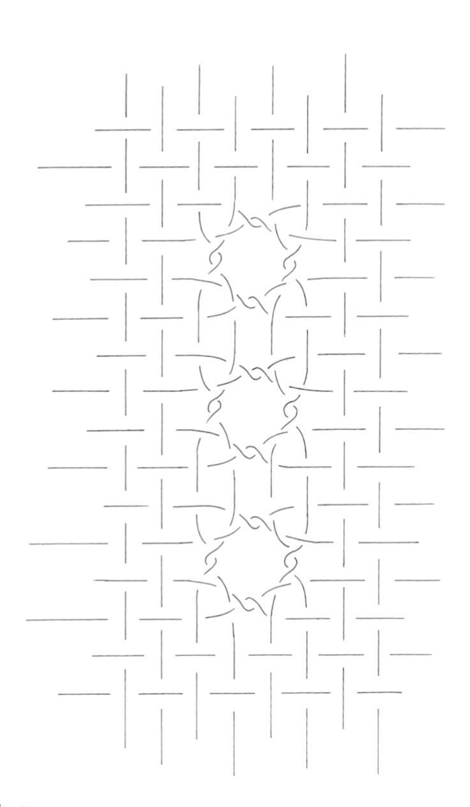

Diags. 119 & 120 *Decorations used in leaves of Modesty*

Pattern 44 – Curly duck
Thread 160/2

Work a Round setting up (diags. 28–30) at (*) and add a double gimp pair, adding more pairs as the pattern becomes wider. When the eye (**1**) is reached, lay the edge pair aside and twist the runners round the gimp pair (diag. 121).
Use the edge pair that was put aside to roll along the setting up to (**2**), and leave it there ready to be used as an edge pair later. When the end of the eye is reached, make top sewings and include the gimp pair again. Pairs have to be added as the braid becomes wider. Pick up the edge pair at (**2**) and continue the braid. At (**3**) the braid is divided (diag. 118). Roll with some picots (diag. 24). The decorations on the head are worked as ribs with picots (diag. 60).

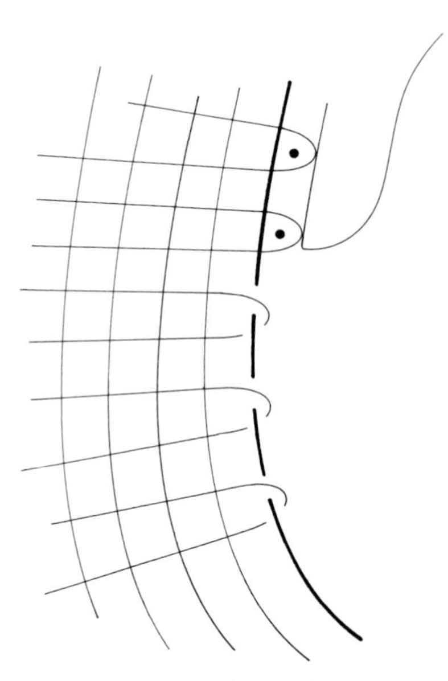

Diag. 121 *Eye of Curly Duck*

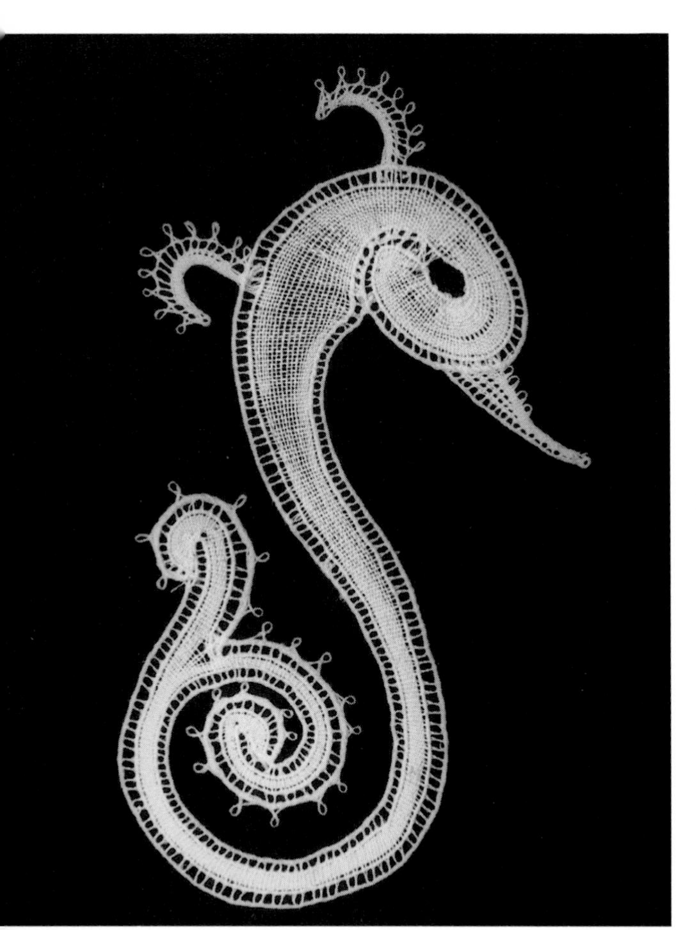

5. Circles

Pattern 45

Thread 120/2

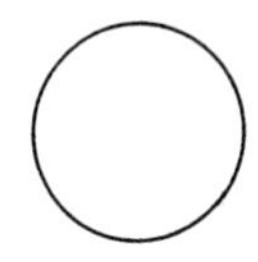

Pins have to be set on a horizontal line from the centre to the edge (diag. 122). Set up as usual adding a gimp pair between the 2nd and 3rd pairs on a support pin set outside the work. Work the centre curve as shown, decreasing 1,2,3, and take sewings in the centre when needed (diag. 123). Try to achieve a neat, even weave, without holes or bulging threads.

When the circle is almost finished (about one eighth still to work), work the runners to the inside and leave them there. Sew the next passives in the centre and use them as new runners. Repeat this until the circle is closed. Take care to work the last used runners to the outside if they are required for the bundle. Sew in one pair at a time and tie them (diag. 124).

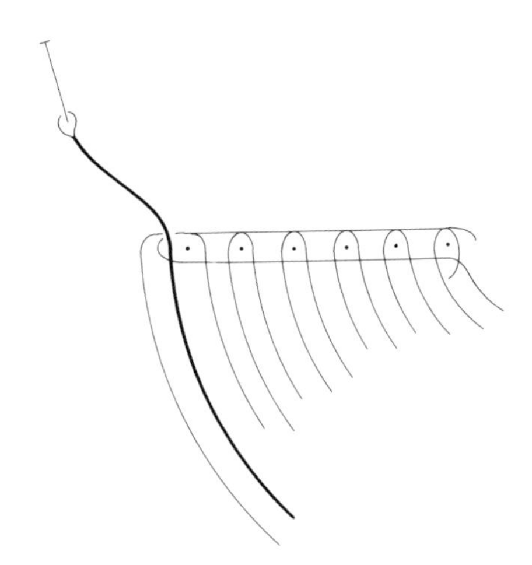

Diag. 122 *Setting up for the circle*

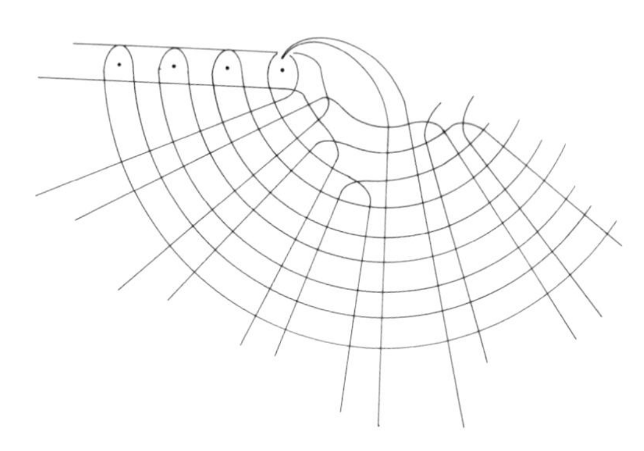

Diag. 123 *Decreasing 1,2,3 and making sewings when necessary*

This circle may be worked in either whole stitch or half stitch (see photograph of cotoneaster, p.82).

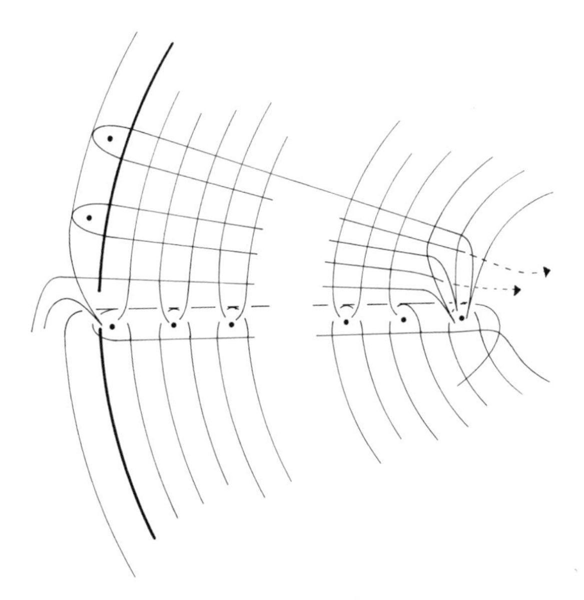

Diag. 124 *Finishing of a circle*

Pattern 46

Thread 120/2

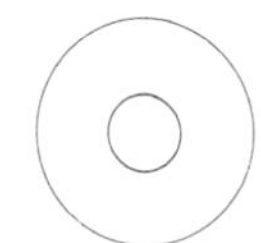

This is another method for working a circle. The pattern is drawn with one smaller circle inside the outer one. Make sure that there is enough space for at least 2 setting up pins between inner circle and centre. The setting up of this circle is similar to that of the first one, but having set the 1st pin on the outer edge, work back to the inner circle. Do not work the 4 pairs in the centre circle. Set a support pin in front of the last worked passives. Use these passives as runners and work back to the outside. Make an edge stitch and work back to the centre. Work the curve by decreasing 1,2,3 where necessary. Every alternate row is worked right to the centre and the row in between only to the inner circle. When a new support pin is set on the inner circle the last pin is taken out (diag. 125). In this way, fewer sewings have to be made. Finish the circle in the same way as the 1st one.

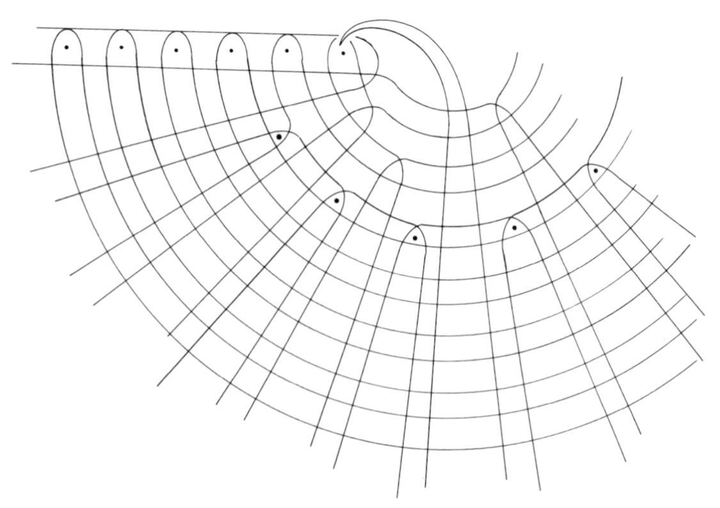

Diag. 125 *Circle, decreasing decoratively*

As the circle is divided into 2 parts, a combination of whole stitch and half stitch is possible. This method can also be applied to an oval. The pins are set on the narrow side (diag. 126) and, because of its shape, the inner side is best worked in half stitch.

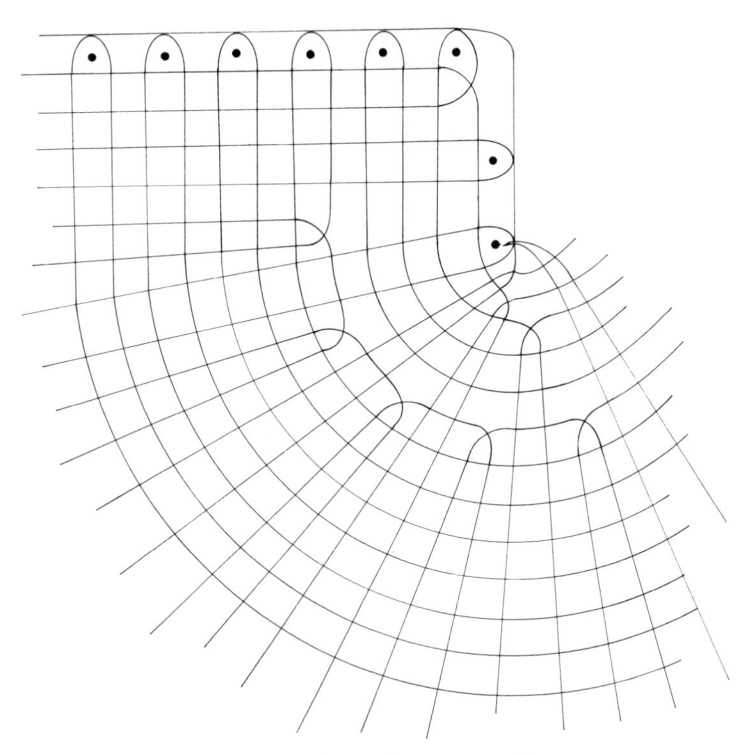

Diag. 126 *Oval, setting up on the narrow side*

Pattern 47 – Teddy
Thread 100/2

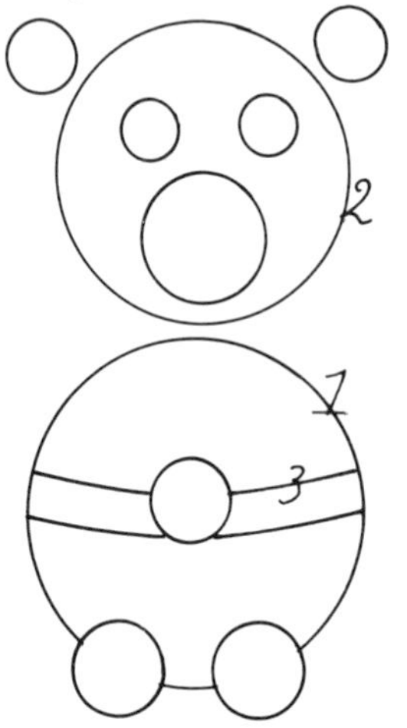

Work a variety of circles, smaller ones as in Pattern 45 (diags. 122–124) and larger ones as in diag. 125. Use either whole stitch on the inside and half stitch on the outside, or any combination of these. When the circles are finished, the ribs (**1**) and (**2**) have to be worked. Roll these with picots and attach where necessary. Then the belt can be worked (**3**) and the filling (point ground) is worked last.

The finished teddy can be seen on the jacket of this book.

Pattern 48 – Cotoneaster
Thread 160/2

Start with the circles (diags. 122–124) and roll them. The leaves can be worked as in diags. 55–57 and sewn into the circle. Roll.

Pattern 49 – Holly
Thread 120/2

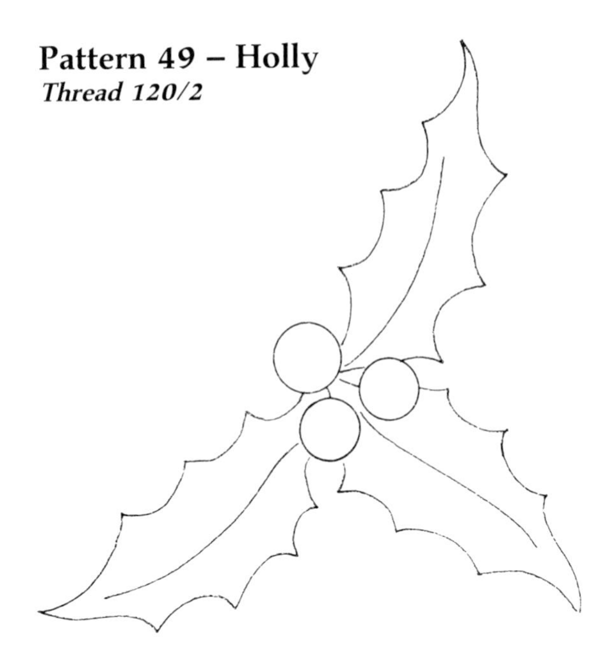

Begin by working the 3 circles (diags 122–124). Roll them. Continue with one of the 3 leaves setting up at the points (diags. 33–35). Work all the leaves in half stitch because of the shape. Add more pairs straight away. For the leaves see diags. 55–57. The veins are made as in diags. 103–104. Sew into the circles but do not work on top of them. Roll, with a picot at the points.

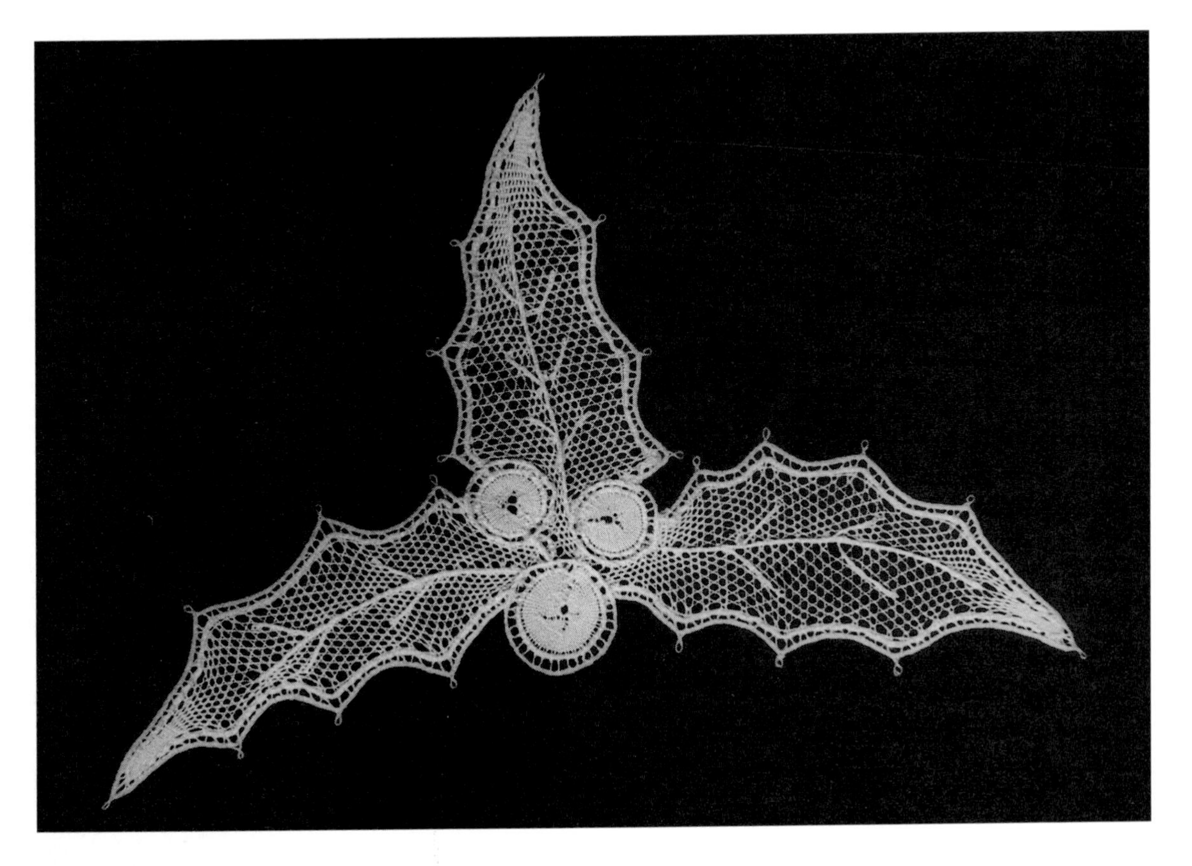

Pattern 50 – Honeysuckle

Thread 160/2

Start with the centre (**1**) of each flower. Work this as an oval (diag. 126); half in whole stitch, half in half stitch. Roll. Use the round setting up (diags. 28–30) for the petals, starting with (**2**) because this one is in front. Work them in numerical order. The small flower at the top is started with a rib. Study the petals of this to find out with which one to start.

Small stamens: Set 2 pins together (or one thicker pin). Hang 2 pairs around these (this), twist them 8 times and work a plait (diag. 127).
Large stamens: Hang 2 pairs around a pin; twist 4 times and work – whole stitch, twist, picot, whole stitch, twist, picot, whole stitch, twist, picot, whole stitch, twist.

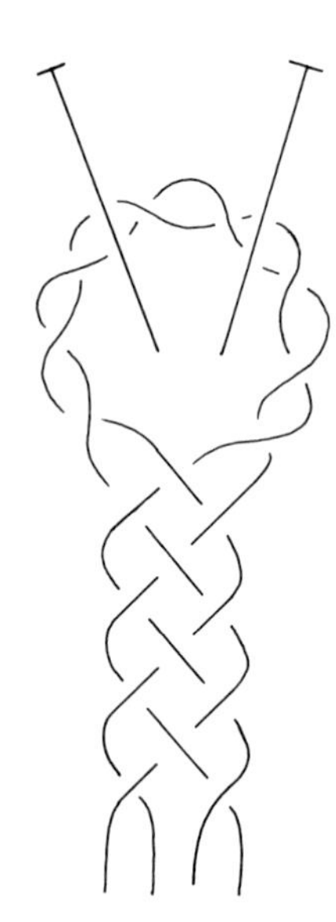

Diag. 127 *Small stamens in Honeysuckle*

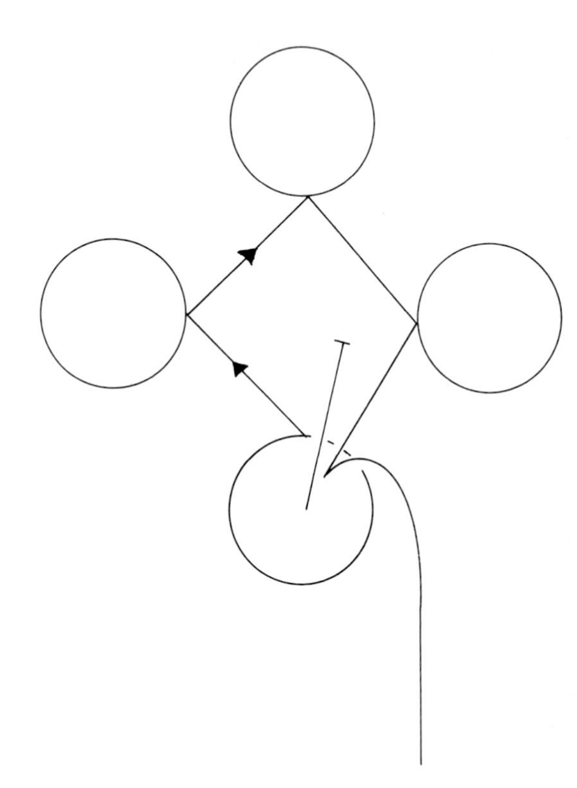

Diag. 128 *Large stamens in Honeysuckle*

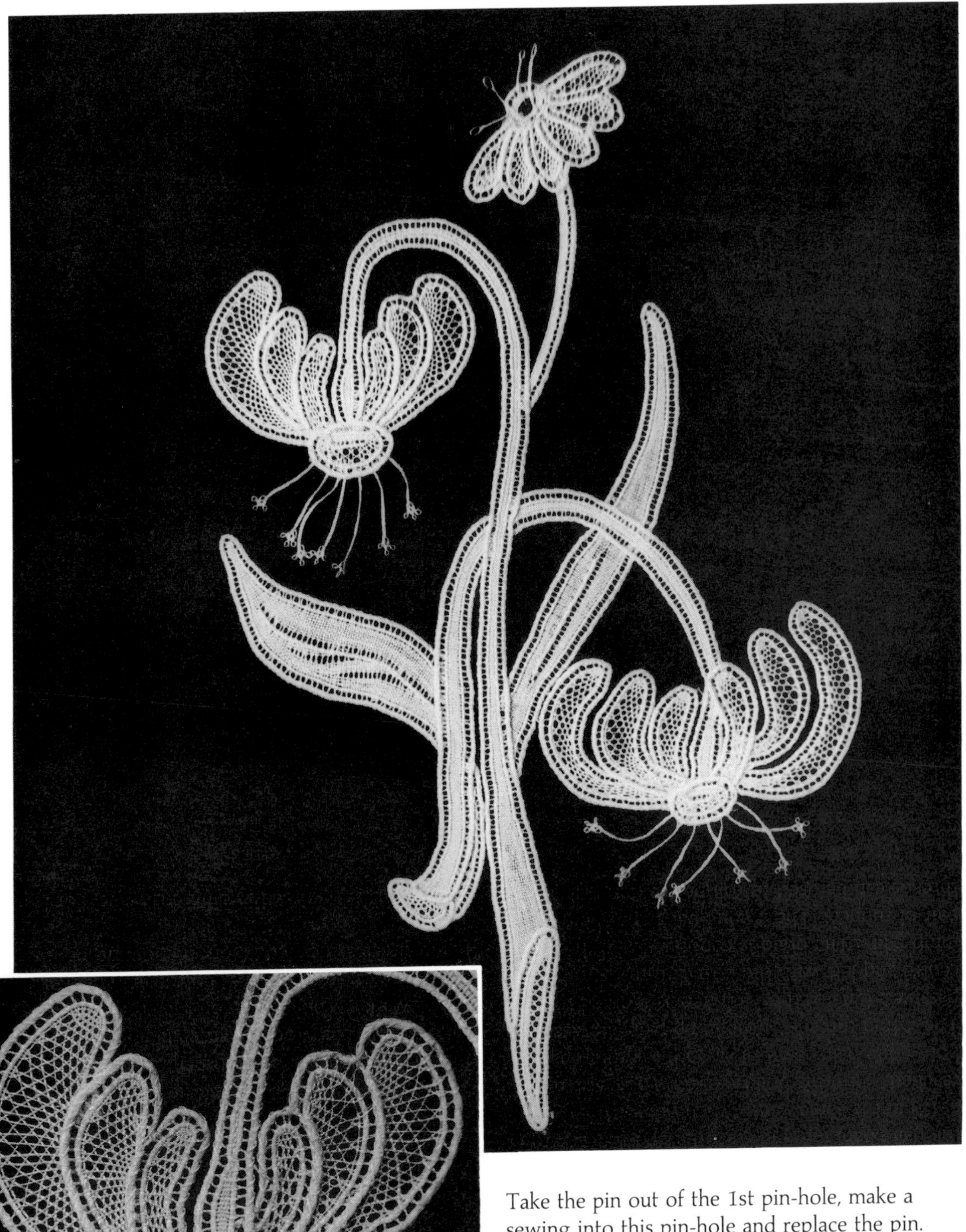

Take the pin out of the 1st pin-hole, make a sewing into this pin-hole and replace the pin. Work a plait and sew into the centre of the flower (diag. 128). Work the bottom side of the stems first. Roll them. Then the stems can be worked. Finish with the leaves.

Pattern 51 – Moulin Rouge
Thread 160/2

(for actual size see p.151)

Start with scroll (**1**) (diags. 108–110); finish (diag. 112) and roll. Work scroll (**2**). Finish as in diag. 52. Set up pairs for braid (**3**). On one side a straight edge stitch is used. On the other side there are 4 twists round the pin. Work the curve decoratively as in diag. 50. Then work the little rib (**4**) using 4 or 5 pairs only.

The oval (**5**) is worked as in diag. 126. The scroll (**6**) is not rolled but has picots on the edge (diag. 60).

For leaf (**7**) see Pattern 36 (Reverse side). Hang pairs for rib (**8**), and work, sewing the runners of the rib to the scroll on every other row. For the raised vein (**9**), see diags. 140–142. Braid (**10**) is worked in the same way as Braid (**3**) Add raised vein (**11**).

Pattern 52 – Easter egg
Thread 160/2

(for actual size see p.151)

Start with circle (**1**) (diags. 122–124). Roll. Set up at the point of (**2**) and work the braid. Sew into circle and roll. The other one is worked in the same way. Set up at point (**3**). Add as many pairs as necessary in the same way as for the flower (diag. 63). Finish at point (**o**). Roll only the top of this detail and leave the bundle. Set pins to work the 'inside' of the braid (see Pattern 36, Reverse side). Work it in half stitch. Finish in the circle. Pick up the bundle and continue rolling along this last worked piece. Also roll between (**o**) and (**3**). The other side is worked in the same way.

Braid (**4**) can be worked now, as well as the rib (**5**). Sew in pairs to work the outside rib. Roll. The top decorations are braids, ribs and flower petals. Once these have been worked, the filling (point ground) can be made.

Pattern 53 – Lapel motif

Thread 100/2

Start with a Round setting up (diags. 28–30) at (**1**). Add as many pairs as necessary. Continue to (**2**), then roll back to (**3**) with the edge pair and the gimp pair (diag. 56). Make 2 sewings in the last pin-hole. Set 2 pins in the curve and hang 2 pairs round each pin. Work the narrow setting up (diags. 25–27) from right to left, starting with the edge pair of the bundle. Work the gimp pair in whole stitch and leave it next to the edge pair. Continue in whole stitch, adding pairs. At the end of the vein the runners are sewn and used as passives. Pick up the runners from the other side (diag. 59) and continue.

On the outside curve, set the pins a little wider apart, but on the inside put them head to head. Take pairs out as the braid narrows. When the braid becomes a leaf, pairs have to be added again. Finish at the point and roll on both sides. Each side finishes at (**3**).

Set 3 pins for a rolled scroll (**4**). Add a double gimp pair (diags. 108–110 and 113–115). When (**5**) is reached, leave the edge pair and the gimp pair, sew the runners and continue the braid. Each time a sewing has to be made, leave the runners, sew in the last used passives and use those as new runners. This is a neat way of gradually losing pairs. Finish with a pair of runners, gimp pair and edge pair. Work the runners to the inside, twist the edge pair one more time, work it through the gimp pair and sew it one pin-hole lower to ensure a flowing line. Use the edge pair and the gimp pair to roll.

Set up at point (**6**) (diags. 33–35). Work according to the lines indicated on the pattern, setting the pins further apart on the outside curve. Finish this part in the same way as the rolled scroll (**4**). (**7**) and (**8**) are set up at their points and worked in the same way as (**6**). Start leaf (**9**) also at its point. The circles (**10**) and (**11**) can be worked as in diags. 122–124. Set 3 pins for a rolled scroll (**12**). When (**13**) is reached roll back to (**14**) with the edge pair and the gimp pair (diag. 56), making 2 sewings in the last pin-hole. Set 2 pins in the curve and hang 2 pairs round each pin. Work the narrow setting up. etc. (see start of this pattern). Continue to (**15**), roll back, etc. Work to (**16**) making sure the work flows according to the line of the pattern, turning the pillow as the work progresses. At (**16**) take the gimp pair and the edge pair and roll back to where the scroll starts. Finish by making a top sewing, tie the pairs and cut them off (diag. 20).

Set 3 pins for a rolled scroll (**17**) and work to (**16**). Sew the runners into the end of the vein and use them as passives (diag. 59). Pick up the runners from the other side and continue. When (**18**) is reached, pairs have to be added as the braid becomes wider and separates. At (**19**) add a double gimp pair and divide (diag. 118), using a pair of passives as the edge pair (diag. 55). Continue this part and finish in the point. Roll back. Leave the bundle half way. Add a new edge pair and a pair of runners to continue the braid, and finish in the point of the leaf. Roll. Add the other motifs in the same way as in the 1st half of this pattern.
The filling consists of snow flakes.

Pattern 54 – Scroll square
Thread 140/2

Every motif in this pattern has to be set up and finished with a scroll (diags. 108–112). Follow diags. 48–50a for the braids. Set up and finish the fillings at their points. Roll. Add pairs for the braids. Sew in on the other side. Work the circles between the motifs as ribs.

6. Berries

Pattern 55
Thread 140/2

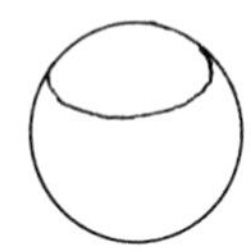

Start the rib as indicated (diag. 129). After the rib is closed it is then rolled (diag. 130). Put its pairs in the correct order when back at the start. Make an edge stitch and add a gimp pair. Apart from using all the pairs from the rib, add new pairs

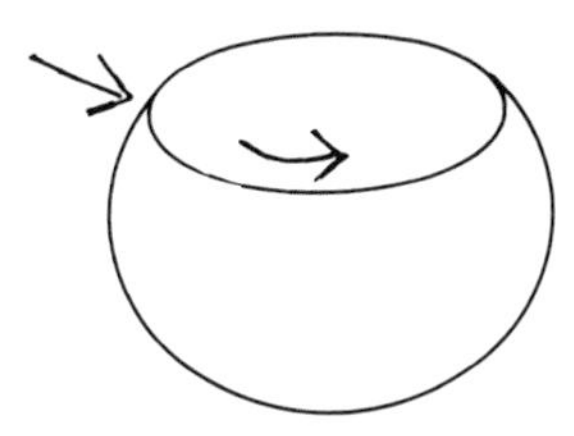

Diag. 129 *Starting point of the berry's rib*

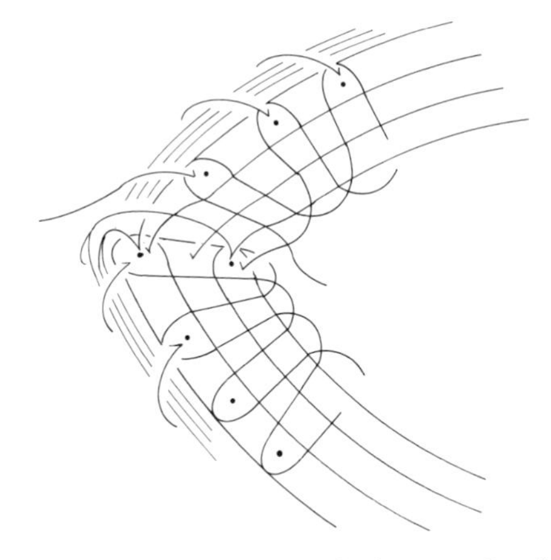

Diag. 130 *The rib of the berry is closed and then rolled*

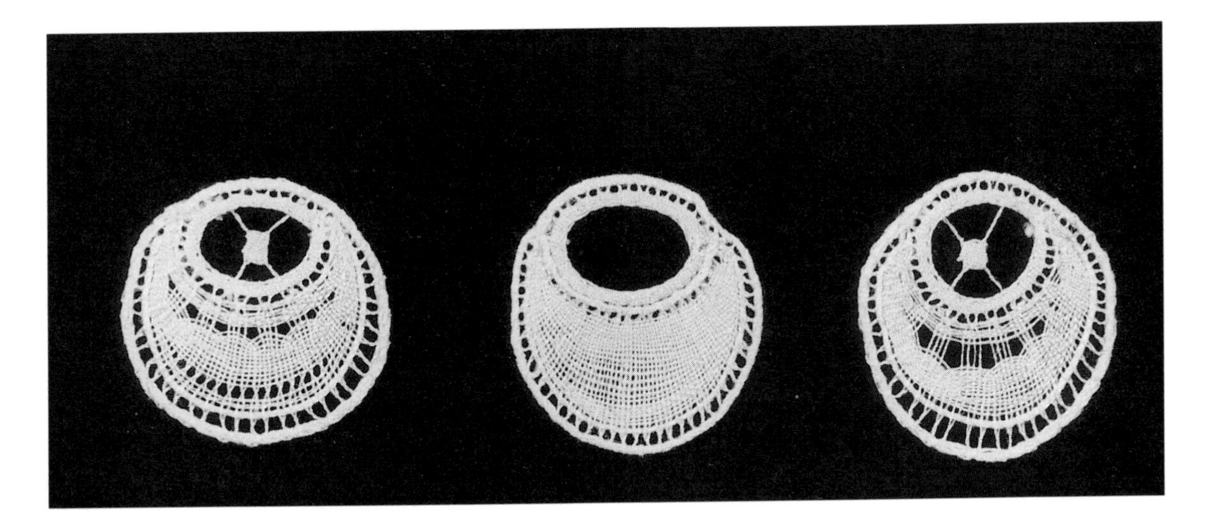

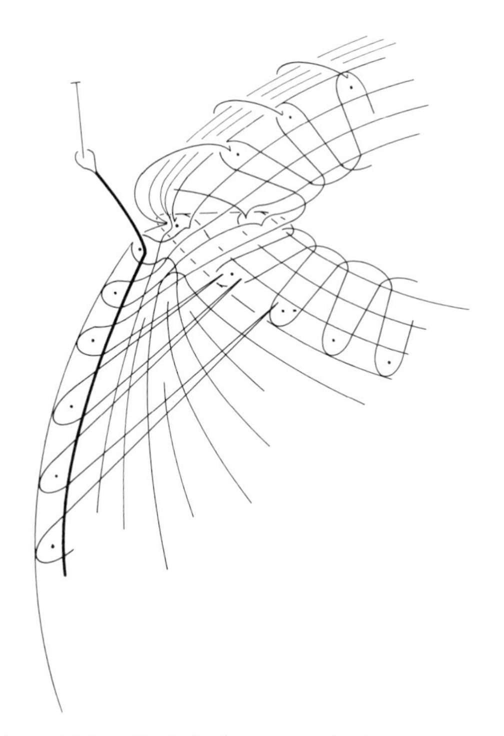

Diag. 131 *Start the bottom of the berry in the point, adding new pairs (roll not shown)*

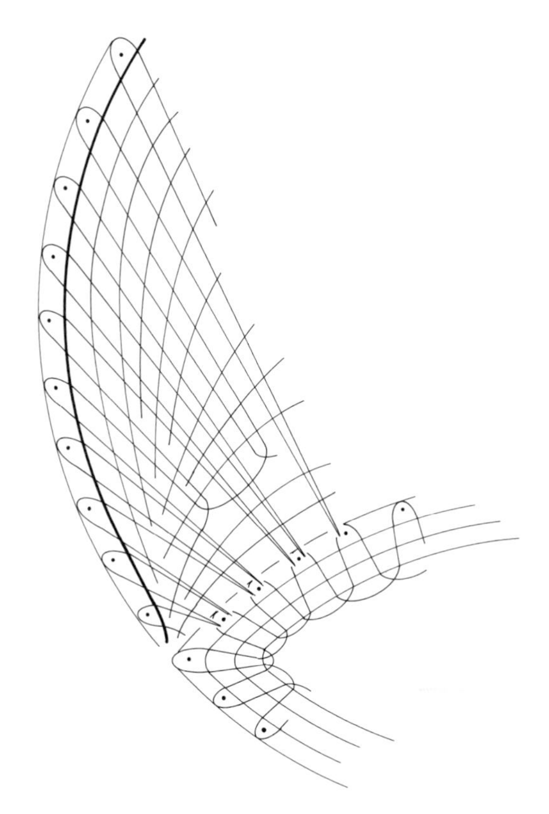

Diag. 132 *Taking out pairs when finishing in the point (roll not shown)*

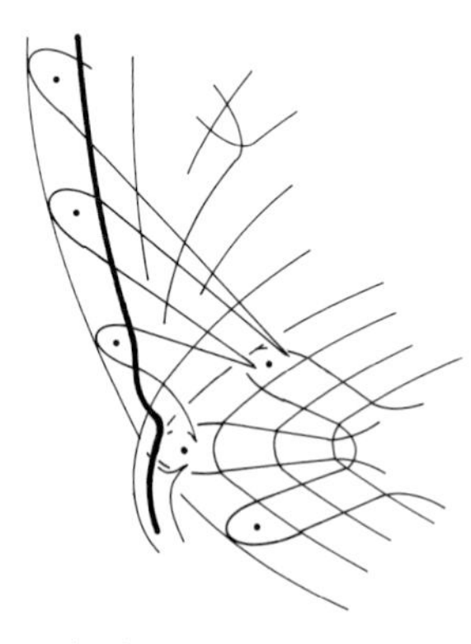

Diag. 133 *The berry is rolled, started at the top over the first roll (roll not shown)*

straight away. Make sure the runners create a flowing line of work (diag. 131). Work a decorative curve on the inside. As the pattern narrows, pairs have to be put aside (diag. 132). Finish at the point in such a way that the line flows into the rib. Bundle and roll (diag. 133).

Pattern 56 – Christmas bell

Thread 160/2

Work the berries and the circle first. Leaf (**1**) can be worked next. Because of the shape, half stitch gives the best finish. See diags. 55–56 for the vein. Finish at the circle. Work the stem (**2**) in whole stitch and sew into the berries. Then leaves (**3**) and (**4**) can be worked. Before the bell is started, the stem (**5**) must be worked as far as the loop of the bell. Leave the pairs hanging and start rolling both sides of the stem so that pairs for the loop can be sewn in (**6**). Work the loop and continue with the ribs of the bell [(**7**) and (**8**)]. Roll. Work rib (**9**) on the other side and the bottom one (**10**). Roll these and work the ribs [(**11**) and (**12**)]. Finish the stem (**5**) at the loop of the bell. Work the stem between the loop and berry (**13**). Sew in pairs to work the filling of your choice for the bell. Now work the last leaf (**14**) to finish the pattern.

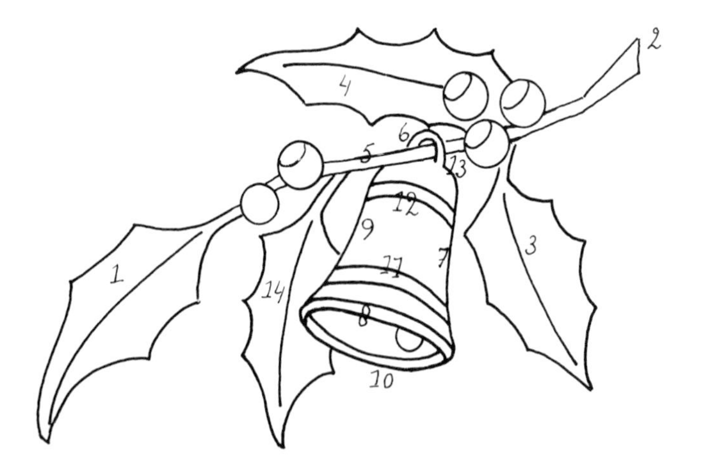
1
2
3
4
5
6
7
8
9
10
11
12
13
14

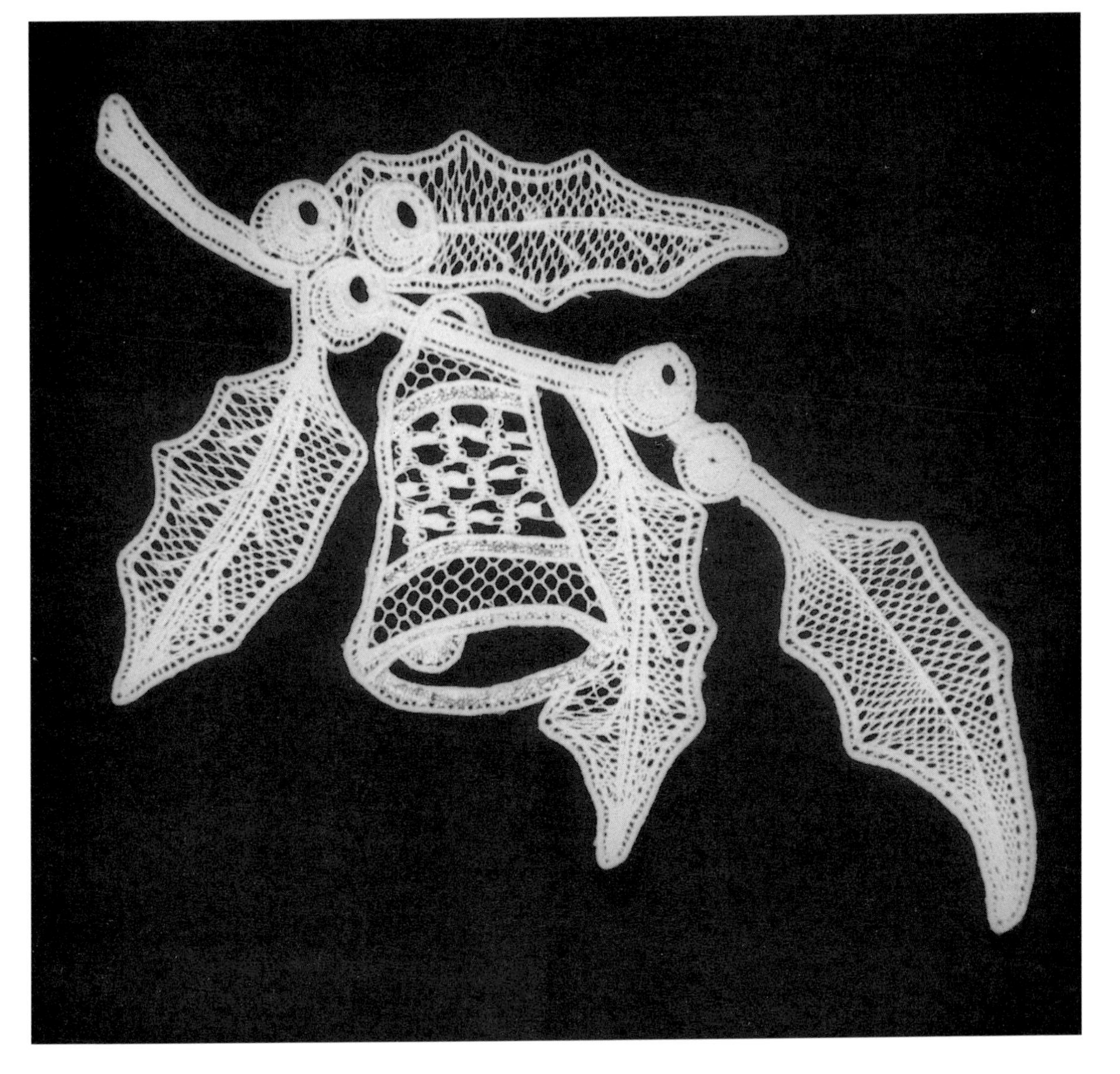

Pattern 57 – Yew
Thread 180/2

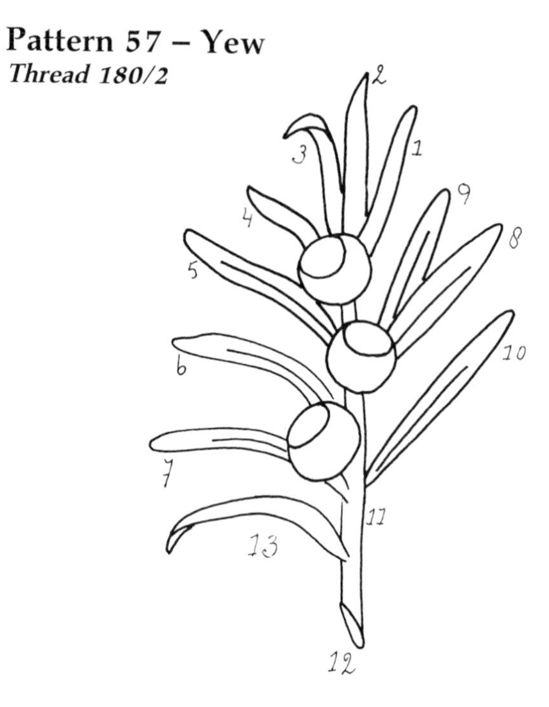

Start with the berries and then work the leaves in the order indicated on the pattern. Work variations as in diags. 100–102 or twist the runners. The bottom of the stem (**12**) is worked as in Pattern 36, to show the reverse side.

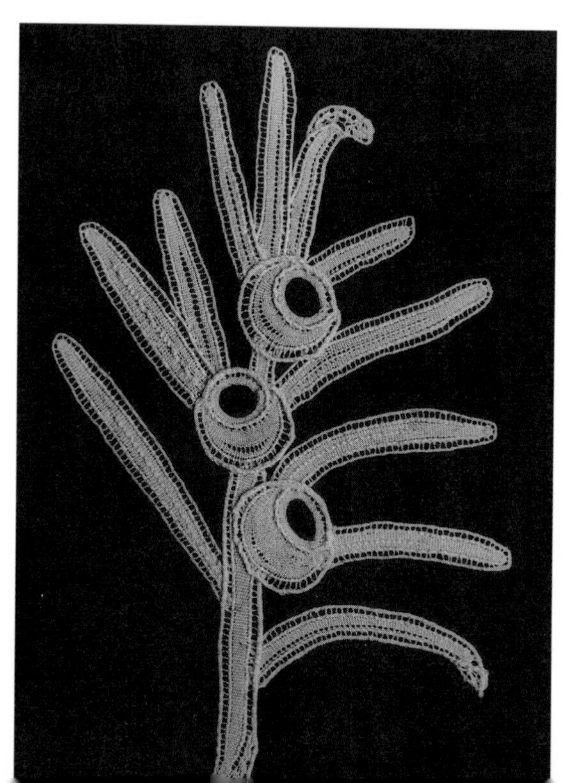

Pattern 58 – Buttercup flower
Thread 140/2

Work the berry as in diags. 130–133 but add a gimp pair in the rib to make it wider. Roll the berry. Work the stem, sewing pairs into the berry, and finish at the tip. Roll on both sides.

The leaf is started at the point (diags. 33–35). Work it in half stitch and make a vein as in diags. 55–56 sew into the stem and roll. Work the rib from the point and add 2 extra pairs in the first pin-hole for rolling (diag. 54).

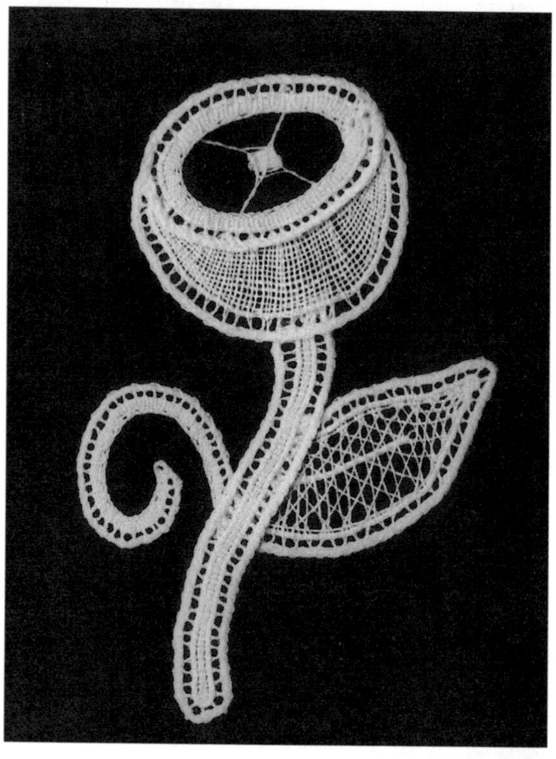

Pattern 59 – Dahlia

Thread 160/2

Reverse side of Dahlia

Set up and work the rib and roll (diag. 61). Continue with the petals around the rib, using a Round setting up (diags. 28–30). Pairs have to be taken out towards the point. Finish at the point (diag. 40) and roll.

The second row of petals is started at each point (diags. 33–35) in whole stitch. Gradually change into half stitch, adding more pairs at the same time, starting with one half stitch. In each row one more half stitch is added. Make top sewings into the first circle of petals. See photograph above for reverse side.

Bud: Set up at point (**1**) and add pairs straight away. This is worked like the berry (diags. 131–133) without the rib. Finish at the point and roll. For the top of the bud, set up at point (**2**) and work in the same way as the outer petals of the flower.

Work the scroll (**3**) (diags. 108–110) and continue into the braid (diag. 111), sewing into the flower. Roll. Add the rib and sew into the scroll at regular intervals.

The leaves (**4**) can now be worked, setting up at their points. The rib at the side (**5**) is made with picots (diag. 60).

Pattern 60 – Lily

Thread 140/2

Start the flower at (**1**) with Round setting up (diags. 28–30). Pairs are taken out on the sharp curve and added again when the braid becomes wider. Finish at (**2**) in the same way as for finishing at a point (diag. 38), but set the pins on the curve. Roll.

The centre petal is set up at (**3**) (Round setting up). Set the pins a little apart so that not too many pairs are needed. Work as far as the centre vein. Set a pin and hang a double gimp pair round this (diags. 134a & b). Continue the work, twisting twice between the gimp pairs of this centre vein. Take out pairs at the sides (see Round setting up). Sew into the part that has already been worked and roll. Continue with the petals [(**4**) and (**5**)].

Set up (**6**) at the point (diags. 33–35). Add pairs as they are needed. A straight edge stitch is worked on the centre vein. Work one side first (diags. 55–59). As the leaf is sewn into the stem (**8**), roll leaves (**6**) and (**7**) (take care when rolling the point (diag. 39). Put all these pairs aside and now start on stem (**8**). Set up at the point. Sew into leaf (**6**) and roll. Now leaf (**6**) can be finished.

The bud is set up at point (**9**) and finished at the point. Roll on both sides. Use the pairs of the bundle to set up the two side leaves.

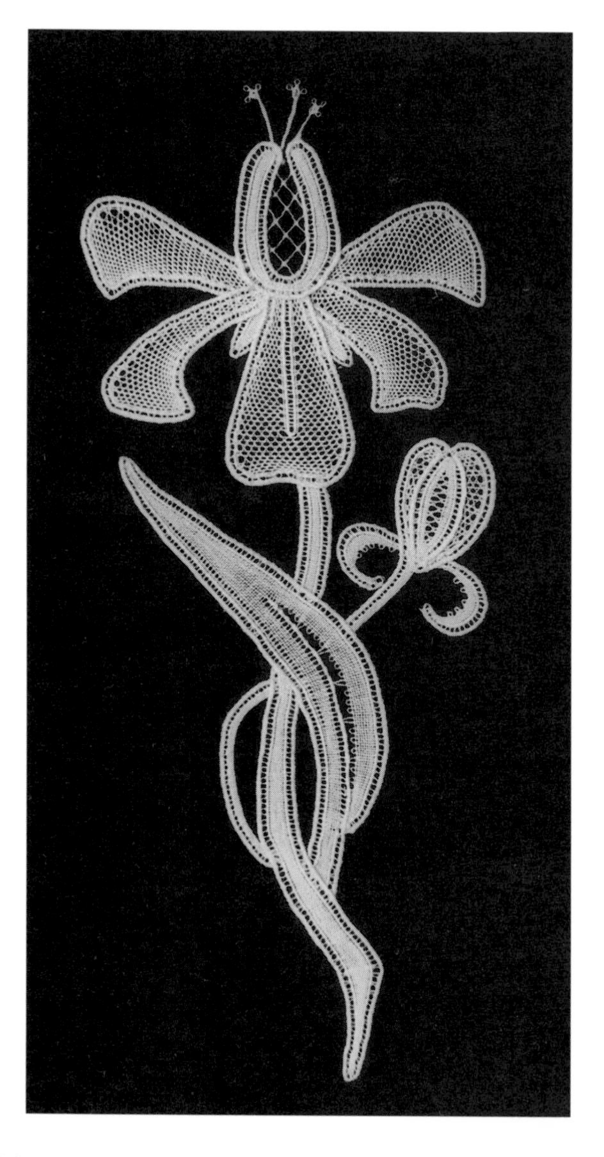

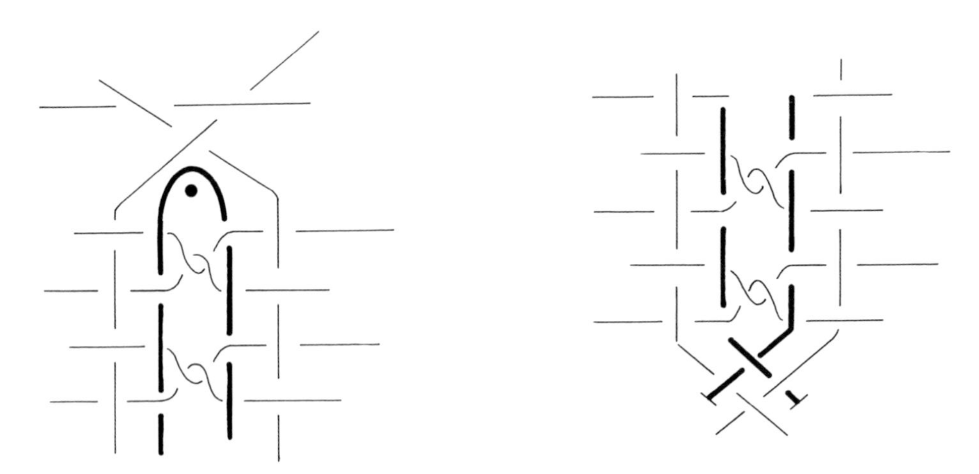

Diags. 134a & b *Decorations in centre leaf of Lily*

Pattern 61 – Flower garland
Thread 140/2

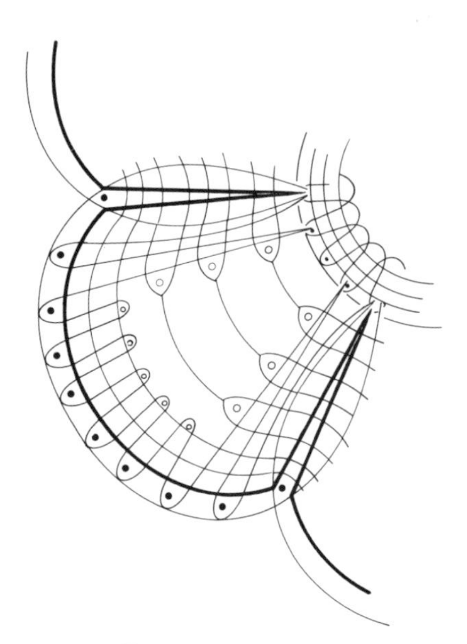

Diag. 135 *Decoration in the big flower of Flower Garland*

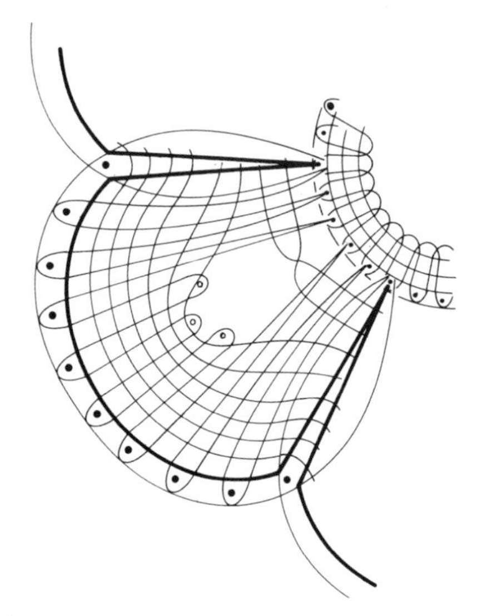

Diag. 136 *Decoration in flower (3) of Flower Garland*

Start with the big flower at the bottom. Work this in half stitch with plaits (diag. 135). The leaves (**1**) are then worked. Choose from the variety of possibilities. The circles (**2**) are worked next (diags. 122–124). Flower (**3**) is worked as in diag. 136.

Study the pattern carefully and continue to work the motifs that are foremost before the ones that are partly hidden. Each part is joined by a braid.

Pattern 62 – Dragon

Thread 140/2

(for actual size see p.151)

Start the eye (**1**) as a rib, changing into half stitch (diag. 137). Close the ring and roll. Work the nose (**2**) as a circle (diags. 122–124). Roll the circle and use the pairs for the head. Add enough pairs to work the head and the neck, turning the pillow with the direction of work. Work a sharp curve decoratively where necessary (diag. 50). Work as far as (**3**) and roll back with the gimp and edge pairs to the eye. Work round the corner (**3**) as in diag. 96. Make top sewings on the other side and sew to finish. Use pairs to roll the outside, finishing at the nose. Work the 2nd eye with an edge pair, gimp pair, one pair of passives and runners. Roll.

Work the wing (**4**). Start from the point (diags. 33–35) working in half stitch and adding pairs on one side. Sew into the neck and roll. Each part of the wing falls behind the previous one. Set up at point (**5**). Sew into the neck and roll. Add pairs to work (**6**). Twist, whole stitch, twist in the centre. Sew into the first wing part and roll. Then add pairs to work (**7**). Each section is worked in this order. The other wing (**8**) is started at its point and rolled.

Start (**9**) at its point, and then (**10**) at its point. Roll back and use narrow setting up to start (**11**). Make a straight setting up at (**12**), work in half stitch and add plaits as a decoration (diags. 103–104). The parts (**13**) and (**14**) are worked in the same way. Sew in pairs for the leg (**15**) and add more pairs when needed. Continue to (**16**). Roll back on both sides of the leg, to the neck (**17**). Put aside the remaining pairs.

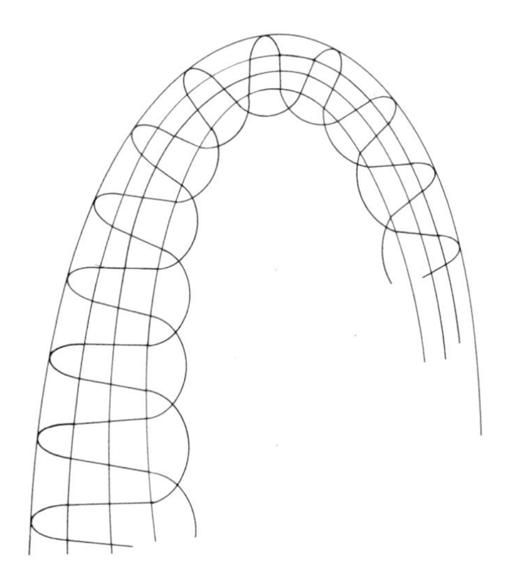

Diag. 137 *The eye for the Dragon is started as a rib, changing into half stitch*

Diag. 138 *Grain of the Dragon's body*

Set up at the point of the tail, adding pairs straight away and taking them out when it becomes narrower. Then add them again, working towards the leg and the body (diag. 138). Sew pairs into the leg and continue working the body, picking up pairs that were put aside. It may be necessary to add a few pairs at (**16**) to prevent a hole forming. From (**17**) work around the sharp bend (diag. 96). Some of the pairs have to be sewn into the wing. Continue to work towards the neck. Roll the tail.

Pattern 63 – Nurse's buckle

Thread 160/2

Start and finish each of the 4 braids in scrolls (diags. 108–110 and 112). Join them when rolling (diag. 21). Sew in pairs to work the ribs of the flowers. Roll the ribs and use the pairs to work the petals. Work the circles (diags. 122–124). Roll and join. Work the rib in the centre. Roll and join.
The filling is a snowflake.

7. Raised Veins

Pattern 64
Thread 80/2

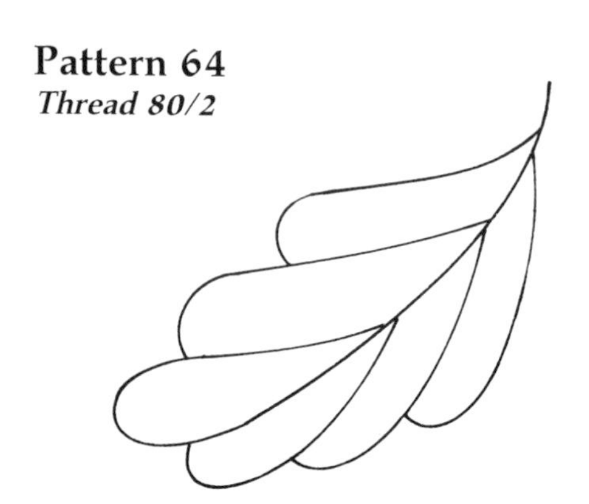

Set up for the rib. When this becomes the top of the leaf, the runners become passives on the inside. Work back with the last used passives, edge stitch and pin. Whole stitch to the inside and also leave these runners (diag. 139). Whole stitch back to the outside; edge stitch; pin. Add a gimp pair and passives round a support pin. Work through all pairs and make a top sewing into the top bar of the pin-hole. Work back to the outside. Decide whether there are enough passives. The next sewing is made in the bottom bar of the same pin-hole (diag. 140).

Mark the grain (direction of work) on the pattern in order to ensure that all the leaves are worked in the same direction. (**N.B.** By sewing into the top and bottom bar at the top of each leaf, the grain can be adjusted.) When the leaf narrows, put pairs aside until there are only 6 and the

Raised vein and raised vein with interrupted rib (see p.122)

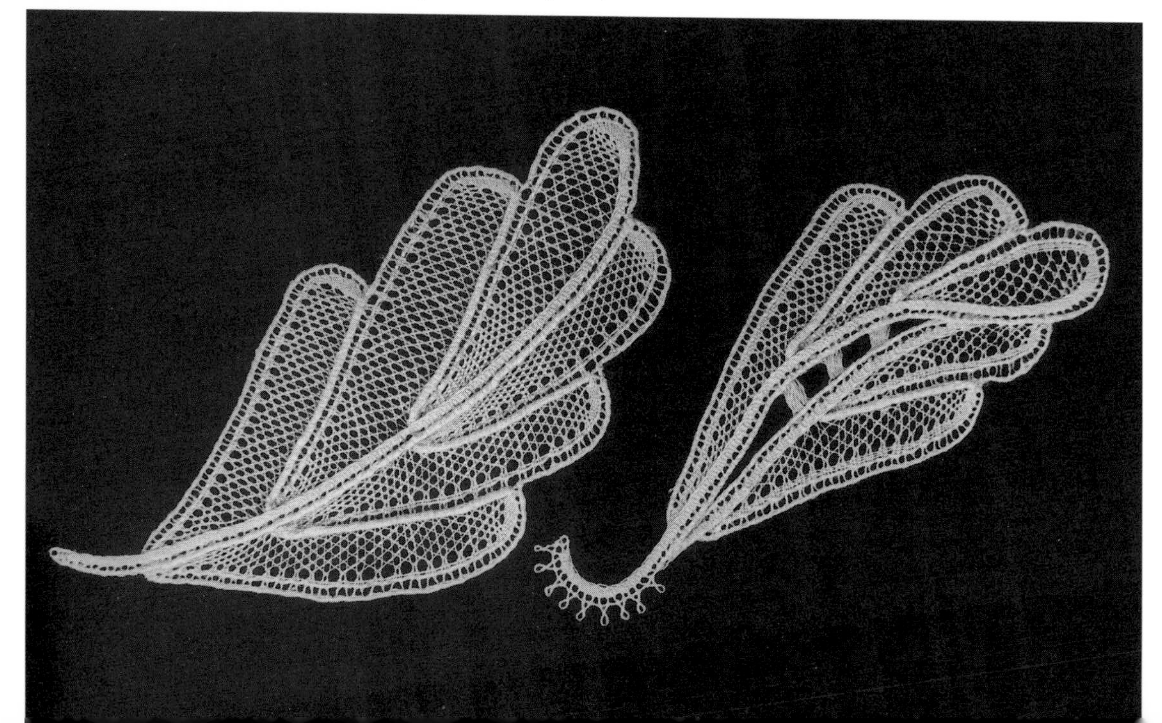

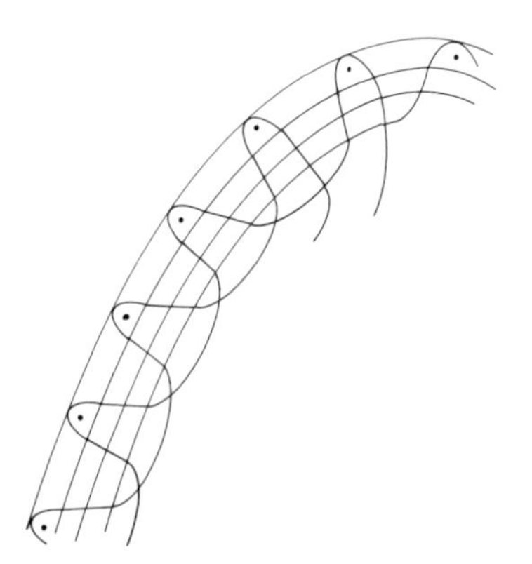

Diag. 139 *At the top of the rib the runners become passives on the inside*

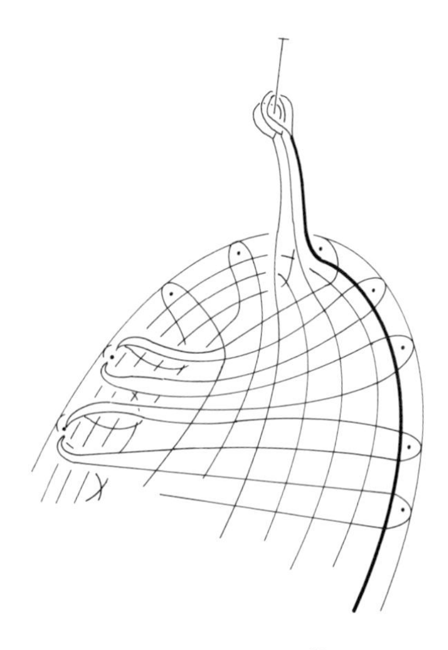

Diag. 140 *A gimp pair as well as passives are added*

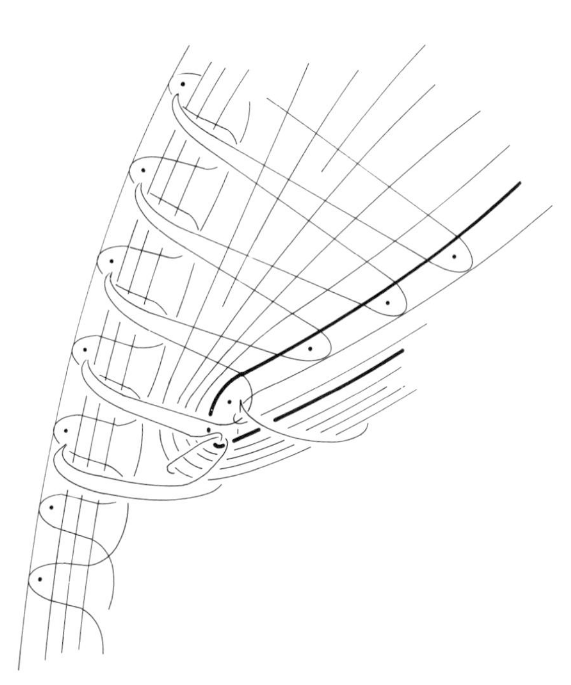

Diag. 141 *Start rolling in the pin-hole underneath the last sewing*

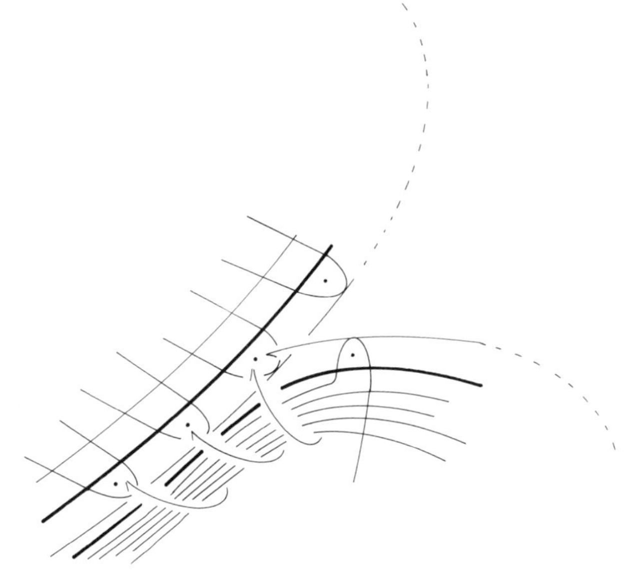

Diag. 142 *2 sewings are made in the last pin-hole*

gimp pair left. Bundle these and start rolling, in the pin-hole underneath the last sewing. By doing this, you will ensure that the vein comes right from the rib (diag. 141). Make two sewings in the last pin-hole (diag. 142).

Put the pairs in order so that from right to left, they are: edge pair, gimp pair, and another 5 pairs. Take the 3rd pair from the right, work through the gimp pair, make an edge stitch, pin. Work the runners through all pairs and leave them on the left. Continue the leaf as described. When the last leaf on this side is finished, bundle the pairs and roll along the rib until the leaf on the other side is reached.

Pattern 65 – Swan
Thread 160/2

(for actual size see p.151)

Start with round setting up at (**1**) (diags. 28–30) and work the wing as far as the end of the vein. Leave the pairs. Roll back with the edge pair and the passives next to this pair (diag. 56). At the top sew twice in the top pin-hole and add pairs to work a narrow setting up (diags. 25–27). Add pairs and make sewings into the vein as the work progresses. At the end of the vein sew the runners into the bottom pin-hole and use them as passives. Pick up the runners from the other side (diag. 59). Continue the wing in this way. Finish with the scroll (diag. 112). Roll.

Work a rolled scroll as the head (**2**) (diags. 108–110 and 113–114) and change to the braid. At (**3**) leave the runners; sew the edge pair; continue the row and work back (omitting the gimp pair). Leave the runners and decrease the number of pairs as in diag. 52. After the side of the scroll has been passed, more pairs have to be added (**4**). The vein can be worked as in diags. 55–57.

The tail parts (**5**) and (**6**) have to be worked in the same way as the wing. (**7**) is filled with whole stitch. (**8**) and (**9**) are worked as a braid with a straight edge stitch on one side and picots on the other.

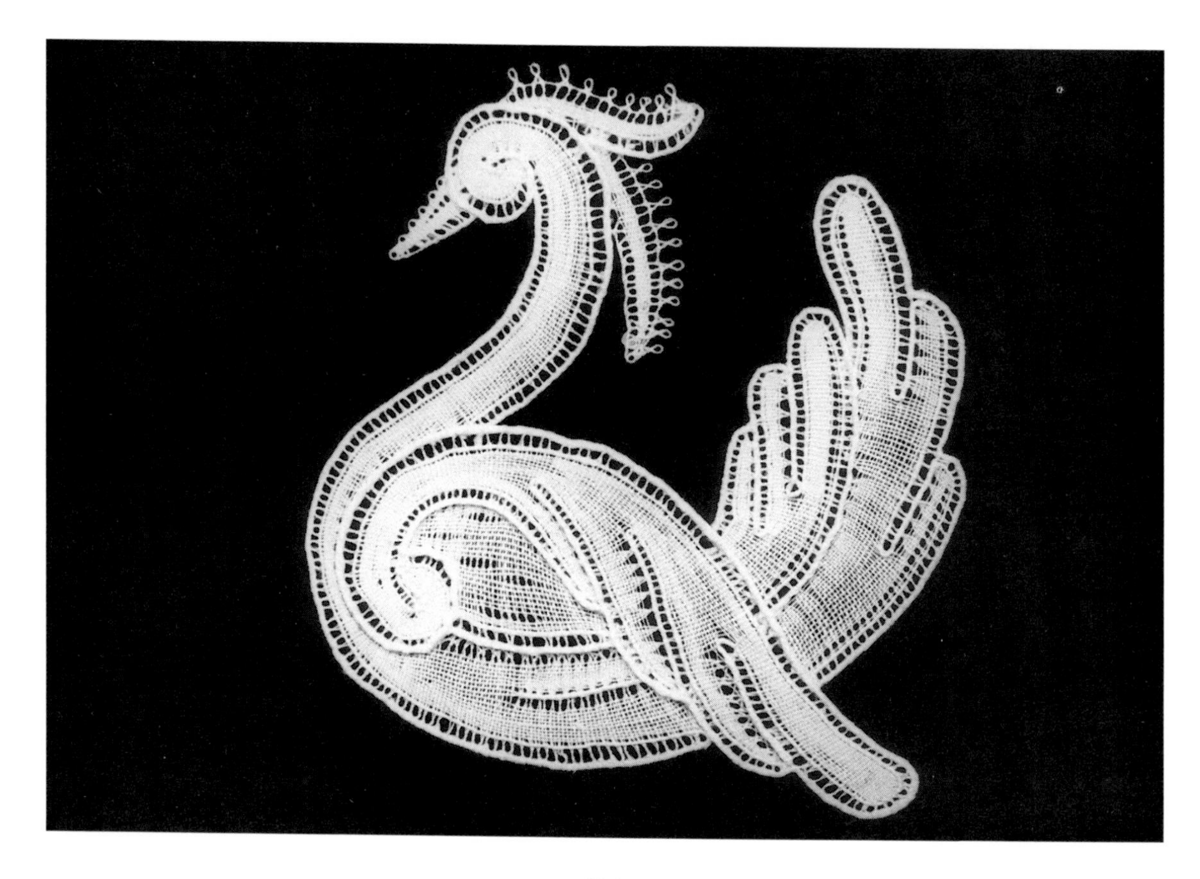

Pattern 66 – Baby's collar
Thread 180/2

Begin with the flowers (**1**). Set up to work the rib. Roll this. Use the 6 pairs for the rib of the first petal (diags. 139–140). Sew pairs into the rib to finish the petal. Plait them (see waves – diags. 155–156). Work the next petal by rolling the pairs (diag. 142) and using them again. Work all the petals in this way. Roll. The clover leaves are started by working the scroll (**2**). Work the circles and the ribs. The motifs have to be attached by joining as in diag. 21.

See jacket for a picture of the collar.

Pattern 67 – Queen crane
Thread 160/2

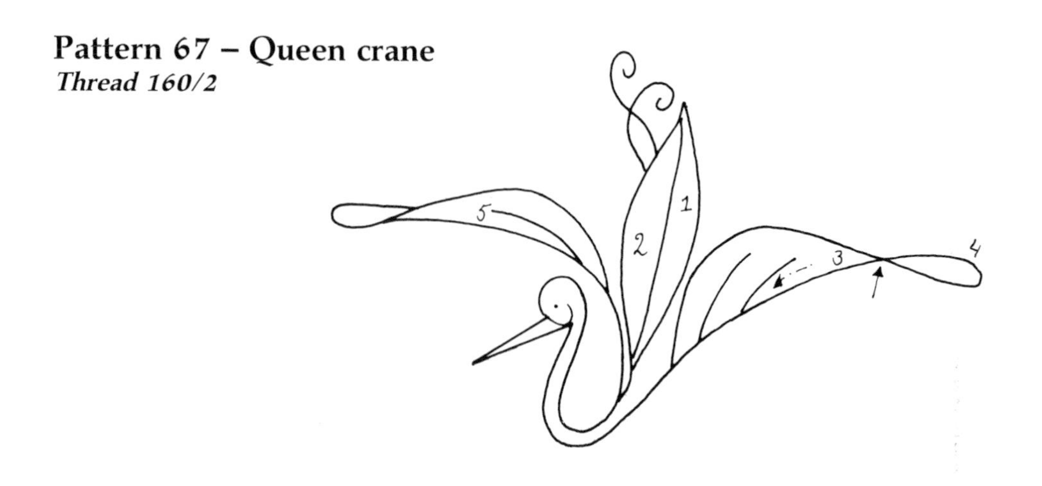

Queen crane and King crane

Start this pattern at (**1**). Work the 1st half of the body and roll. Set up in the tip for the 2nd half. Work a straight edge stitch on the inside and every 4th row sew this into the 1st half. Work the ribs on this section. Work leaf-shape (**3**). Set up at the tip of the wing. Work this section to the 1st vein. Leave the pairs hanging as in diag. 55. Finish at the point; roll and pick up the other pairs. Continue the work. Roll and leave the bundle of the bottom side hanging.

Set pins in the tip (**4**) and work this as a reverse side (Pattern 37). Work the third wing section (**5**) in the same way.

The head is worked as a scroll. Set up on 2 pins. Add pairs where necessary. Start the beak with a single pin (diag. 143).

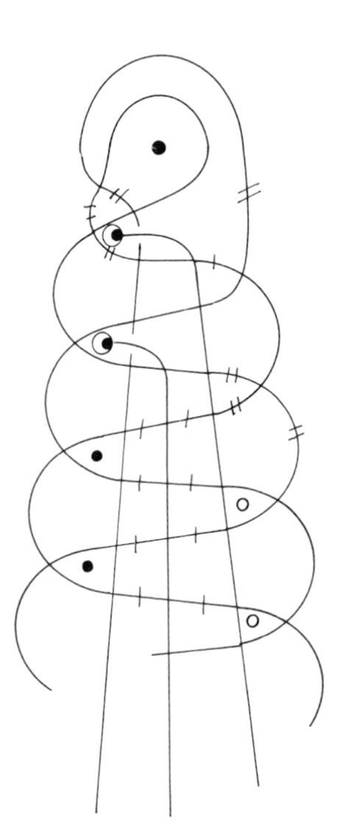

Diag. 143 *Setting up for the beak on a single pin, adding pairs on the 2nd and 3rd pin*

Pattern 68 – King crane

Thread 160/2

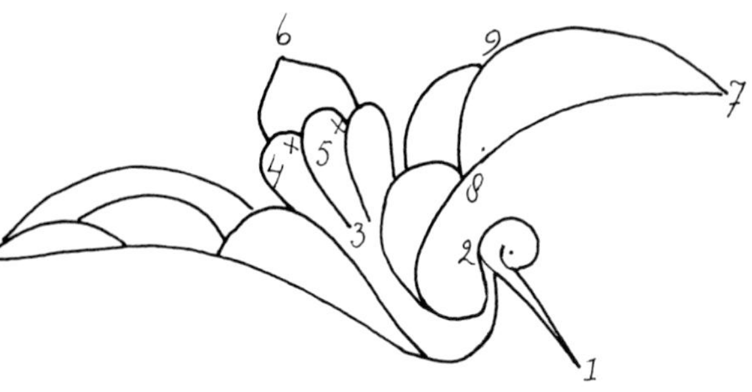

Set up at point (**1**) using one pin and 4 pairs (diag. 143) and finish with a scroll. Roll. Sew in pairs at (**2**) and add extra pairs where the braid widens. Work round the corner decoratively, leaving some pairs at (**3**), and finish in corner (**4**). Roll back with 2 pairs (diag. 56) and pick up the required number of pairs to work (**5**) and finish in the corner (*). Roll back, etc. Finish by rolling.

Set up point (**6**). Add as many pairs as needed. Sew into the part below and roll with picots. Set up at point (**7**). Add pairs where necessary. There are 2 half stitches in each whole stitch row. They move by one stitch every 2nd row. Take out pairs at (**8**) and add them again. Finish at the point and roll. Sew in pairs at (**9**). Add more when necessary and finish at the point. Roll. Work the other side in the same way, with the addition of a braid added to the edge of the wing.

Pattern 69 – Flower crane
Thread 160/2

Start the centre flower with a rib and roll. Take pairs into the petals (diag. 62). Because of the peculiar shape of the petals it is necessary to work them in half stitch and work the curve as in diag. 50a, as many times as needed. Roll the flower. Work the round setting up at (**1**). Roll and then work (**2**) and (**3**). The head is started as a scroll adding pairs for the neck. Finish the neck at the flower, except for the edge pair, gimp pair, runners and a few passives. Continue with these pairs as a rib. The wing is worked as the raised vein. The other side is worked in the same way. Start with the rib at (**4**).

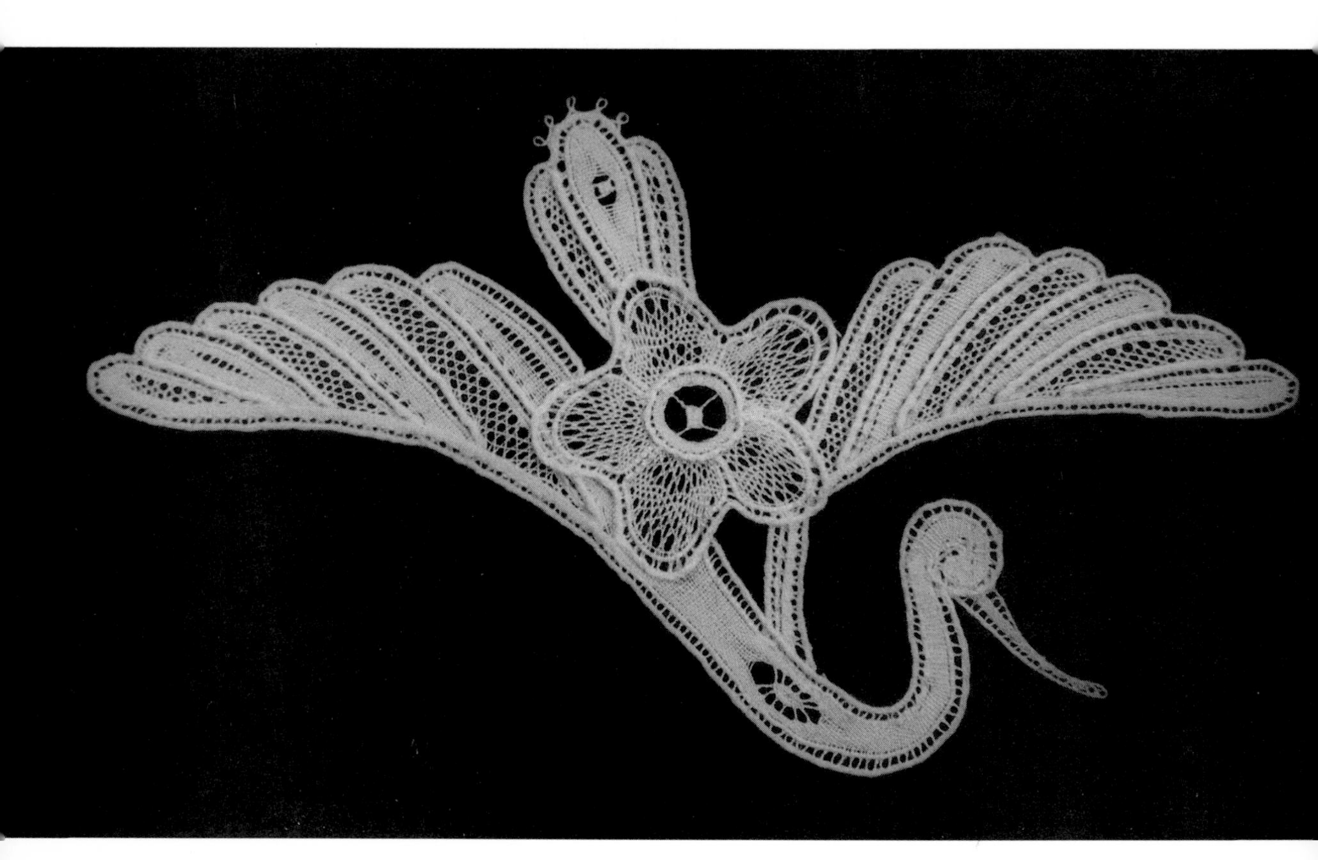

Pattern 70 – Orchid

Thread 160/2

(for actual size see p.152)

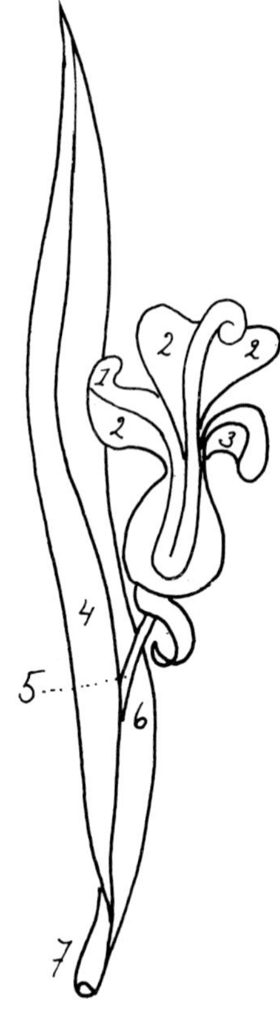

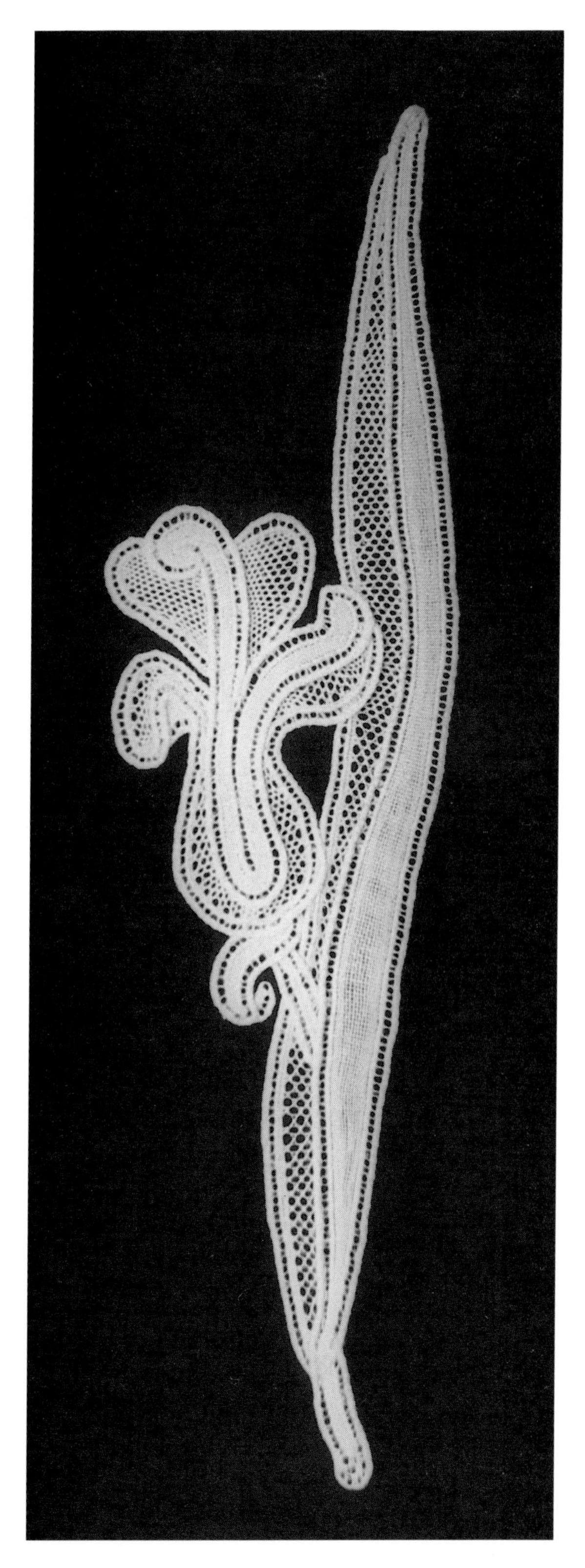

Work a round setting up for the flower at (**1**) (diags. 28–30). Turn round at the bottom and work it in the same way as the clover leaf (diag. 93). Finish with a scroll (diag. 112) and roll. Work a Round setting up for the petals at the side (**2**) and finish at the point (diag. 37) taking out as many pairs as necessary (see round setting up). Add pairs for the petal (**3**). Sew on one side, adding and taking out pairs when necessary, and finish at the other side. Roll. Set up at the point to work the whole stitch part of the leaf (**4**). Then add the leaf at the bottom of the flower starting from the point. Work the stem (**5**). Add the shadow of the leaf (**6**). Add the stem (**7**).

Pattern 71 – Butterfly
Thread 160/2

Start with a rib at (**1**), roll. Add the body, starting from the point (diags. 33–36). Sew into the rib, roll. Start the wing (**2**) as a scroll (diags. 108–110). Sew and roll. Work braid (**3**) starting at the rib and roll. Use some of the pairs of the bundle to work the bottom wing. The filling is a snowflake.

Set up at (**5**), work to (*) and roll back. Set up at (**6**) sewing into the vein of (**5**) and finish at the body.

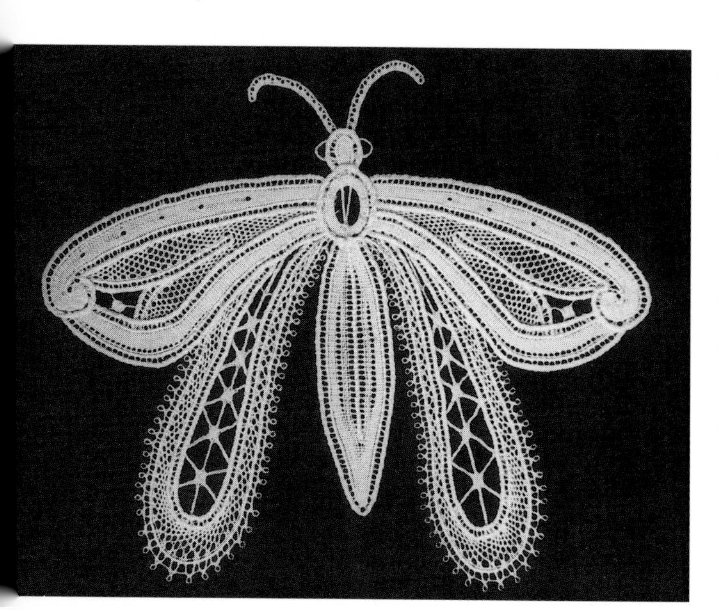

Pattern 72 – Crane ballet
Thread 160/2

Set up on one pin (**1**) with 4 pairs (diag. 143). Gradually add pairs and gimp pairs on both sides. See diag. 144 for the curve and the eye in the head. Take out pairs in the neck as it narrows and curves and add them again when it becomes wider.

The wings at the bottom of the body are worked reverse to the raised vein (diags. 145a–145b). The feet are started as plaits. Work them separately to the heel; work the point where they join together, and the legs, as ribs.

(Opposite): Crane ballet and Lords awaiting

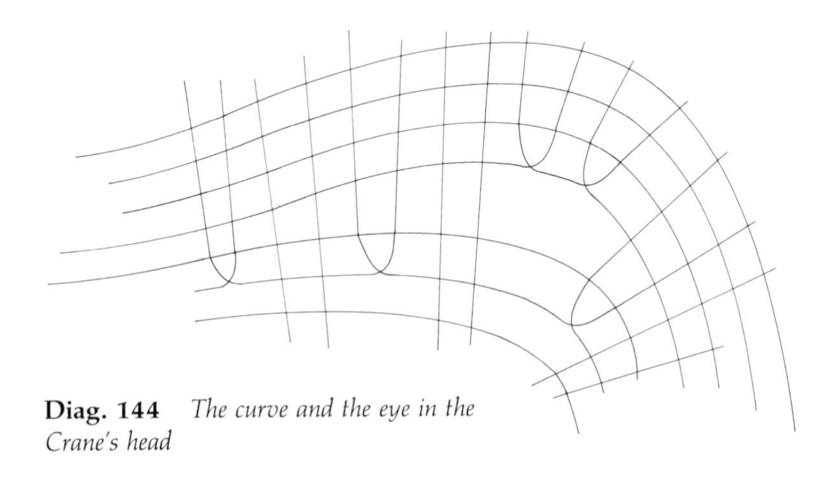

Diag. 144 *The curve and the eye in the Crane's head*

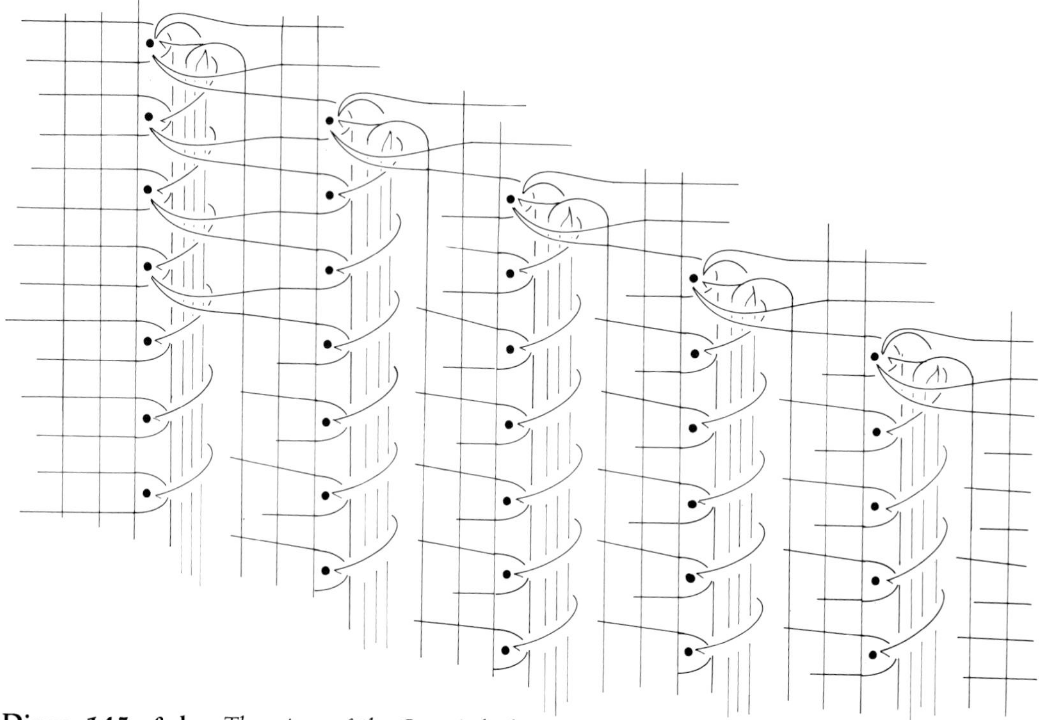

Diags. 145a & b *The wings of the Crane's body*

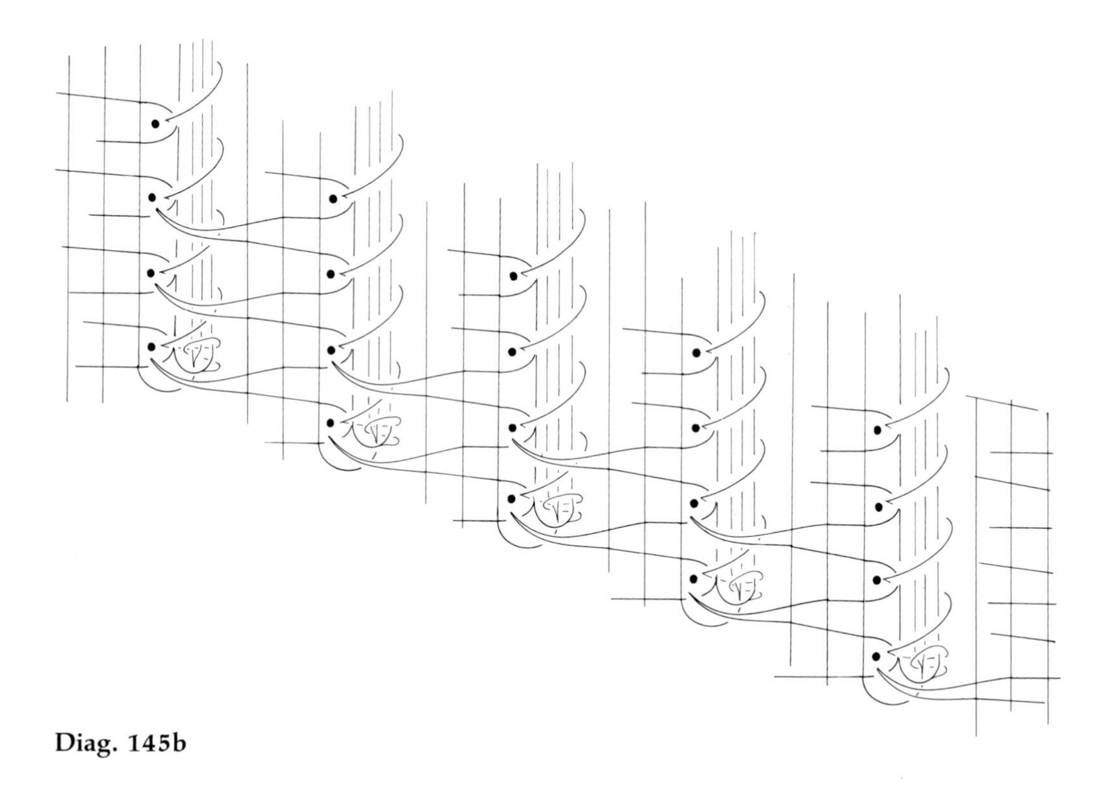

Diag. 145b

Pattern 73 – Lords awaiting
Thread 160/2

and

Pattern 74 – Crane couple
Thread 160/2

All these cranes are worked in the same manner. Look carefully to see which part to work next. Make sure the line flows with the direction of the pattern. Turn the pillow as the work progresses.

Pattern 75 – Caddis fly
Thread 140/2

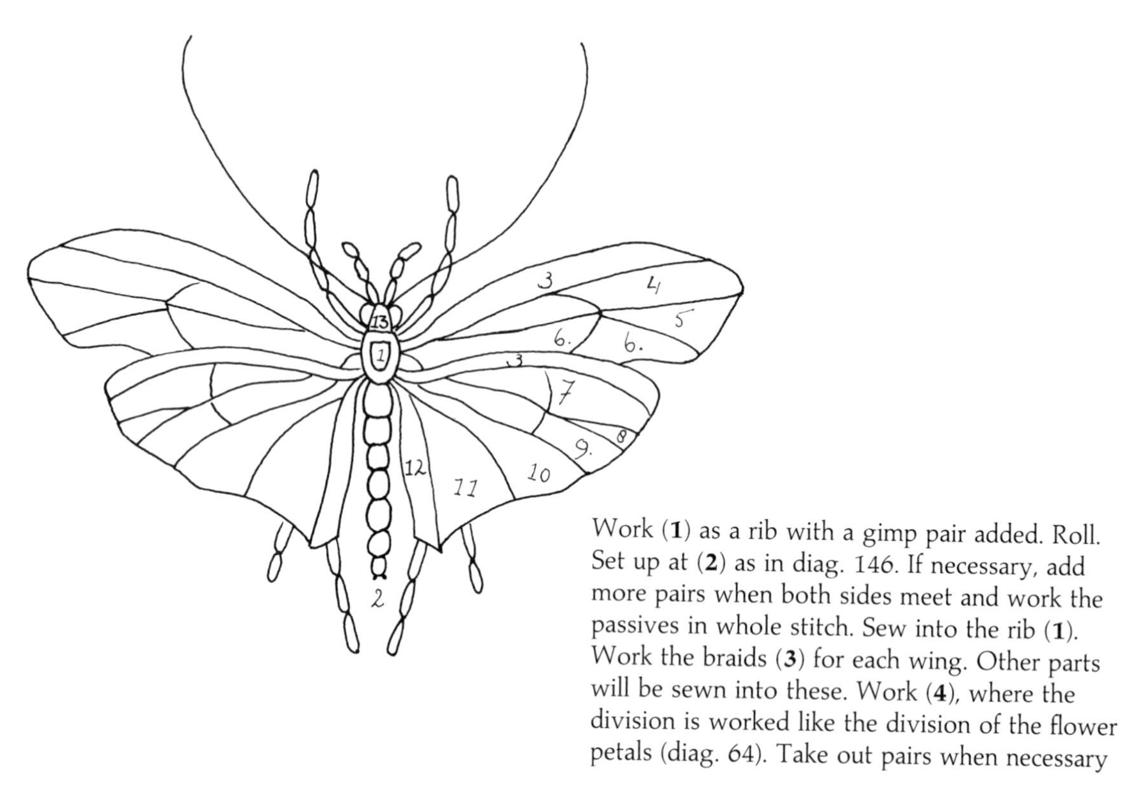

Work (**1**) as a rib with a gimp pair added. Roll. Set up at (**2**) as in diag. 146. If necessary, add more pairs when both sides meet and work the passives in whole stitch. Sew into the rib (**1**). Work the braids (**3**) for each wing. Other parts will be sewn into these. Work (**4**), where the division is worked like the division of the flower petals (diag. 64). Take out pairs when necessary

and sew into the braid. Roll back and use the pairs to set up at (**5**). Finish at the point, make sewings on both sides. Set up at (**6**). The division is the same as in (**4**).

Work the bottom wings in numerical order. Start the feelers as in diag. 147. Join them at (**13**) and add a gimp pair to work the head. Finish with eyes and legs.

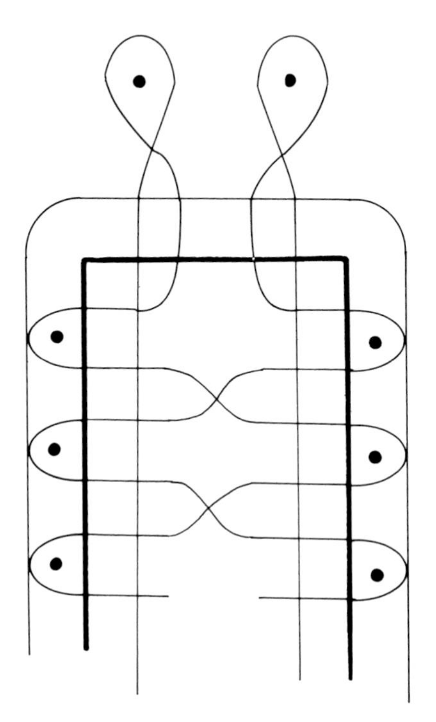

Diag. 146 *Setting up for the body of Caddis fly*

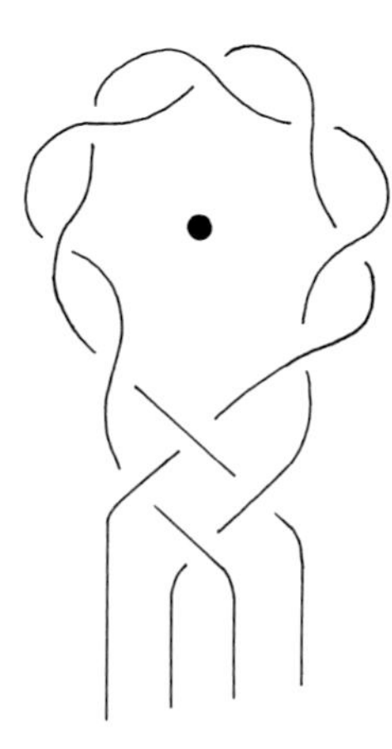

Diag. 147 *The feelers are started as a false picot*

Pattern 76 – Golfer

Thread 140/2

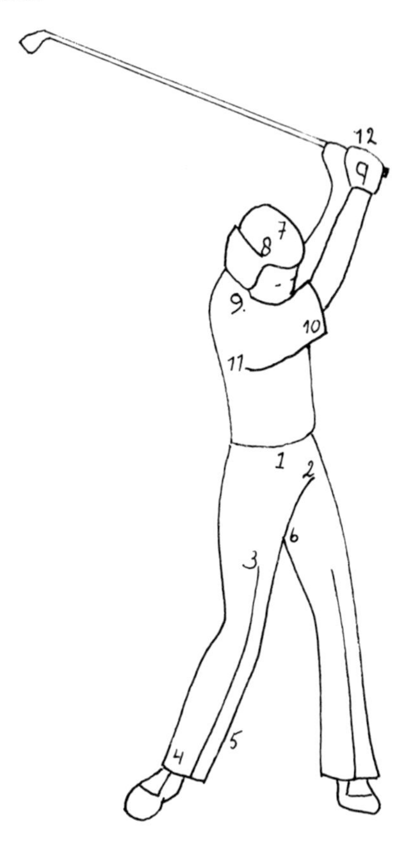

Work a straight setting up at (**1**), the waistline at the top of the trousers. Continue to the division of the two legs (**2**). Divide the pairs; add a gimp pair and an edge pair (diag. 55). Work the foremost leg, taking out pairs when necessary. The crease in the trousers (**3**) is made by working as shown in diag. 101. Finish at (**4**) with a straight edge (diag. 17) and roll the inside of the leg from (**5**) back to (**2**). One of the pairs of the bundle will be used as runners (diag. 56) for the other leg. Add extra pairs straight away and work from the outside to the inside. Sew the runners into the top loop (top sewing) of the pin-hole and leave this pair as passives (diag. 148). Add a new pair to the bottom loop and use this pair as the new runners. Repeat this as often as necessary. Add a new edge pair and gimp pair at (**6**) and work to finish this leg in the same way as

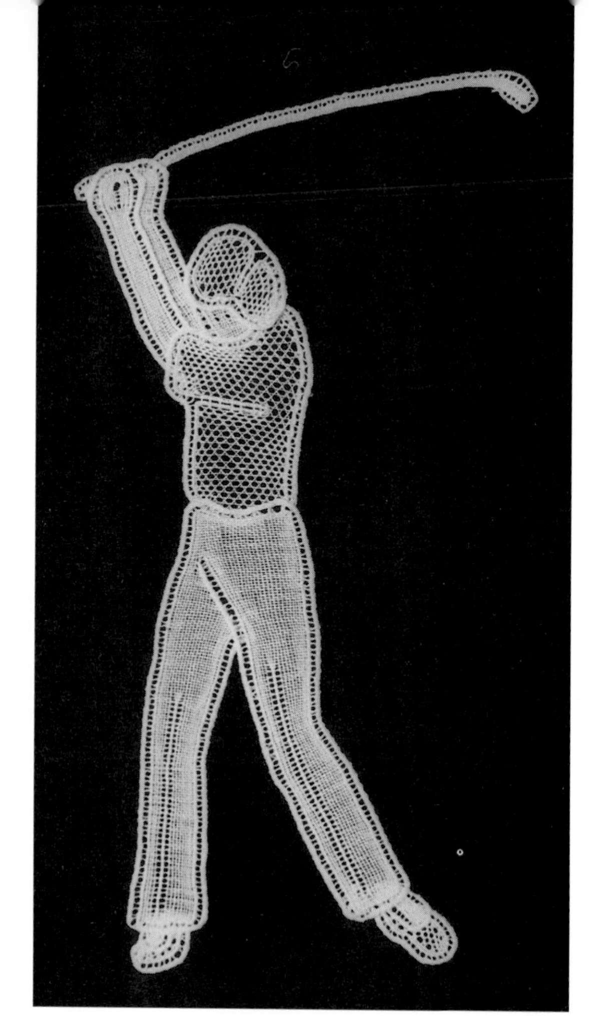

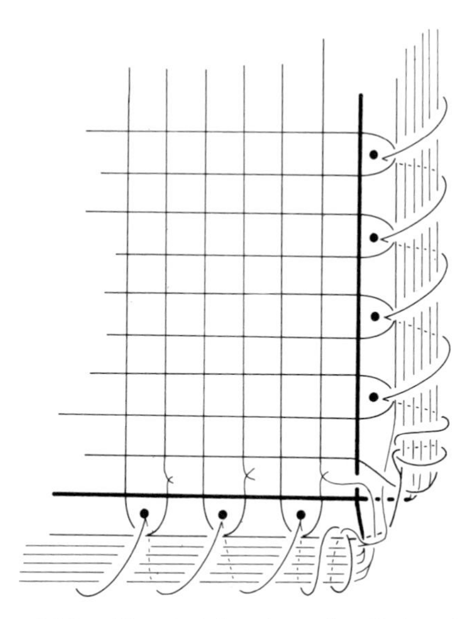

Diag. 149 *The straight edge is bundled on both sides and rolled on both sides*

the other one. Bundle on both sides (diag. 149). On one side, roll to (**6**). The rest of the trousers are rolled with the other bundle.

Set up at (**7**) to work the hair in half stitch. The

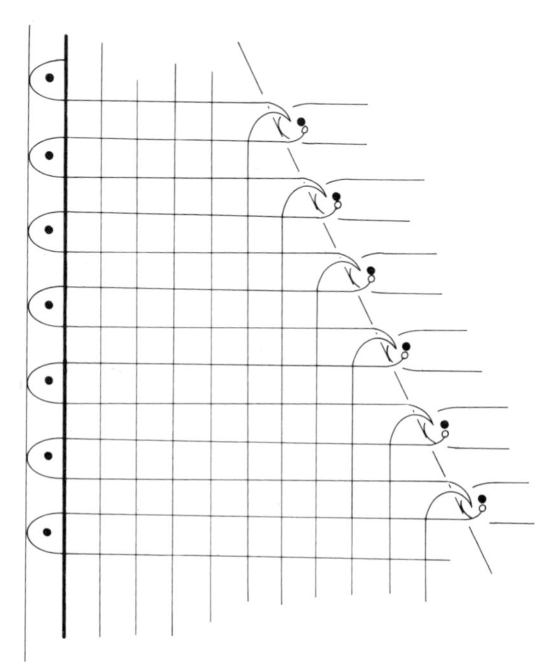

Diag. 148 *Adding pairs on a diagonal line*

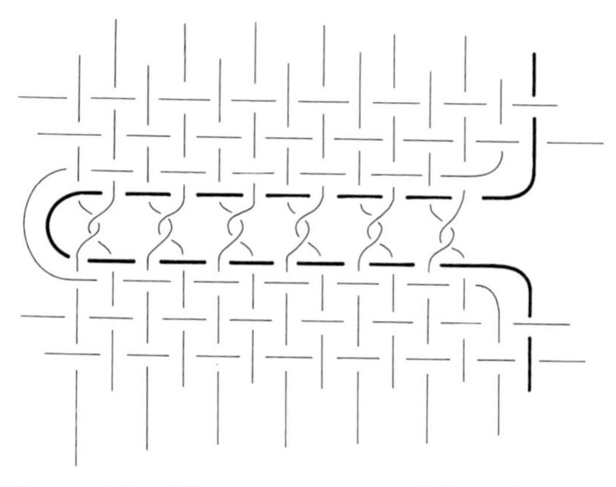

Diag. 150 *The gimp pair is worked inside to denote the parting in the hair*

gimp pair to denote the parting is worked inside (diag. 150). Set a support pin (**8**), twist the passives twice, and go back to the side. Finish the hair as a straight edge. Roll.
Use some of the pairs for the shirt. Work an edge stitch on both sides. Hang in pairs to work the shoulder and sleeve. Work as far as (**10**) taking out some pairs (diag. 17). Work the gimp pair to (**11**), twist the passives twice, and work the gimp pair back to the edge. Finish the shirt and sew into the trousers. Roll.
Start the hand (**12**) using the Round setting up method (diags. 28–30). Change into the arm, finish and sew it into the sleeve. Roll. Sew in pairs to work the face. Then the second arm can be made. The golf club is started at its head. Take out some pairs and continue with a rib, sewing in to the rear hand.

Pattern 77 – Sunflower

Thread 80/2

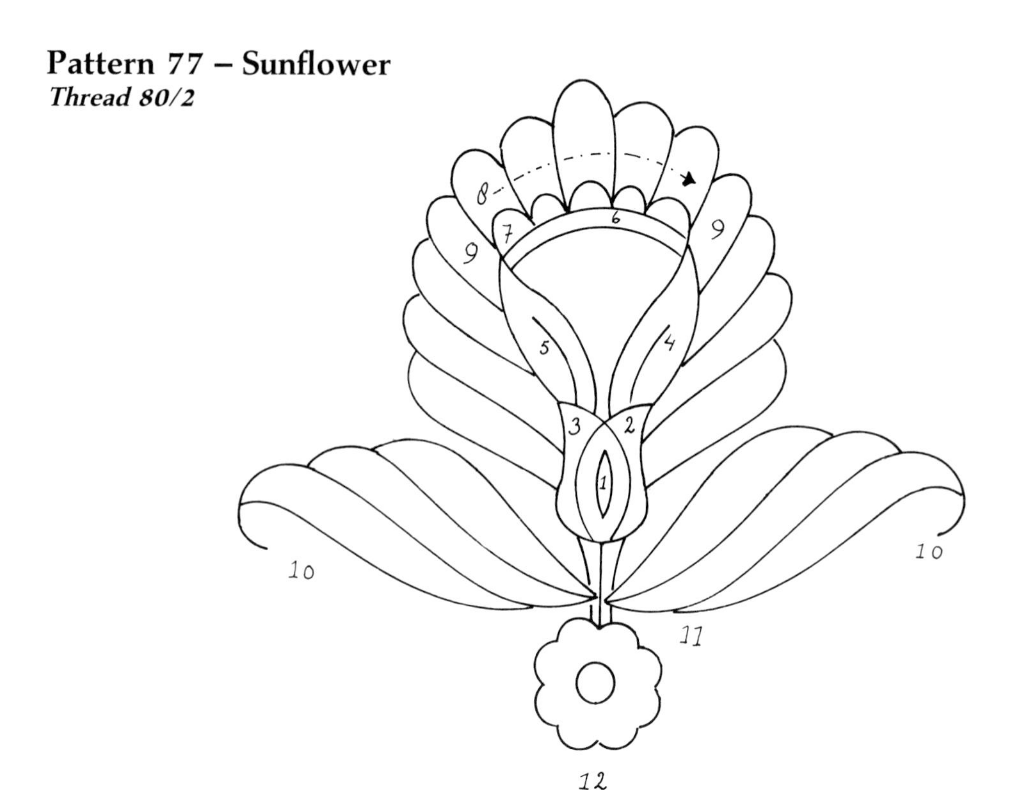

Set up with a rib (**1**), roll and fill this rib with whole stitch. The outside is worked in half stitch ((**2**) and (**3**)). Work the leaves (**4**) and (**5**) as in diags. 55–59. Hang in pairs to work the braid (**6**). Roll both sides. A picot is made in the centre of each rib on the top edge (diag. 24). Sew in pairs for rib (**7**). When the rib has to be joined to rib (**6**), sew the runners and the last used pair of passives that will become the runners. Roll the rib. Use the pairs of the bundle and add new pairs to work the petals (**8**). They are worked as waves (diags. 155–156) and rolled. Sew in pairs to work the side petals at (**9**). Start with a rib, by sewing pairs at the top of the petal, and work according to diag. 139, adding as many pairs as are needed. Work the petal and finish at a point (diag. 141) rolling back with the remaining 6 pairs and the gimp pair. Work the remaining petals as in diag. 142.

Start the rib (**10**), on one pin hung with 4 pairs. Add one pair on both the 2nd and 3rd pins. Add a gimp pair and work an edge stitch on both sides (diag. 143). Roll back at (**11**). Leave the

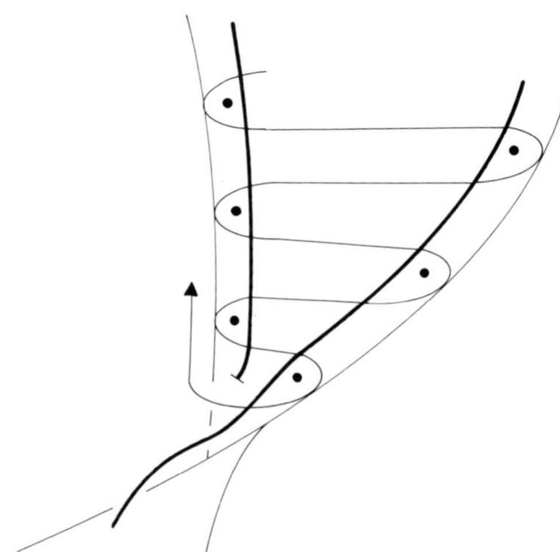

Diag. 151 *Leaving gimp pair and edge pair behind to pick them up later*

gimp pair and the edge pair (diag. 151). These are picked up when the 2nd leaf reaches this point, to keep the line flowing.

The flower at the bottom is worked as a circle (diags. 122–124).

Pattern 78 – Stylized leaf

Thread 160/2

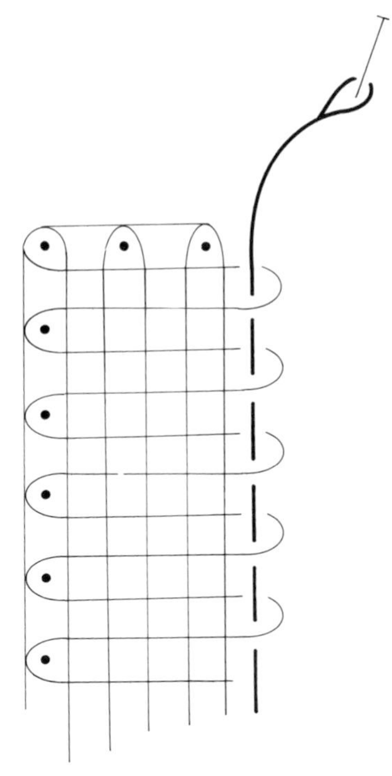

Diag. 152 *The runners are twisted round the gimp thread*

Start with the circle in the centre. Set 3 pins; hang the pairs around them and set up. Add a gimp pair which is put on a pin outside the work (diag. 152) and twist the runners round this gimp thread. When the ring is closed, the gimp thread can be cut off and the circle rolled.

Add pairs for the rib (**1**) and roll the rib. Work the petals as raised veins (diags. 141–142) in the order indicated. Work the other two leaves in the same way. Add the tallies.

Work the rolled scroll (diags. 108–110 and 113–114). Change into a braid and sew into the leaf. Roll.

Pattern 79 – Christmas angel

Thread 160/2

(for actual size see p.152)

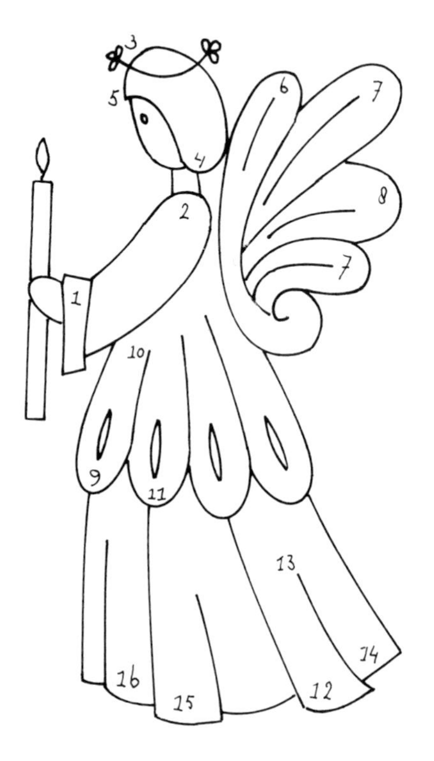

Start with the cuff of the sleeve (**1**). Use a straight setting up and work a braid, finishing with a straight edge (diags. 17–19). Use a round setting up (diags. 28–30) at the top of the sleeve (**2**). Sew into the sleeve cuff and roll. Work the crown next (diag. 153).

To start the hair, use a round setting up (**3**). Take out pairs at (**5**) and leave them to work the face. Finish the hair at the bottom and roll. Work the face, roll, and use some of the pairs to work the neck. Roll.

Work the wing, starting at (**6**) with a round setting up and finish with a scroll (diag. 112). Work the other parts in numerical order.

Use a round setting up to work the dress, starting at (**9**) and working in half stitch. The decoration in the dress is a gimp thread worked as shown in diags. 134a–134b. Continue to (**10**). Roll back right to the sleeve. Again, set up at (**11**) and work this section in the same way as the previous one. Pick up all the pairs, sew in and finish at the top.

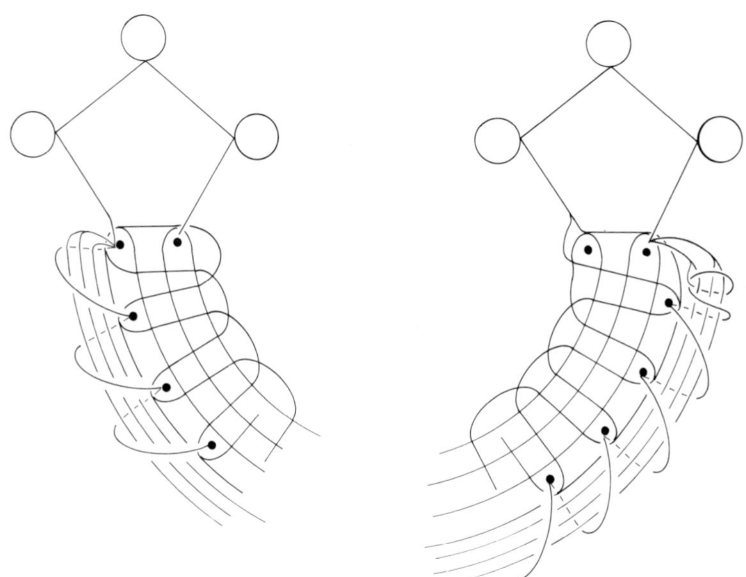

Diag. 153 *The crown of the Christmas angel*

Work a straight setting up for the skirt at (**12**). Choose a decorative stitch and work as far as (**13**). Roll back with the edge pair and the gimp pair. Use these pairs to set up again at (**14**). Pick up the pairs left at (**13**) and sew into the top. Roll. The other 2 sections of the skirt are worked in the same way, in numerical order.

Pattern 80 – Raised vein with interrupted rib
Thread 80/2

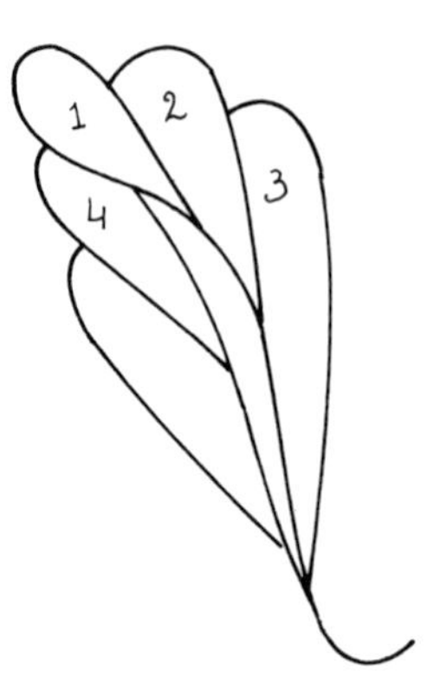

The 1st half of this leaf is worked as in diags. 139–142. If the leaf is worked in half stitch, 6 pairs and a gimp pair are sufficient. Roll back using all these pairs and continue according to the diagram. When the 3rd section is finished, roll all the way round and finish where the picots start. It is not necessary to use all the pairs to roll back with, but leave them there, and pick them up to work the 2nd rib together with the pairs from the bundle. The 2nd rib 'disappears' behind the first leaf (diag. 154). Sew the rib into the leaf and hang in new pairs where it appears again. Work section (**4**). As it is not completely visible, use only 5 pairs and add another one when the whole of it is visible. Finish this half as the previous one. Roll. Roll the inside of the 2nd rib and add the tallies. (Photograph p.102.)

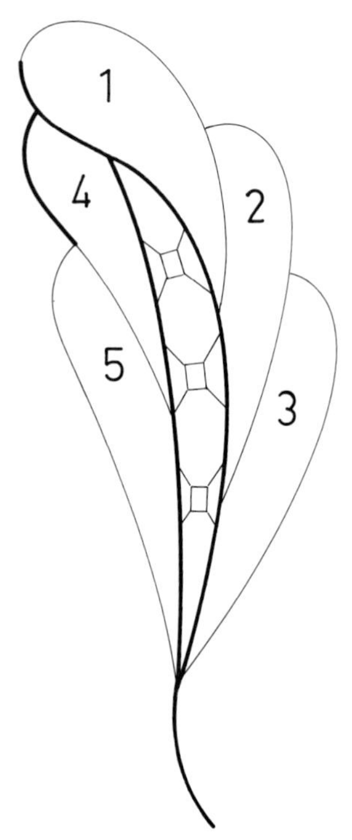

Diag. 154 *Working order as well as the disappearing of the 2nd rib*

8. Waves

At first sight, waves look like the petals of a flower. However, they are worked in a different way. Each wave is started and finished on the same basis. Instead of cutting off the pairs, they are plaited and transferred to the next wave (diags. 155–156).

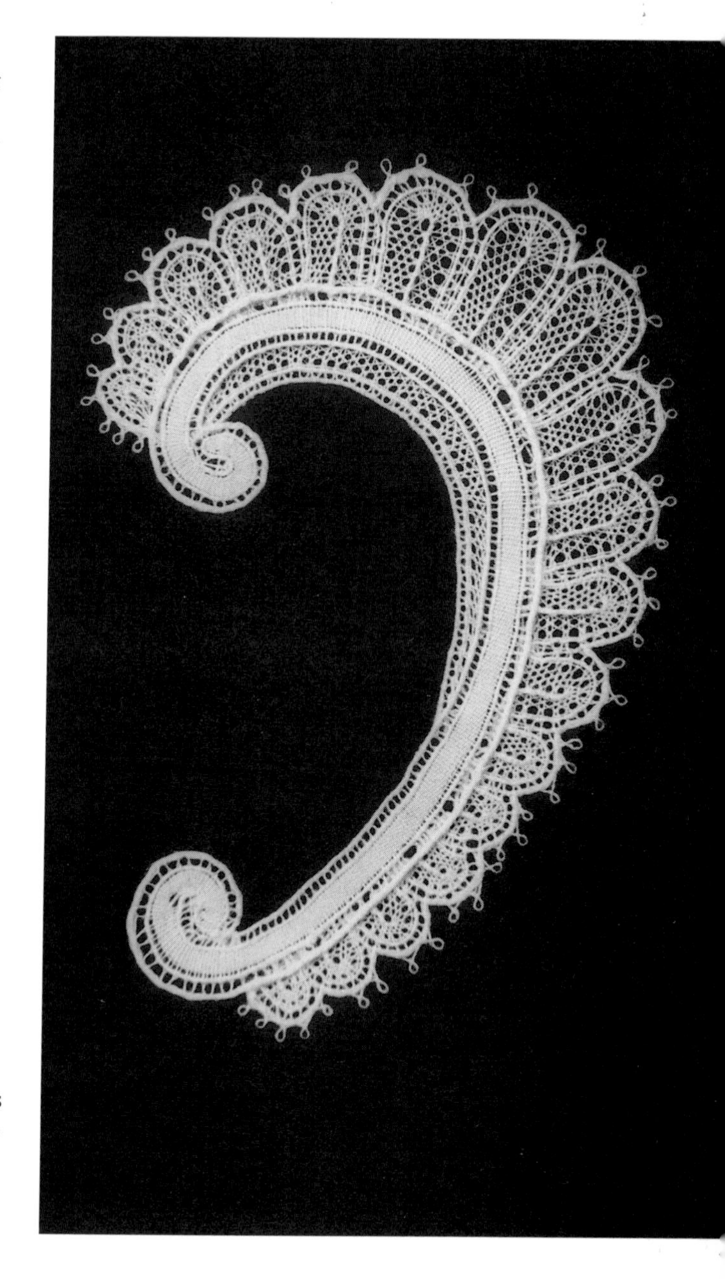

Pattern 81 – Cock's comb

Thread 160/2

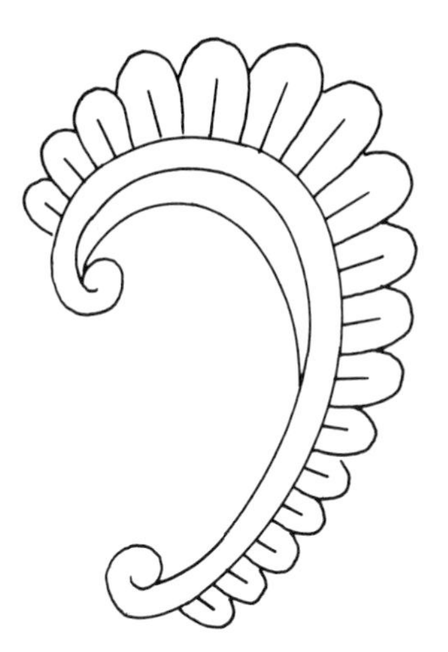

Start with a scroll (diags. 108–111) and finish with another scroll (diag. 112). Roll the outside first, and then the inside, so that the pairs are on the right side to work the inside in half stitch. Roll back with only a few pairs. The petal shapes on the outside are worked as waves (diags. 155–156). When rolling, add a few picots.

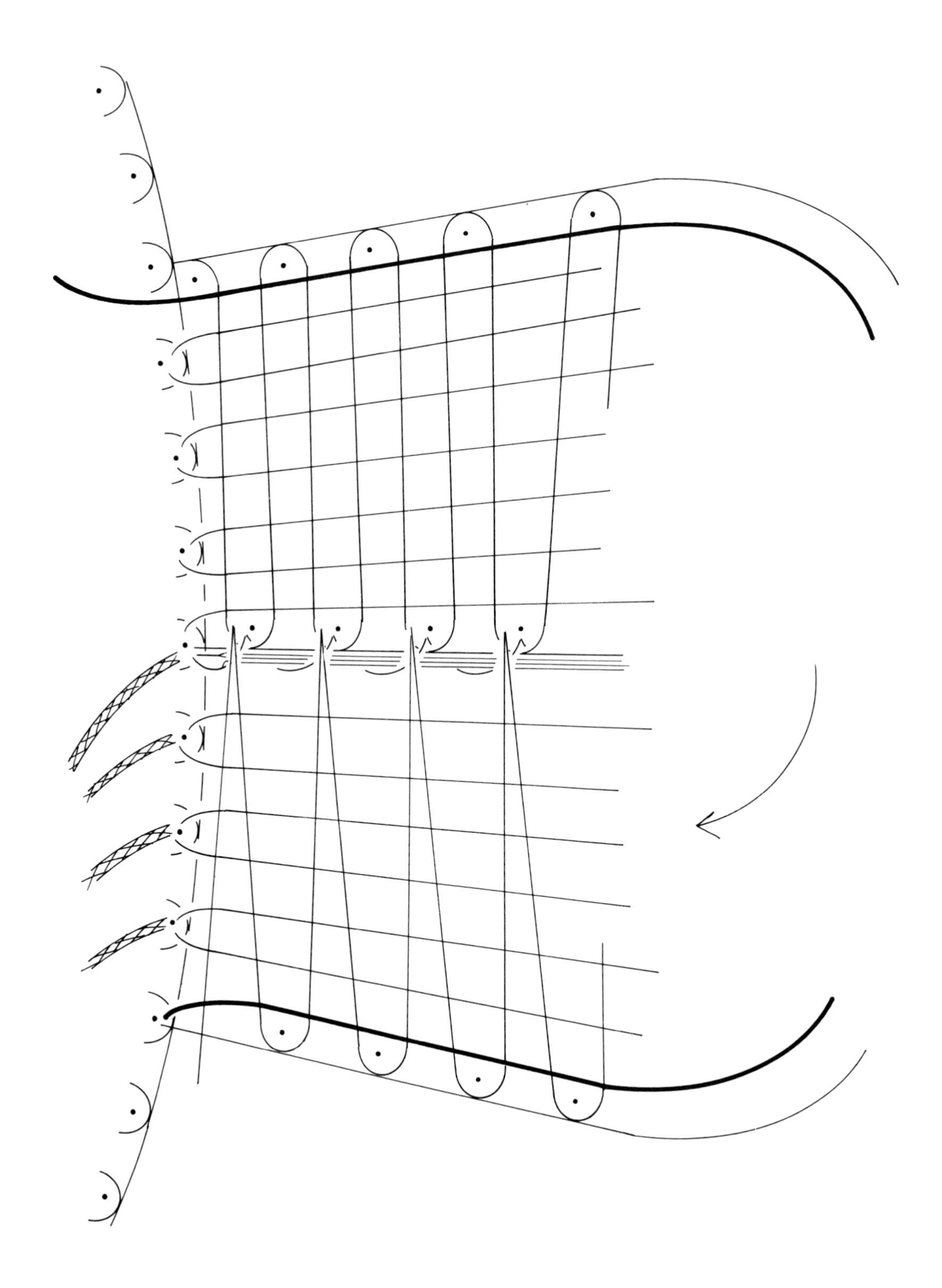

Diag. 155 *In waves the pairs are sewn in and plaited*

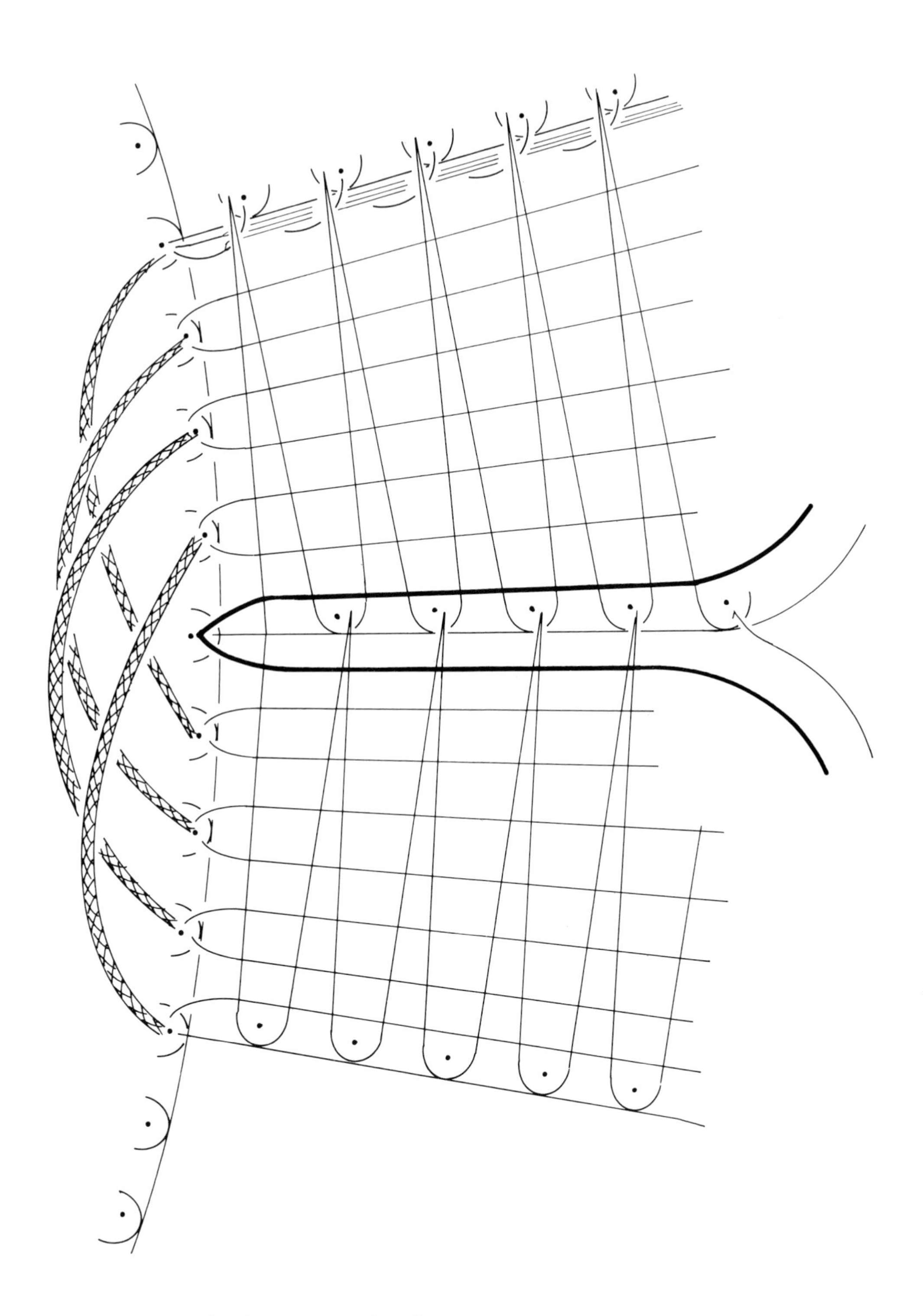

Diag. 156 *The plaits are carried to the next wave*

Pattern 82 – Snail

Thread 140/2

(for actual size see p.152)

Start with a rolled scroll (diags. 113–115) in the centre of the snail. When the scroll becomes braid (**1**) do not make top sewings every time, but set a pin, twist the runners twice round this, and go back to the edge (diag. 157). Another way of decreasing is to leave the runners and take the last used passives as runners (see the same diagram).

When (**2**) is reached, make sewings on every row and add more passives. Continue as far as the eye. Follow diag. 158 for the eye and finish. The petal shapes are worked as waves (diags. 155–156). Roll with picots (diag. 24).

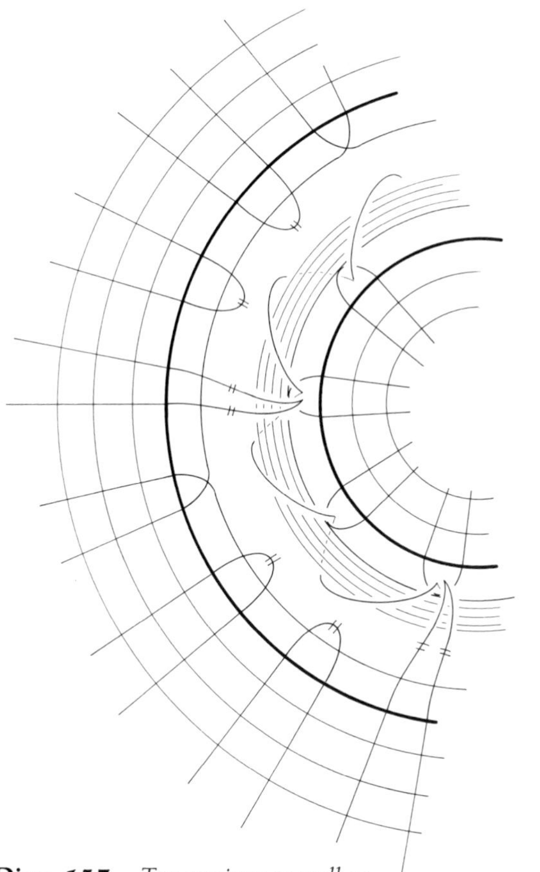

Diag. 157 *Top sewings as well as decreasing decoratively*

Reverse side of the Snail

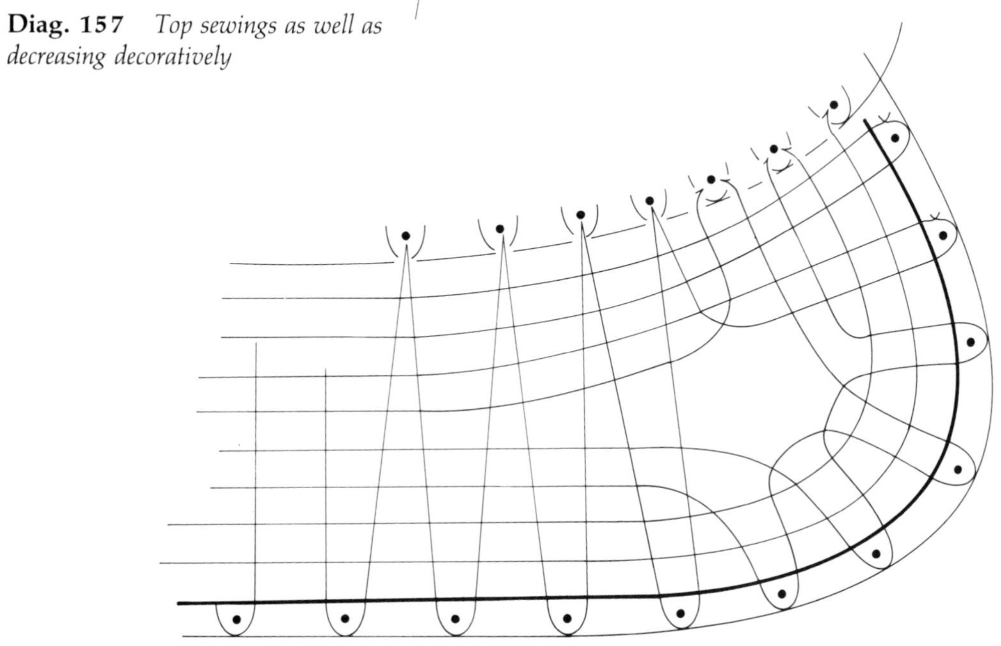

Diag. 158 *The Snail's eye*

Pattern 83 – Crown
Thread 160/2

(for actual size see p.152)

Work the flower, clover leaves and circles. Join them together while they are being rolled (diag. 21). Waves are worked on the outside of the scrolls (diags. 155–156). Start with the centre one and work to left and right.

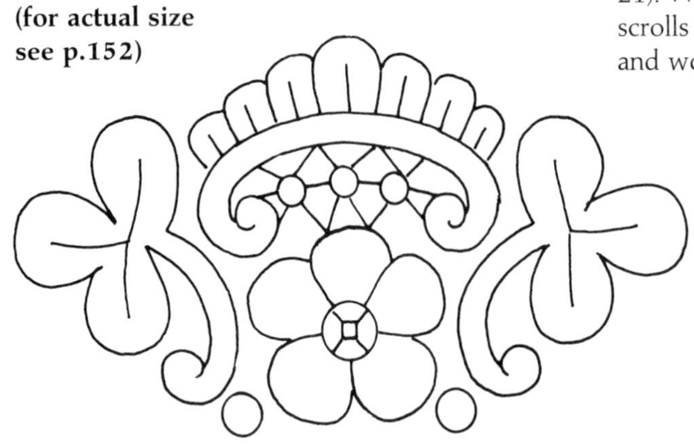

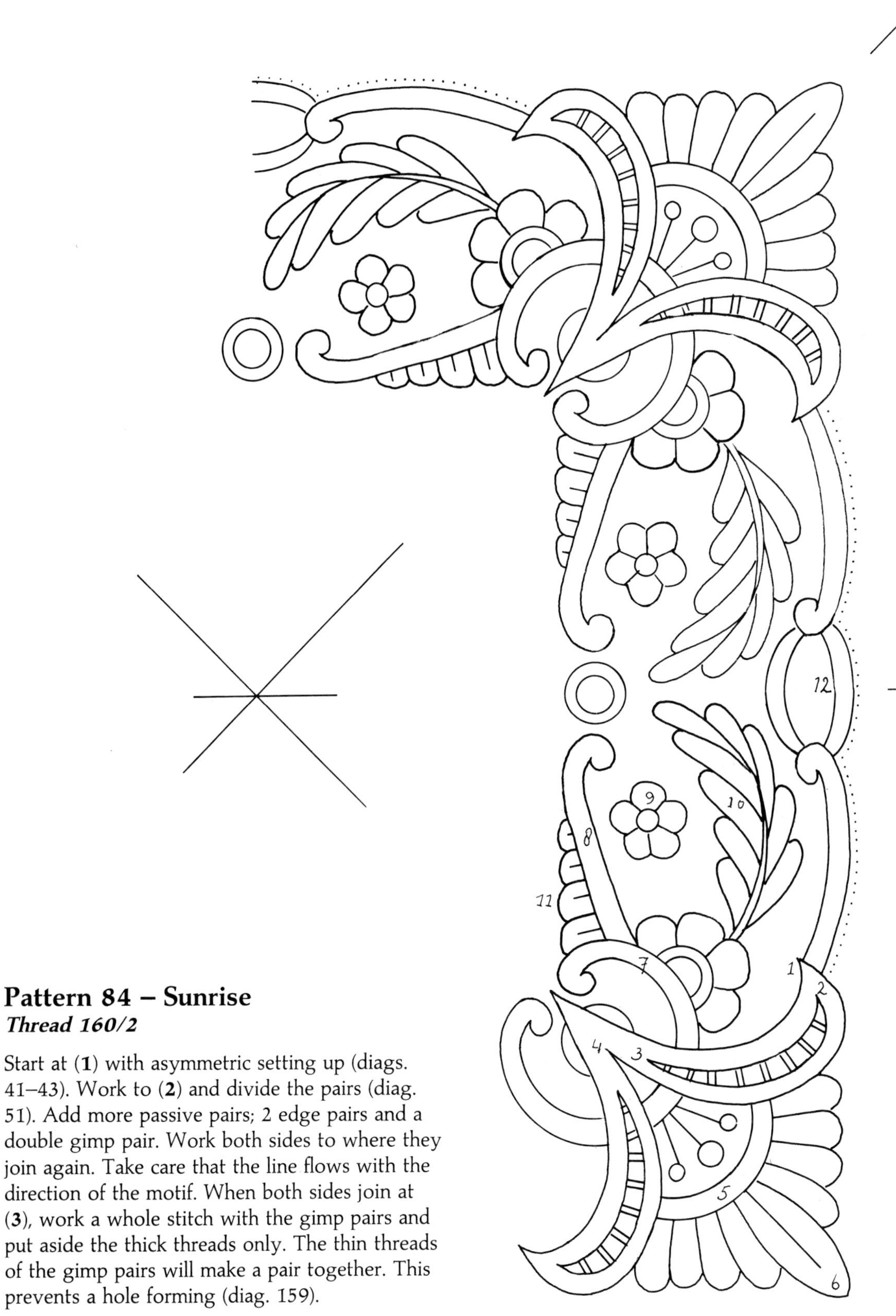

Pattern 84 – Sunrise
Thread 160/2

Start at (**1**) with asymmetric setting up (diags. 41–43). Work to (**2**) and divide the pairs (diag. 51). Add more passive pairs; 2 edge pairs and a double gimp pair. Work both sides to where they join again. Take care that the line flows with the direction of the motif. When both sides join at (**3**), work a whole stitch with the gimp pairs and put aside the thick threads only. The thin threads of the gimp pairs will make a pair together. This prevents a hole forming (diag. 159).

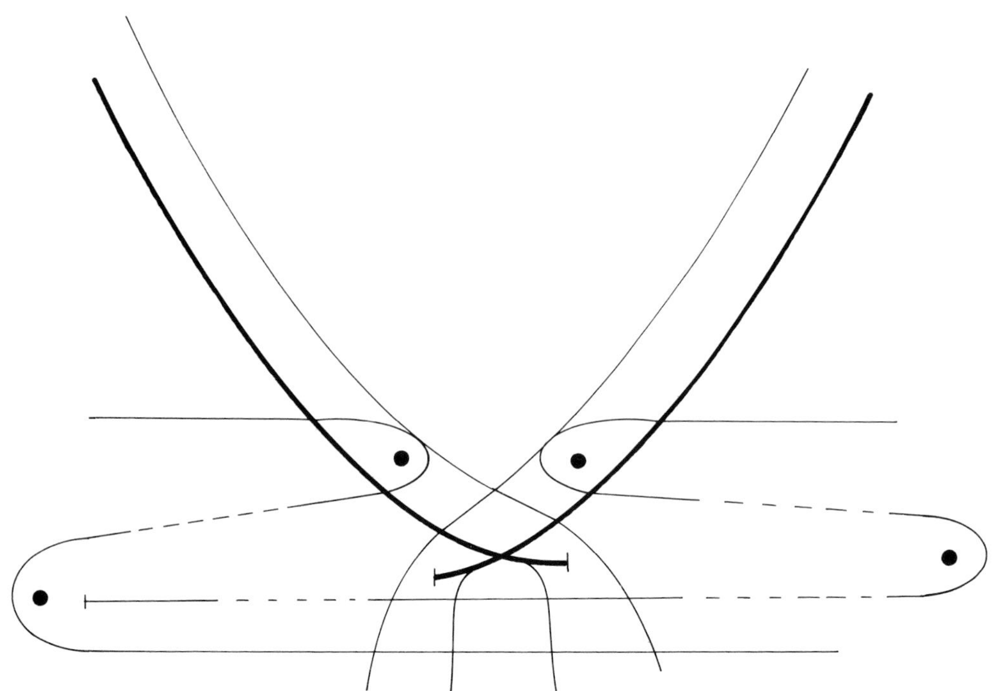

Diag. 159 *Joining of 2 sides*

Continue until the next join at (**4**). Take out pairs where necessary. Leave the pairs and start on the other side. Work in exactly the same way as the first half. Before the 2 sides are joined, make a few sewings on the opposite edge (diag. 95). Then join the 2 sides (**4**) as just described. Finish at the point (diag. 37). Roll and make picots on the top outside edge. Add pairs to work the braid (**5**).

Work the corner leaf shape (**6**) using a round setting up (diags. 28–30) following the diags. 55–57. Roll back on both sides to where the next leaf starts and work this like the raised vein (diags. 141–142). Add pairs where necessary. When they have all been worked, roll with picots (diag. 24). Work the scrolls (**7**) and (**8**) and the braid. Sew and roll. The petals on the braid (**11**) are worked as the petals of a flower. Work the rib of the flower and add pairs for the petals. The smaller flower (**9**) can now be worked and the leaves with the raised veins added (**10**), starting with the rib (diags. 139–142). Work the ring as a rib.

Work all 4 corners. Join them by a braid (**12**) of which the top one is rolled with picots. The filling is point ground.

Pattern 85 – Spray of Kerria

Thread 160/2

Start with rib (**1**) where indicated (*). Roll. Use these pairs to work the rib of the centre petal (**2**) (diags. 140–142). Sew the petal into the rib (diags. 155–156). Roll one side of this petal, using the same pairs. Change into rib (**3**) to work the top of the petal and finish it. The other petals are worked likewise. Roll with picots.

The other 2 flowers are worked in the same way. The leaves are worked differently. Starting at the tip (**4**), set up at a point (diags. 33–35) and add pairs. The centre vein is worked according to diag. 100. One half stitch is added on one side. There is one twist in the runners on the other side.

Work the next group of leaves (**5**) as in diags. 55–57. The vein of the next group downwards (**6**) is worked as follows: 2 twists; whole stitch; 2 twists. The runners are twisted for the bottom group.

Start and finish the buds (**8**) at their points. Roll on one side and work the other half as in diags. 141–142. Finish with rib.

Pattern 86 – Bridal handkerchief

Thread 180/2

Start the corner flower with rib (**1**), add pairs (**2**), take out pairs towards (**3**) and add them again on the other side. You should finish with the same number of pairs as you started, since the ring has to be closed now (diag. 61). Roll. Work the top petals first (**4**) as waves. Roll these petals.

Sew pairs at (**5**) adding as many as needed. Divide the pairs at (**6**) and work one side at a time. Finish in the point (diag. 37). Roll. Add tallies. Sew in pairs for petals at (**7**). Work the petals on one side. Finish them off at (**5**) and roll. Work the petals on the other side in the same way.

Flower (**8**) can now be worked. Start with rib where indicated, roll the rib, and finish it by tying and cutting off the pairs. Sew in pairs for the petals as indicated and finish on the other side (**9**). Roll and add a tally in the centre. Work scrolls (**10**) and (**11**) and circle (**12**) (diags. 124–126). Work a lattice filling, sewing into the sides of the circle (see the photograph on p.95 which shows the reverse side of the dahlia). Repeat on the other side. Sew in pairs for the rib (**13**) and work this as the raised vein. Add the leaf (**14**) in half stitch. Different veins are used in each of the 4 corners: plaits (diags. 103–104); twists in the runners; whole stitch and twist in the centre of the leaf; one half stitch which changes place every other row. (**15**) is started with a rib and the leaves are worked in half stitch.

The centre heart is started at (**16**) as a braid. Sew in when it reaches the other side (**17**), take out pairs and continue the centre rib. Work this central leaf motif (see raised vein). Roll this as well as the braid. Fill the area with half stitch. Alternatively, start at (**16**) and work a rib all the way round, changing into the raised vein.

Set up from point (**18**). Divide the pairs as in diag. 118. Finish both sides. Add circles.

Pattern 87 – Horn of Plenty

Thread 180/2

Start from the point of leaf (**1**) at (**o**) as in diags. 55–59 and 103–104. Roll. Start leaf (**2**) in the same way. Leave the pairs used for rolling at (*****). They can be used when the petals are made. Leaf (**3**) is made in the same way. Add pairs for the braid (**4**) at leaf (**2**), roll and add pairs to work the petals. Roll with picots (diag. 24). Start leaf (**5**). Work a plaited vein. Set up ribs (**6**) and work a straight edge stitch with picots (diag. 60). Work the leaves (**7**) in the same way as the raised vein (diags. 139–140).

Start the top flower with a rib (**8**) and fill with half stitch. Add pairs for braid (**9**). Work decoratively round the curve. Add pairs to work the petals. Start the other flower at the centre (**o**) with rib (**11**) and fill the centres. Work the braid (**12**) and finish the flower with the petals.

The three small flowers (**13**) can now be worked. Start with a rib; roll it and finish the flowers in the usual way, attaching them when rolling. Add the leaves (**14**) (diags. 55–59). Start leaf (**15**) at its tip and work it in the same way as leaf (**14**).

After rolling, use the pairs to work a rib. The

small circles are worked with picots. When the circle is closed, use some of the pairs to work the rib.

The oval (**17**) is now worked and closed. Use a double sided setting up for rib (**18**) (diags. 44–45) and work it with picots. When the oval (**17**) is reached, use the pairs of the rib for rolling the oval. Pairs are taken out towards the bottom. With the 6 remaining pairs work the rib. Rib (**19**) is set up double sided. Finish with the rib and roll. Start circle (**20**). Roll. The rib can be made with the pairs of the bundle, together with some pairs of the circle.

Start the last 3 flowers from point (**21**) (*). Roll and use pairs to work the centre (**22**). Roll. Start each of the petals at their tips, beginning with (**23**). The leaves (**24**) are worked as in Pattern 37 with a reverse side.

Horn: Set up at rib (**25**) and roll. Add pairs to work the ribs, starting at (**o**). Roll the ribs. It is necessary to leave pairs hanging for the next rib to be worked and rolled before sewing and finishing any rib. After the ribs are worked, the filling can be made, using point ground with some tallies.

9. Eyes

Pattern 88 – Eye

Thread 160/2

Set pins on the line shown and hang pairs double-sided. Add a double gimp pair on the outside. The inside may be worked either as a rib or with a straight edge stitch. It is necessary to work the curve decoratively. When both sides meet, work the pairs through one another, starting from the centre. Take care that the line of the threads flows smoothly. Put aside pairs where they are not needed any more and add pairs in other places to get a nice even weave.

It is very difficult to give a good description of this! Passives may become runners and runners passives. Decide as the work progresses which is the best way to work the pairs to give the neatest appearance (diag. 160).

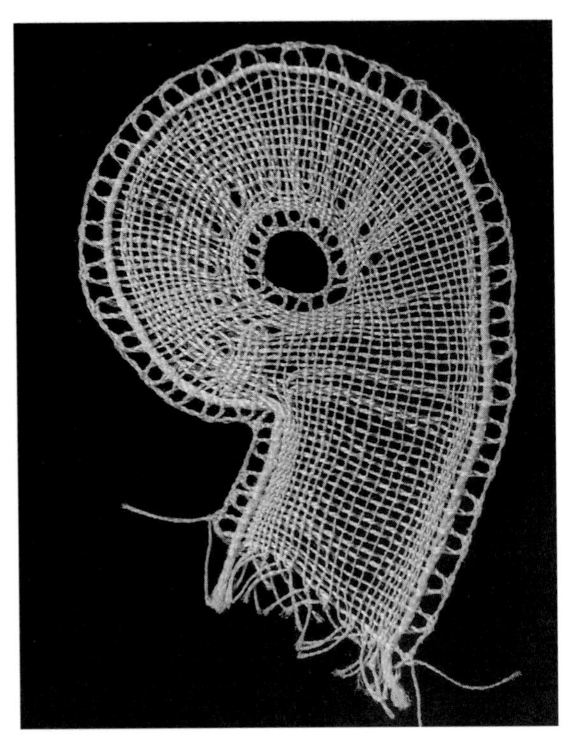

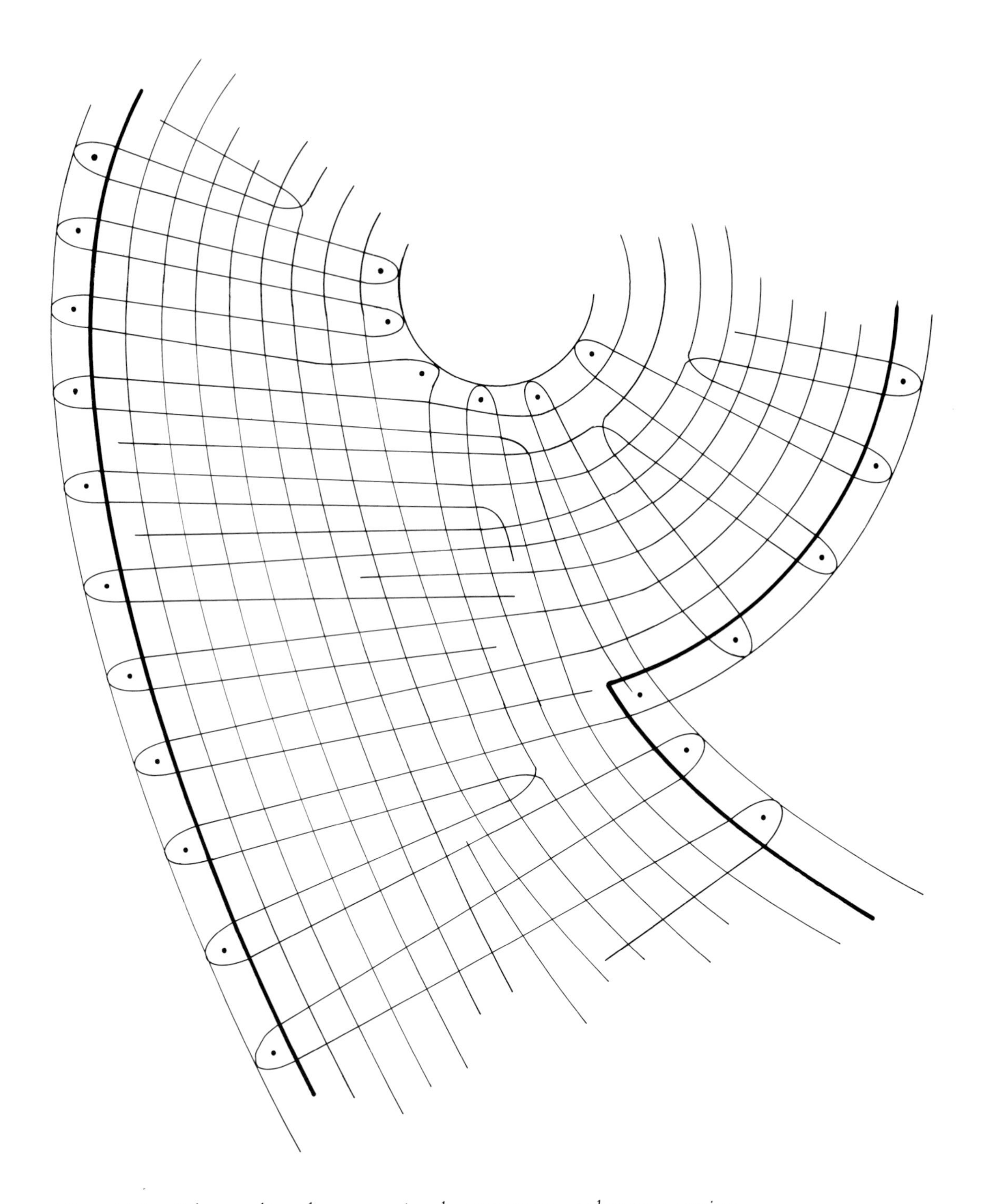

Diag. 160 *When working the eye, passives become runners and runners passives*

Pattern 89 – Bib
Thread 80/2

Start the head as indicated in Pattern 88. When the neck gets narrower, end with 6 pairs and a gimp pair. All other pairs are taken out and changed into a rib (*). At the start of the rib, the pins are set on the inside of the curve. To prevent the rib 'falling over' twist the runners twice before the last used passives are worked as runners. Work the wings in the same way as raised veins (diags. 139–141). Roll the whole bird and add the beak as follows.

Set one pin at the tip (**1**) and hang 4 pairs round this pin (diag. 143). Work whole stitch and 2 twists with the 1st and 2nd pairs. Twist the 3rd and 4th pairs twice. The edge stitch of the rib will be formed at the bottom of the beak. Take the 3rd pair from the edge stitch; work a whole stitch with the pair next to the edge stitch; then an edge stitch and set the pin. Add a new pair round this pin. Continue the rib. Add another pair round the 3rd pin. There are now 6 pairs.

Widen the beak by adding an edge stitch on the other side. Do this as follows. Twist the runners twice before working the last passive; make a whole stitch; twist both pairs twice and put in a pin to make the edge. Continue to make an edge stitch on either side. To make the beak even wider, twist the runners between the passives once. Sew into the head and roll with one thread. Finish with top sewing in the last pin-hole.

Continue with one of the 2 centre birds. Work this bird to where the ribs cross (**2**). Leave the pairs here and start the head of the other centre bird, until the ribs meet. Work whole stitches with the passives (**33**) (diag. 46) and continue the ribs on either side until they meet; work the edge stitch as usual, but twist both edge pairs (diag. 161). Again the wings are worked as raised veins. One of the wings is partly hidden. Make sure that motifs are rolled before another part is sewn in.
Set 3 pins for the ribs (**4**). Work them as ribs, but set support pins to keep the rib wide (diag. 162).

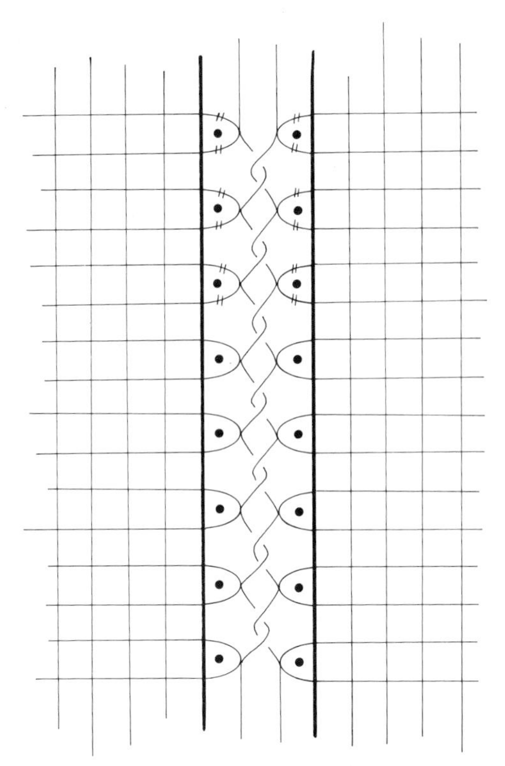

Diag. 161 *The edge pairs of both wings are twisted together*

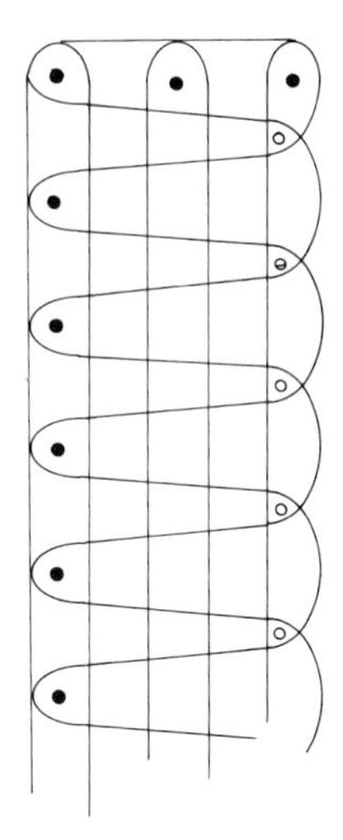

Diag. 162 *To keep the rib wide, support pins are set*

Pattern 90 – Turkey
Thread 160/2

Work a round setting up at (**1**) (diags. 28–30) and finish at the point (diag. 37). Start the wings (**2**) and work these as raised veins (diags. 139–142). Work the leg (**3**) and the feathers (**4**), again as raised veins.

The head is started with a rib (**5**). Roll and use these pairs to work the feathers on the head. To work the head, sew in pairs on both sides of the feather and join both sides. It is necessary to work the curve in diag. 50a. Work the pairs as shown in diag. 160 and finish the neck with several raised veins. Work (**6**), making sewings on one side; the tail (**7**), starting with a scroll; and the second leg (**8**). Choose from the variety of decorations.

Pattern 91 – Summer swirl
Thread 160/2 **(for actual size see p.152)**

To work the braids in this pattern, it will be necessary to leave hanging the pairs used to work the previous braid. Add pairs to roll and start other braids before any sewing can be made. As the braids are only narrow, use 2 pairs to roll them.

Start with braid (**1**), work to (*) and roll as far as possible. Work braid (**2**), sew into (**1**) and roll. Work braid (**3**) and sew into (**1**), roll. Continue braid (**1**) and finish it at braid (**3**). Roll braid (**1**). Plait the pairs of the roll and transfer them to braid (**4**).

Set up for (**5**) and roll to halfway down the stem (*). It is is now possible to work braid (**6**) and flower (**7**). Sew stem (**5**) into the flower. Work braid (**8**) to (*) and roll, so that braid (**9**) can be worked. Sew braid (**8**) into (**9**) and transfer the pairs as plaits to the other side of braid (**9**). Finish braid (**8**) and sew into the scroll. Study the pattern carefully to decide in which order to work. If possible, try to transfer pairs from one motif to the other.

The fillings are point ground twin picots and tallies.

Pattern 92 – Corner motif

Thread 120/2

Start this pattern with the flower. For the decoration in the petals work the runners from the outside (**0**) in whole stitch through the gimp pair and one passive pair and twist the runners.* Now take a passive pair through the runners and lay aside, twist the runners*.

Repeat this a few times to reach (**1**) and set a support pin. Twist the runners and bring them in the same way (* to * as above) back to the outer edge.

Start with a scroll (diags. 108–110) and work the braid (**2**) (diag. 111). Sew into the flower. Roll and work the 2nd scroll and braid (**3**) and sew into the flower.

The petals round the corner are worked as waves (diags 155–156). Start with the centre one (**4**) working to one side (follow arrow). Sew in pairs to work the other side (**5**). Roll. The leaves between the two braids can now be worked, starting at the tip (diags. 33–35). Finish the pattern with the ribs and roll them.

10. Fillings

SNOWFLAKE

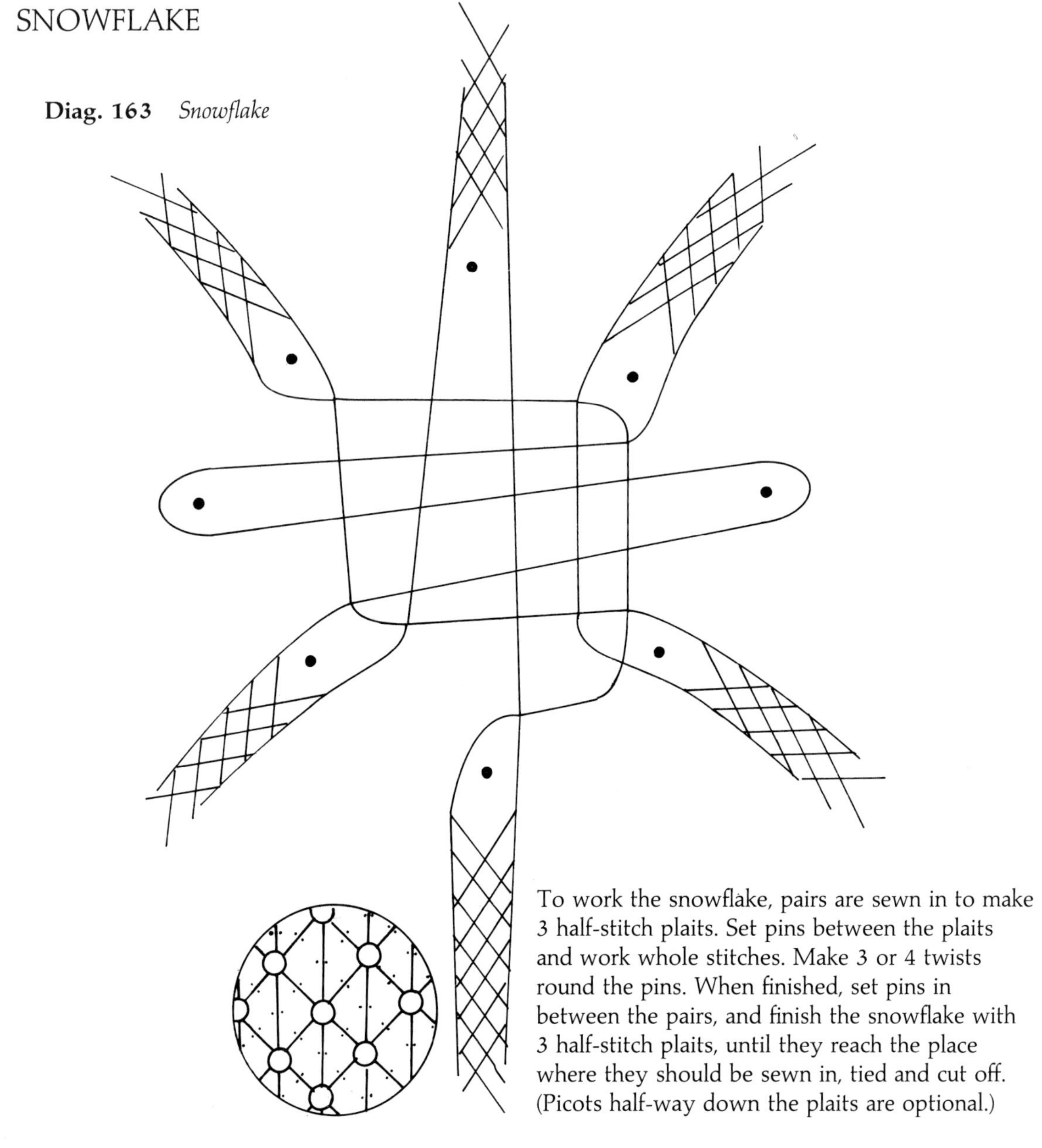

Diag. 163 *Snowflake*

To work the snowflake, pairs are sewn in to make 3 half-stitch plaits. Set pins between the plaits and work whole stitches. Make 3 or 4 twists round the pins. When finished, set pins in between the pairs, and finish the snowflake with 3 half-stitch plaits, until they reach the place where they should be sewn in, tied and cut off. (Picots half-way down the plaits are optional.)

TWIN PICOT

The twin picot can be worked where two half-stitch plaits meet. The crossings are worked in whole stitch in numerical order. Work a picot on both sides and continue the whole stitches before working the 2 half-stitch plaits.

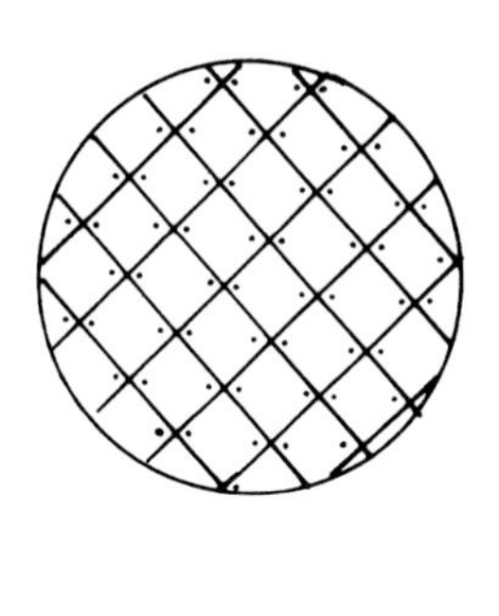

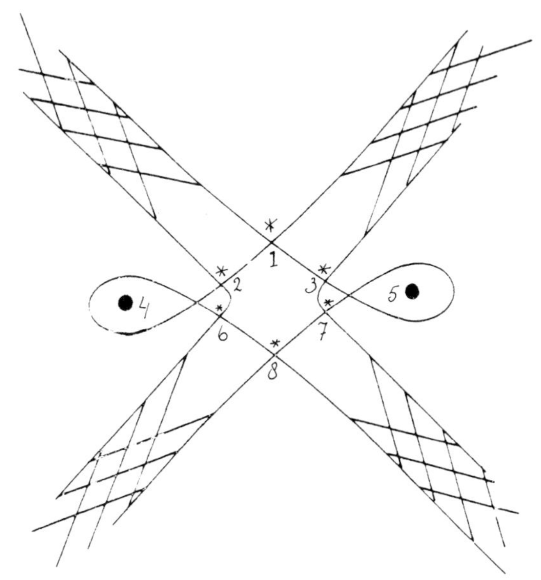

Diag. 164 *Twin picot*

LATTICE

The squares are usually drawn a little smaller than those of the twin picots, because single pairs are sewn in. Twist these pairs until they meet. Then work a whole stitch with a pin in the centre of the stitch.

Diag. 165 *Lattice*

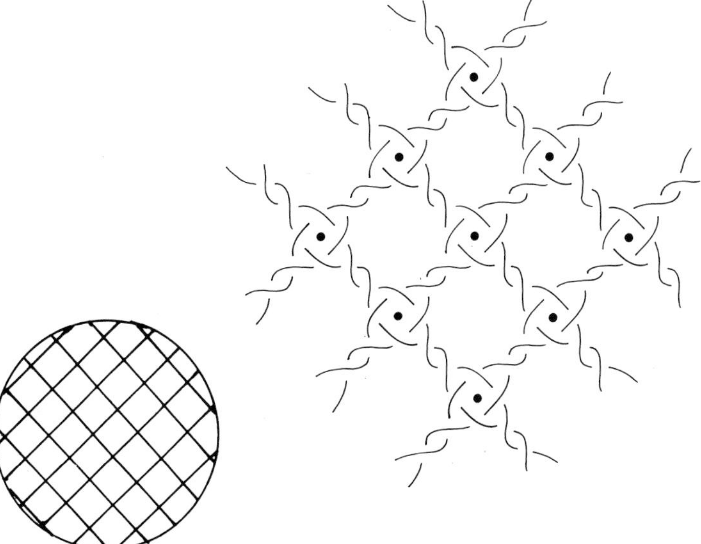

WHOLE STITCH TWIST

This filling can be worked on the same squares as the lattice: single pairs are sewn in. Twist the pairs. On the crossing work a whole stitch and twist, set a pin, and again whole stitch and twist.

Diag. 166 *Whole stitch – twist*

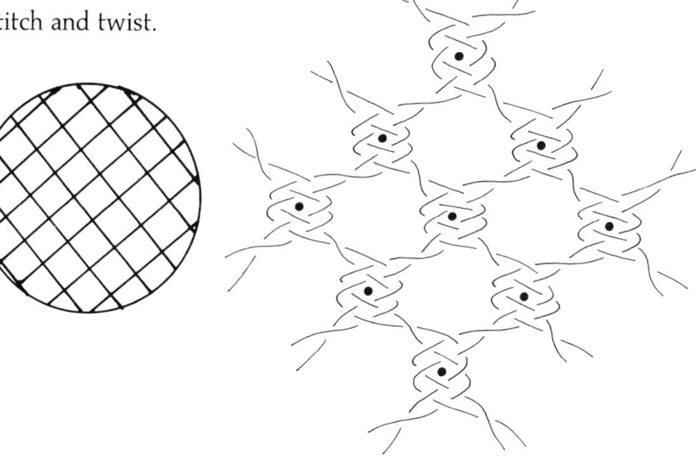

POINT GROUND

Two scales of point ground are given. Choose the scale according to the thickness of the thread being used.

Diag. 167a

Diag. 167b

Text sources

Mrs L.W. van der Meulen-Nulle: *Met Naald en Klos en Speldenbos Handleiding tot het vervaardigen van Duchessekant*
Patricia Wardle and Mary de Jong: *Catalogue: Lace in Fashion/Fashion in Lace*
Mrs E.M. Depape: *History of the Royal Lace School 'Koningin Sophie der Nederlanden' at Sluis*

Finished pieces, shown actual size

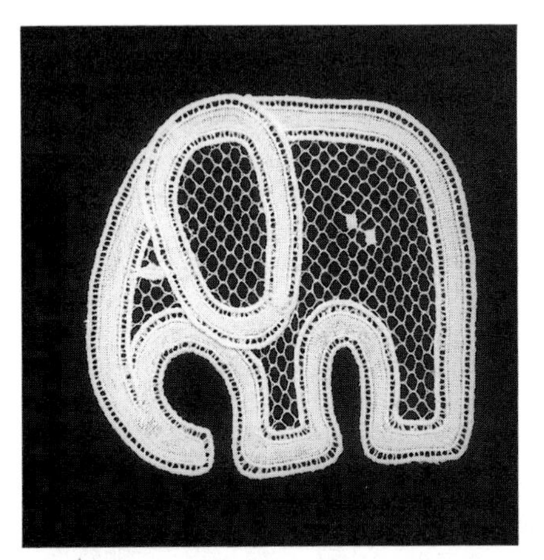

Pattern 5 – *Elephant*
(working instructions on p.28)

Pattern 12 – *Pram*
(working instructions on p.35)

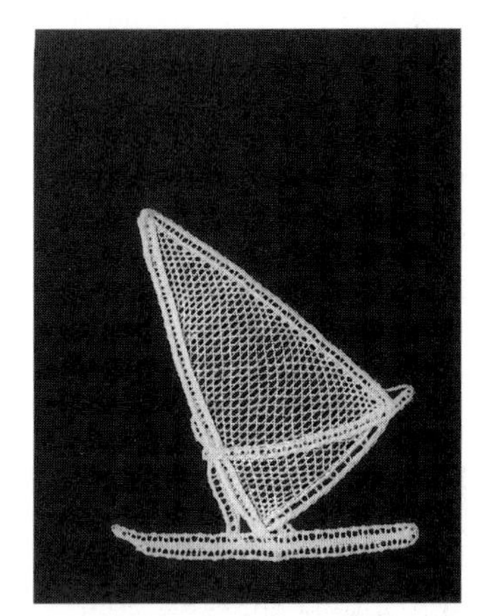

Pattern 13 – *Surfer*
(working instructions on p.36)

Pattern 21 – *Chinese flower*
(working instructions on p.49)

Pattern 32 – *Elegant swan*
(working instructions on p.67)

Pattern 51 – *Moulin Rouge* (working instructions on p.86)

Pattern 62 – *Dragon* (working instructions on p.99)

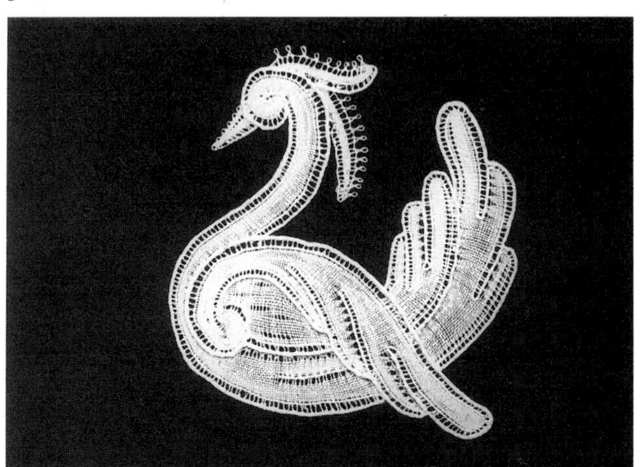

Pattern 65 – *Swan* (working instructions on p.104)

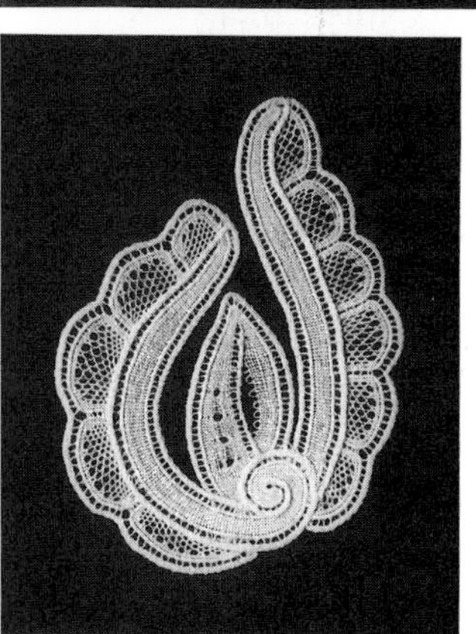

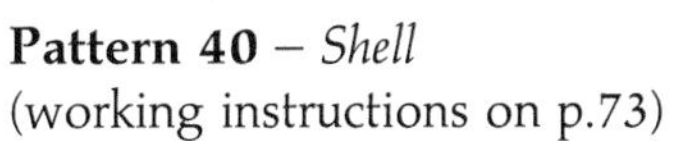

Pattern 40 – *Shell* (working instructions on p.73)

Pattern 52 – *Easter egg* (working instructions on p.87)

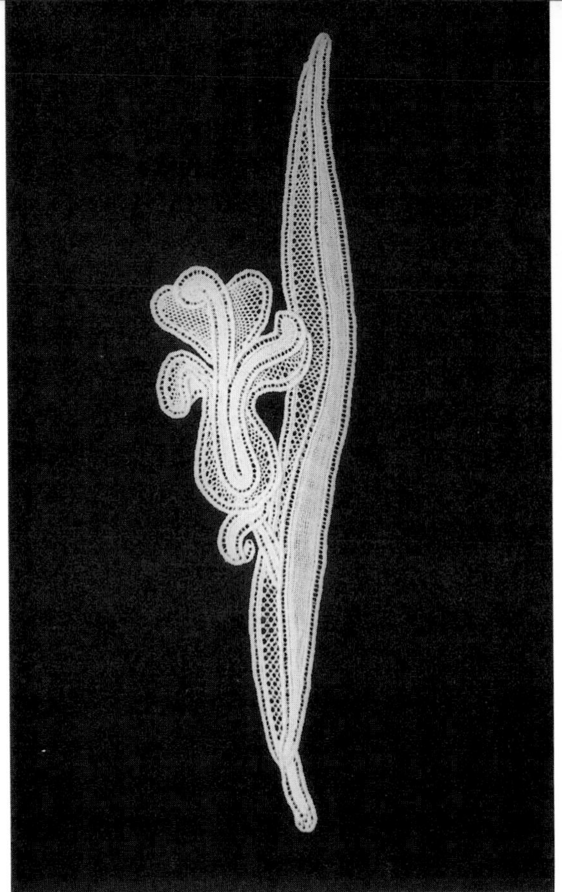

Pattern 70 – *Orchid*
(working instructions on p.109)

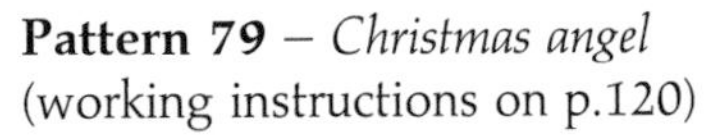

Pattern 79 – *Christmas angel*
(working instructions on p.120)

Pattern 83 – *Crown*
(working instructions on p.128)

Pattern 82 – *Snail*
(working instructions on p.126)

Pattern 91 – *Summer swirl*
(working instructions on p.142)

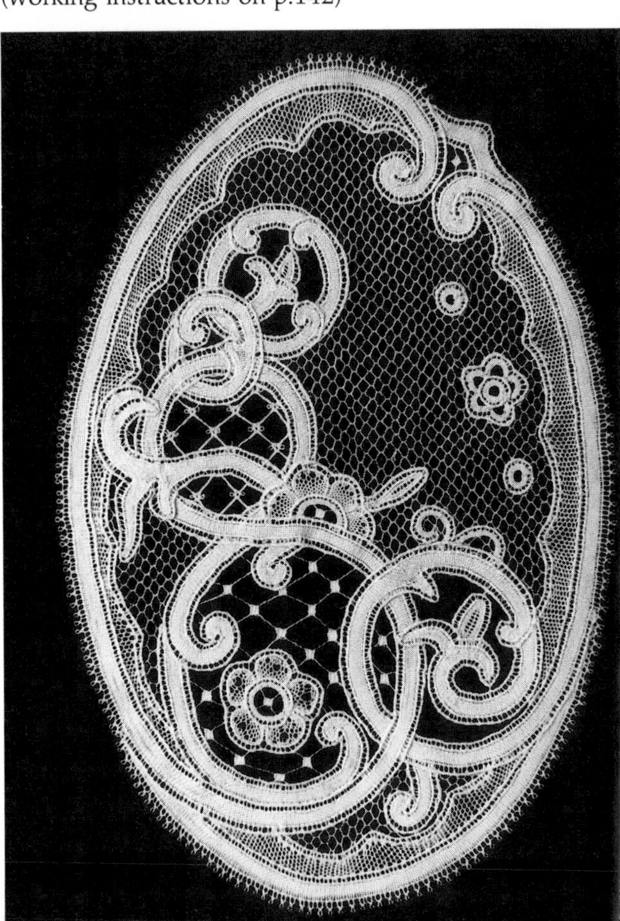

Suppliers and sources of information

UNITED KINGDOM

General Suppliers

Alby Lace Museum
Cromer Road
Alby, Norwich
Norfolk NR11 7QE

Busy Bobbins
Unit 7
Scarrots Lane
Newport
IOW PO30 1JD

Chosen Crafts Centre
46 Winchcombe Street
Cheltenham
Glos GL52 2ND

Jo Firth
Lace Marketing &
Needlecraft Supplies
58 Kent Crescent
Lowtown
Pudsey
W Yorks LS28 9EB

J. & J. Ford
October Hill
Upper Way
Upper Longdon
Rugeley
Staffs WS15 1QB

Framecraft
83 Hampstead Road
Handsworth Wood
Birmingham B2 1JA

Doreen Gill
14 Barnfield Road
Petersfield
Hants GU31 4DQ

R. Gravestock
Highwood
Crews Hill
Alfrick
Worcs WR6 5HF

The Handicraft Shop
47 Northgate
Canterbury
Kent CT1 1BE

Frank Herring & Sons
27 High West Street
Dorchester
Dorset DT1 1UP

Honiton Lace Shop
44 High Street
Honiton
Devon

D. J. Hornsby
149 High Street
Burton Latimer
Kettering
Northants NN15 5RL
also at:
25 Manwood Avenue
Canterbury
Kent CT2 7AH

Frances Iles
73 High Street
Rochester
Kent ME1 1LX

Jane's Pincushions
Unit 4
Taverham Crafts
Taverham Nursery
Centre
Fir Covert Road
Taverham
Norwich NR8 6HT

Loricraft
19 Peregrine Way
Grove
Wantage
Oxon

Needlestyle
5 The Woolmead
Farnham
Surrey GU9 7TX

Needlestyle
24–26 West Street
Alresford
Hants

Needlework
Ann Bartleet
Bucklers Farm
Coggeshall
Essex CO6 1SB

Needle and Thread
80 High Street
Horsell
Woking
Surrey GU21 4SZ

The Needlewoman
21 Needles Alley
off New Street
Birmingham B2 5AE

T. Parker
124 Corhampton Road
Boscome East
Bournemouth
Dorset BH6 5NZ

Jane Playford
North Lodge
Church Close
West Runton
Norfolk NR27 9QY

Redburn Crafts
Squires Garden Centre
Halliford Road
Upper Halliford
Shepperton
Middx TW17 8RU

Christine Riley
53 Barclay Street
Stonehaven
Kincardineshire
Scotland

Peter and Beverley Scarlett
Strupak
Hill Head
Cold Wells
Ellon
Grampian
Scotland

Ken & Pat Schultz
134 Wisbech Road
Thornley
Peterborough

J. S. Sears
Lacecraft Supplies
8 Hillview
Sherington
Bucks MK16 9NY

Sebalace
Waterloo Mills
Howden Road
Silsden
W Yorks BD2 0NA

A. Sells
49 Pedley Lane
Clifton
Shefford
Beds

Shireburn Lace
Finkle Court
Finkle Hill
Sherburn in Elmet
N Yorks LS25 6EB

SMP
4 Garners Close
Chalfont St Peter
Bucks SL9 0HB

Southern Handicrafts
20 Kensington Gardens
Brighton
Sussex BN1 4AC

Spangles
Carole Morris
Cashburn Lace
Burwell
Cambs CB5 0ED

Stitchery
Finkle Street
Richmond
N Yorks

Stitches
Dovehouse Shopping Parade
Warwick Road
Olton
Solihull
W Midlands

Teazle Embroideries
35 Boothferry Road
Hull
N Humberside

Lynn Turner
Church Meadow Crafts
15 Carisbrooke Drive
Winsford
Cheshire CW7 1LN

Valley House Craft Studios
Ruston
Scarborough
N Yorks

George Walker
The Corner Shop
Rickinghall
Diss
Norfolk

West End Lace Supplies
Ravensworth Court
Road
Mortimer West End
Reading
Berks RG7 3UD

Christopher Williams
19 Morrison Avenue
Parkstone
Poole
Dorset

George White Lacemakers' Supplies
40 Heath Drive
Boston Spa
W Yorks L23 6PB

Bobbins

A. R. Arches
The Poplars
Shetland
near Stowmarket
Suffolk IP14 3DE

Bartlett, Caesar and Partners
12 Creslow Court
Stony Stratford
Milton Keynes
MK11 1NN

Bartlett, Caesar and Partners
The Glen
Shorefield Road
Downton
Lymington
Hants SO41 0LH

T. Brown
Temple Lane Cottage
Littledean
Cinderford
Glos

Chrisken Bobbins
26 Cedar Drive
Kingsclere
Bucks RG15 8TD

Malcolm J. Fielding
2 Northern Terrace
Moss Lane
Silverdale
Lancs LA5 0ST

Richard Gravestock
Highwood
Crews Hill
Alfrick
Worcs WR6 5HF

Larkfield Crafts
Hilary Ricketts
4 Island Cottages
Mapledurwell
Basingtoke
Hants RG25 2LU

Loricraft
19 Peregrine Way
Grove, Wantage
Oxon

T. Parker
124 Corhampton Road
Boscombe East
Bournemouth
Dorset BH6 5NZ

Bryan Phillips
Pantglas
Cellan
Lampeter
Dyfed SA48 8JD

D. H. Shaw
47 Lamor Crescent
Thrushcroft
Rotherham
S Yorks S66 9QD

Sizelands
1 Highfield Road
Winslow
Bucks MK10 3QU

Christine & David Springett
21 Hillmorton Road
Rugby
War CV22 5DF

Richard Viney
Unit 7
Port Royal Street
Southsea
Hants PO5 3UD

West End Lace Suppliers
Ravensworth Court
Road
Mortimer West End
Reading
Berks RG7 3UD

Lace pillows

Newnham Lace
Equipment
15 Marlowe Close
Basingstoke
Hants RG24 9DD

Bartlett, Caesar and
Partners
12 Creslow Court
Stony Stratford
Milton Keynes
MK11 1NN
(tel. 0908 566026)

Bartlett, Caesar and
Partners
The Glen
Shorefield Road
Downton
Lymington
Hants
SO41 0LH
(tel. 0590 644854)

Books

Christopher Williams
19 Morrison Avenue
Parkstone
Poole
Dorset BH17 4AD

Silk embroidery and lace thread

E. & J. Piper
Silverlea
Flax Lane
Glemsford
Suffolk CO10 7RS

Silk weaving yarn

Hilary Chetwynd
Kipping Cottage
Cheriton
Alresford
Hants SO24 0PW

Frames and mounts

Doreen Campbell
Highcliff
Brenisham Road
Malmesbury
Wilts

Matt coloured transparent adhesive film

Heffers Graphic Shop
26 King Street
Cambridge CB1 1LN

Linen by the metre (yard) and made up articles of church linen

Mary Collins
Church Furnishings
St Andrews Hall
Humber Doucy Lane
Ipswich
Suffolk IP4 3BP

Hayes & Finch
Head Office & Factory
Hanson Road
Aintree
Liverpool L9 9BP

UNITED STATES OF AMERICA

Arbor House
22 Arbor Lane
Roslyn Hights
NY 11577

Baltazor Inc.
3262 Severn Avenue
Metairie
LA 7002

Beggars' Lace
P.O. Box 17263
Denver
Colo 80217

Berga Ullman Inc.
P.O. Box 918
North Adams
MA 01247

Frederick J. Fawcett
129 South Street
Boston
MA 02130

Frivolité
15526 Densmore N.
Seattle, WA 98113

Happy Hands
3007 S. W. Marshall
Pendleton
Oreg 97180

International Old Lacers
P.O. Box 1029
Westminster
Colo 80030

Lace Place de Belgique
800 S. W. 17th Street
Boca Raton
FL 33432

Lacis
2150 Stuart Street
Berkeley
CA 9470

Robin's Bobbins
RTL Box 1736
Mineral Bluff
GA 30559

Robin and Russ
Handweavers
553 North Adams Street
McMinnvills
Oreg 97128

Some Place
2990 Adline Street
Berkeley
CA 94703

Osma G. Todd Studio
319 Mendoza Avenue
Coral Gables
FL 33134

The Unique And Art
Lace Cleaners
5926 Delman Boulevard
St Louis
MO 63112

Van Scriver Bobbin Lace
130 Cascadilla Park
Ithaca
NY 14850

The World in Stitches
82 South Street
Milford
N.H. 03055

AUSTRALIA

Australian Lace magazine
P.O. Box 1291
Toowong QLD 4066

Dentelles Lace Supplies
c/o Betty Franks
39 Lang Terrace
Northgate 4013
Brisbane
Queensland

The Lacemaker
724a Riversdale Road
Camberwell
Victoria 3124

Spindle and Loom
Arcade 83
Longueville Road
Lane Cove
NSW 2066

Tulis Crafts
201 Avoca Street
Randwick
NSW 2031

BELGIUM

't Handwerkhuisje
Katelijnestraat 23
8000 Bruges

Kantcentrum
Balstraat 14
8000 Bruges

Manufacture Belge de
Dentelle
6 Galerie de la Reine
Galeries Royales St
Hubert
1000 Bruxelles

Orchidée
Mariastraat 18
8000 Bruges

Textiel Scharlaeken
Philip Stockstraat 5–7
B–8000 Bruges

Ann Thys
't Apostelientje
Balstraat 11
8000 Bruges

FRANCE

Centre d'Initiations à la
Dentelle du Puy
2 Rue Duguesclin
43000 Le Puy en Velay

A L'Econome
Anne-Marie Deydier
Ecole de Dentelle aux
Fuseaux
10 rue Paul Chenavard
69001 Lyon

Rougier and Plé
13–15 bd des Filles de
Calvaire
75003 Paris

WEST GERMANY

Der Fenster Laden
Berliner Str. 8
D 6483 Bad Soden
Salmünster

P.P. Hempel
Ortolanweg 34
1000 Berlin 47

Heikona De Ruijter
Klöppelgrosshandel
Langer Steinweg 38
D4933 Blomberg

HOLLAND

Blokker's Boektiek
Bronsteeweg 4/4a
2101 AC Heemstede

Theo Brejaart
Dordtselaan 146–148
P.O. Box 5199
3008 AD Rotterdam

Irma's Sampler
Groot Heiligland 66
2002 RA Haarlem

Magazijn *De Vlijt*
Lijnmarkt 48
Utrecht

SWITZERLAND

Fadehax
Inh. Irene Solca
4105 Biel-Benken
Basel

NEW ZEALAND

Peter McLeavey
P.O. Box 69.007
Auckland 8

SOURCES OF INFORMATION

The Lace Guild
The Hollies
53 Audnam
Stourbridge
West Midlands
DY8 4AE

The Lacemakers' Circle
49 Wardwick
Derby DE1 1HY

The Lace Society
Linwood
Stratford Road
Oversley
Alcester
War BY9 6PG

The British College of
Lace
21 Hillmorton Road
Rugby
War CV22 5DF

The English Lace School
Oak House
Church Stile
Woodbury
Nr Exeter
Devon

International Old Lacers
President
Gunvor Jorgensen
366 Bradley Avenue
Northvale
NJ 076647
United States

O.I.D.F.A.
(The International
Organization for
Bobbin and Needle
Lace)
7 Rue Louis Le Grand
75002 Paris
France

United Kingdom
Director of
International
Old Lacers
S. Hurst
4 Dollius Road
London N3 1RG

Ring of Tatters
Mrs C. Appleton
Nonesuch
5 Ryeland Road
Ellerby
Saltburn by Sea
Cleveland TS13 5LP

BOOKS

The following are stockists of the complete Batsford/ Dryad Press range:

Avon

Bridge Bookshop
7 Bridge Street
Bath BA2 4AS

Waterstone & Co.
4–5 Milsom Street
Bath BA1 1DA

Bedfordshire

Arthur Sells
Lane Cove
49 Pedley Lane
Clifton
Sefford SG17 5QT

Berkshire

West End Lace Supplies
Ravensworth Court Road
Mortimer West End
Reading RG7 3UD

Buckinghamshire

J. S. Sear Lacecraft
Supplies
8 Hill View
Sherringham MK16 9NY

Cambridgeshire

Dillons The Bookstore
Sydney Street
Cambridge

Cheshire

Lyn Turner
Church Meadow Crafts
15 Carisbrook Drive
Winsford CW7 1LN

Devon

Creative Crafts &
Needlework
18 High Street
Totnes TQ9 5NP

Honiton Lace Shop
44 High Street
Honiton EX14 8PJ

Dorset

F. Herring & Sons
High West Street
Dorchester DT1 1UP

Tim Parker (mail order)
124 Corhampton Road
Boscombe East
Bournemouth BH6 5NL

Durham

Lacemaid
6, 10 & 15 Stoneybeck
Bishop Middleham
DL17 9BL

Gloucestershire

Southgate Handicrafts
63 Southgate Street
Gloucester GL1 1TX

Waterstone & Co.
89–90 The Promenade
Cheltenham GL50 1NB

Hampshire

Creative Crafts
11 The Square
Winchester SO23 9ES

Doreen Gill
14 Barnfield Road
Petersfield GU31 4DR

Larkfield Crafts
4 Island Cottages
Mapledurwell
Basingstoke RG23 2LU

Needlestyle
24–26 West Street
Alresford

Ruskins
27 Bell Street
Romsey

Isle of Wight

Busy Bobbins
Unit 7
Scarrots Lane
Newport PO30 1JD

Kent

The Handicraft Shop
47 Northgate
Canterbury

Frances Iles
73 High Street
Rochester ME1 1LX

Lincolnshire

Rippingale Lace
Barn Farm House
off Station Road
Rippingdale Bourne

London

Foyles
119 Charing Cross Road
WC2H OEB

Hatchards
187 Piccadilly W1

Middlesex

Redburn Crafts
Squires Garden Centre
Halliford Road
Upper Halliford
Shepperton TW17 8RU

Norfolk

Alby Lace Museum
Cromer Road
Alby
Norwich NR11 7QB

Jane's Pincushions
Taverham Craft Unit 4
Taverham Nursery
Centre
Fir Covert Road
Taverham
Norwich NR8 6HT

Waterstone & Co.
30 London Street
Norwich NR2 1LD

Northamptonshire

D. J. Hornsby
149 High Street
Burton Latimer
Kettering NN15 5RL

Oxfordshire

Loricraft
19 Peregrine Way
Grove
Wantage

Scotland

Embroidery Shop
51 William Street
Edinburgh
Lothian EH3 7LW

Beverley Scarlett
Strupak
Hillhead
Coldwells
Ellon
Aberdeenshire

Waterstone & Co.
236 Union Street
Aberdeen AB1 1TN

Surrey

Needlestyle
5 The Woolmead
Farnham GU9 1TN

Sussex

Southern Handicrfats
20 Kensington Gardens
Brighton BN1 4AL

Warwickshire

Christine & David
Springett
21 Hillmorton Road
Rugby CV22 6DF

North Yorkshire

Shireburn Lace
Finkel Court
Finkel Hill
Sherburn in Elmet
N York LS25 6EB

Valley House Craft
Studios
Ruston
Scarborough

West Midlands

Needlewoman
Needles Alley
off New Street
Birmingham

West Yorkshire

Sebalace
Waterloo Mill
Howden Road
Silsden BD20 0HA

George White
Lacemaking Supplies
40 Heath Drive
Boston Spa LS23 6PB

Jo Firth
58 Kent Crescent
Lowtown
Pudsey
Leeds LS28 9EB

Index